Cajun AND *Creole*
COOKING
with Miss Edie and the Colonel

Also by Edie Hand

A Country Music Christmas

The Last Christmas Ride

Recipes for Life

All Cooked Up

Emergency Preparedness Handbooks

Quick & Easy Holiday Treats with Style

Quick & Easy Entrees with Style

Quick & Easy Salads & Breads with Style

Precious Family Memories of Elvis

The Presley Family & Friends Cookbook

Cajun AND *Creole* COOKING

with Miss Edie and the Colonel

THE FOLKLORE *and* ART *of* LOUISIANA COOKING

Edie Hand & Colonel William G. Paul

CUMBERLAND HOUSE PUBLISHING

NASHVILLE, TENNESSEE

CAJUN AND CREOLE COOKING
PUBLISHED BY CUMBERLAND HOUSE PUBLISHING, INC.
431 Harding Industrial Drive
Nashville, TN 37211

Cover design: Bruce Gore Studio
Text design: Lisa Taylor
Cover photo and food photos: Keith Dunn
Reenactment photos: Christi Key

Library of Congress Cataloging-in-Publication Data
Hand, Edie, 1951–
  Cajun and Creole cooking with Miss Edie and the Colonel : the folklore and art of Louisiana cooking / Edie Hand & William G. Paul.
      p. cm.
  Includes bibliographical references and index.
  ISBN-13: 978-1-58182-617-3 (hardcover)
  ISBN-10: 1-58182-617-6 (hardcover)
  1. Cookery, American—Louisiana style. 2. Cookery, Creole. 3. Cookery, Cajun. I. Paul, William G., 1954- II. Title.

  TX715.2.L68H355 2007
  641.59763—dc22

                                                                      2007039221

Printed in the United States of America
1 2 3 4 5 6 7 — 12 11 10 09 08 07

Dedication

We would like to dedicate this book to Jennifer O'Dwyer Paul because of the love, support, and talent she brought to this project. *Merci bien!*

A special tribute to the late Sir Jack D. L. Holmes, author, preeminent historian of the Spanish colonial borderlands, world traveler, Rhodes scholar, *bon vivant* of life, and Spanish Knight of the Order of Isabella de Catolica. He was a mentor and friend and taught me, the Colonel, so much about French and Spanish Louisiana. *Muchos gracias mi bien Hermano.*

A portion of the proceeds from the sales of this book will go to the Louisiana Disaster Recovery Foundation (www.louisianahelp.org) and the Edie Hand Foundation (www.ediehandfoundation.org).

Destrehan Plantation

Destrehan Plantation

The sands of Louisiana time seem to stand still for a moment at Destrehan Plantation. This majestic house watches over the banks of the great Mississippi River, just minutes from New Orleans. Listed on the National Register of Historic Places, Destrehan was established in 1787 and remains the oldest documented plantation home in the lower Mississippi Valley. Destrehan Plantation has seen many changes over the last two centuries. First owned by noble French families, the plantation fell into ruins after being sold for industrial use. It has since been fully restored. Destrehan Plantation remains a tribute to the richness of Louisiana history and represents the dedication of a community to which it has been a cornerstone for over 200 years. Visit them on the Web at www.destrehanplantation.org or call toll free (877) 725-1929.

Fort Toulouse

Fort Toulouse / Fort Jackson Historic Site is located at the juncture of the Coosa and Tallapoosa Rivers just south of Wetumpka, Alabama (ten miles north of Montgomery). The park is operated by the Alabama Historical Commission and is open year round. Within the multifaceted park are replicated French buildings representing the last fort during the colonial occupation of 1717–63. Living history presentations are given once monthly throughout the spring and fall with special events being in April with the French & Indian War encampment and in November with Alabama Frontier Days. The park also has a partial replication of Ft. Jackson (1814–17), the Bartram Arboretum, and a campground. For more information contact the park at 2521 West Ft. Toulouse Road, Wetumpka, Alabama 36093, (334) 567-3002 or at Ftedu1@bellsouth.net.

Contents

Acknowledgments xv

Part 1: Equipment, Terms, and Cooking Techniques

The Louisiana Lifestyle 5

Cooking in the Cajun/Creole Manner 6

The Joy of Cast-Iron Cookware 8

Essential Utensils 11

Basic Cooking Tips 14

The 7 Elements of Louisiana Cooking 17

Cajun/Creole Cooking Techniques 32

Cajun/Creole Culinary Terms 33

Louisiana Ingredients 35

Part II: The Evolution of Cajun and Creole Cuisines

The Land of Louisiana 45

Outline of Louisiana Culinary History 46

A Brief History of Cajun and Creole Cuisines 54

The Difference Between Cajun and Creole Cuisines 66

French Cuisine in the Mississippi Valley 68

The Native American Influence 70

The African Connection 73

The Arrival of the Dons 75

The Acadian Migration 76

La Belle Epoque 78

The Italian Influx 80

Acadian to Cajun 81

A Very Creole Breakfast 82

Mardi Gras 84

Boucherie and Fais Do-Do 86

Part III: Cajun and Creole Recipes

Classic Sauces

1. Bordelaise Sauce 92
2. Classic White Cream Sauce 93
3. Rémoulade Sauce 94
4. Creole Sauce 95
5. Béarnaise Sauce 96
6. Béchamel Sauce 97
7. Creole Hollandaise Sauce 98
8. Creole Meuniere Sauce 98
9. Marchand de Vin Sauce 99
10. Sassy Lemon Sauce 99
11. Cajun Sauce Piquant 100
12. Creole Mayonnaise 101
13. Whiskey or Rum Sauce 102
14. Sauce Espagnole 103
15. Lemon Butter Sauce 104
16. Creole Cocktail Sauce 104
17. Praline Sauce 105
18. White Wine Sauce 105

Breakfast Dishes

1. Calas 108
2. Beignets 109
3. Grillades and Grits 110
4. Eggs Sardou 112
5. Eggs Hussarde 113
6. Eggs Creole 114
7. Creole Crabmeat Omelet Filling 115
8. Cajun Coush-Coush 116
9. Pain Perdu 116

Appetizers and Dips

1. Shrimp Rémoulade 118
2. Stuffed Mushrooms 120
3. Louisiana Crab Cakes 121
4. Creole Stuffed Shrimp 122
5. Shrimp or Crawfish Boulettes 124

6. Cajun/Creole Seafood Dip 125

7. Oysters Bienville 126

8. Oysters Mosca 127

9. Spinach & Crab Meat Dip 128

10. Natchitoches Meat Pies 129

11. Crawfish Beignets 130

Stocks

1. Chicken Stock 132

2. Seafood Stock 133

3. Pork Stock 134

4. Beef Stock 135

5. Vegetable Stock 136

Soups and Gumbos

1. Louisiana Turtle Soup 138

2. Oyster and Artichoke Bisque 139

3. Shrimp and Crab Meat Bisque 140

4. Creole Vegetable Soup 141

5. Crawfish Bisque 142

6. Bouillabaisse Louisiane 143

7. Chicken Sausage Gumbo 144

8. Seafood Okra Gumbo 145

9. Gumbo Z'Herbes 146

10. Seafood Filé Gumbo 147

11. Pot-au-Feu à la Creole 148

12. Creole Potato Soup 149

13. Cream of Asparagus Soup 150

14. Cajun-Style Pumpkin Soup 151

15. Corn and Crabmeat Soup 152

16. Creole French Onion Soup 153

17. Duck and Sausage Gumbo 154

Vegetable Dishes

1. Basic Louisiana Tasty Rice 156

2. Brown Rice 157

3. Cajun Maque Choux 158

4. Creole Stewed Okra and Tomatoes 159

5. Beef-Stuffed Bell Peppers 160

6. Cajun "Dirty" Rice 161

7. Cajun Corn Pudding 162

8. Cajun Collard Greens 163

9. Creole Zucchini and Tomatoes 164

10. Fried Okra 165

11. Creole Red Beans and Rice 166

12. Congri 167

13. Pecan Rice 168

14. Cajun Potato Fries 169

15. Fried Sweet Potatoes and Onion 170

16. Creole String Beans 171

17. Roasted Pecan and Sausage Stuffing 172

18. New Year's Day Hoppin' John 173

19. Hush Puppies 174

20. Seafood-Stuffed Bell Peppers 175

21. Stuffed Eggplant 176

22. Brabant Potatoes 177

23. Smothered Cabbage 178

Meat Entrées

1. Steak Louisiane 180

2. Marinated Steak with Mushrooms 182

3. Cotelettes Creole de Cochon 184

4. Pecan-and-Herb-Encrusted Prime Rib Roast .185

5. Cajun-Style Barbeque Ribs 186

6. Creole Panéed Veal 187

7. Cajun Jambalaya 188

8. New Orleans Creole Jambalaya 189

9. Beef Bordelaise 190

10. Daubé Glacé 191

11. Cajun Pork Roast 192

12. Cochon de Lait 193

Chicken

1. Creole Chicken Salad 196

2. Chicken Sauce Piquant 197

3. Chicken Espagnole 198

4. Chicken Étouffée 199

5. Pecan-Crusted Chicken with Cream Sauce 200

6. Chicken Jean Laffite 201

7. Chicken in White Wine Sauce 202

8. Cajun Fried Chicken 203

9. Chicken Florentine 204

Game

1. Alligator Sauce Piquant 205

2. *Lapin au Sauce Piquant* 207

3. Cajun Venison Roast 208

4. Cajun Roasted Duck 209

5. Quail Étouffée 210

Seafood

1. *Pompano en Papillote* 212

2. Shrimp and Crab Meat au Gratin 214

3. Shrimp Creole 215

4. Shrimp Clemenceau 216

5. Creole Barbecued Shrimp 217

6. Trout Marguery 218

7. Creole-Style Tuna Fish Salad 219

8. Redfish Courtbouillon 220

9. Pecan-Crusted Catfish with Mushroom Sauce 222

10. Fried Creole Mustard Catfish 223

11. Shrimp or Crawfish Étouffée 224

12. Blackened Redfish 225

13. New Orleans–Style Spinach and Crab Meat Casserole 226

14. Louisiana-Style Boiled Shrimp 227

15. Boiled Crawfish 228

16. Creole Shrimp and Crab Meat Quiche 229

17. Louisiana-Style Shrimp Stir-Fry 230

18. Trout Amandine 231

19. Crawfish Pie 232

20. Crawfish Fettuccine 233

21. Crab and Shrimp Étouffée 234

22. Shrimp-Stuffed Mirlitons 235

23. Cajun Fried Crawfish Tails 236

24. Trout Meuniere 237

25. Crab Meat Ravigote 238

Desserts and Candy

1. Red Velvet Cake 240
2. Spiced Fig Cake 241
3. Mardi Gras King Cake 242
4. Satsuma Cake 244
5. Cajun Cane Syrup Cake 245
6. Praline Cheesecake 246
7. Pecan Pie 247
8. Sweet Potato Pecan Pie 248
9. Tarte à la Bouillie 249
10. Riz au Lait 250
11. Chocolate Silk 251
12. New Orleans Bread Pudding 252
13. Bananas Foster 253
14. *Oreilles de Cochon* 254
15. Cajun Tac Tac 255
16. Creole Pecan Pralines I 256
17. Creole Pecan Pralines II 257
18. Christmas Creole Toffee 258

Appendixes

Cajun/Creole Resources 259
Cajun and Creole Restaurants, Nightclubs, and Dance Halls 262
Famous Festivals of Louisiana 268
Tables, Measurements, and Equivalents 270
Selected Bibliography 271
Historical Louisiana Cookbook References .273
Index 275
Colonel Paul's Seasoning Blend 281

Acknowledgments

There are so many people who we would sincerely like to thank for all of their help and wonderful assistance with this project. First off to Kathy Goodwin, Wanda McKoy, Dottie Rager, Natalie Kinsaul, Karen Ivey, and Laura Noon. A heartfelt thanks to Jennifer O'Dwyer, who designed the fabulous place settings for the book jacket. We salute the Viking Chefs, Quito McKenna, and Demietriek Scott, for helping make our recipes better!

Thanks to Keith Dunn, who took pictures of all of the place settings and photographed the book cover. Another is Christi Key, who spent time photographing the reenactors at Fort Toulouse to get us some authentically historic pictures. Thank you to John Rouveyrol for driving The Colonel, and Jean Williams for driving Miss Edie. We appreciate Norris Jackson, Mark Aldridge, and Jenny Paul for their editing talents. Thanks to Jim Parker, the director of Fort Toulouse state Park in Wetumpka, Alabama, who was gracious in allowing us to take pictures at this historic site, and to all of the many reenactors who so kindly posed for us in their historically accurate period French and Indian outfits. We appreciate Dr. Tom Paul Jr. for allowing us the use of his home to shoot our pictures for the book jacket. A very special thank you to Colonel Paul's mother, Ann Paul, who showed us unwavering support throughout the writing of this book. We would like to say thank you to all who helped in some way to make this book possible.

A special memory to the late Jerry Yarley, who was an animal right's activist, TV/film producer, and good friend. He so loved this book and TV concept of food history.

A big thank you goes out to the Viking cooking class in Buckhead, Georgia, and their chefs who helped with the testing of these recipes. For more information go to their website www.thevikingstore.net.

We appreciate Ron Pitkin, president of Cumberland House Publishing, and his staff for helping us make such a beautiful book. *Merci bien.*

Cajun AND Creole COOKING

with Miss Edie and the Colonel

Part I

Equipment, Terms, and Cooking Techniques

The Louisiana Lifestyle

Louisiana is a state of mind as much as it is a physical place. The very name "Louisiana" conjures up vivid romantic images. Steamy moonlit Southern nights, lazy flowing bayous, ancient cypress trees covered in Spanish moss, picturesque plantations along the Mississippi River, sultry jazz in a French Quarter café, small town dance halls filled with couples dancing to Cajun music, charmingly feminine Creole Southern belles, and *fabulous* food! The most delicious-tasting food in all of North America. In other parts of the country they may eat, but here in Louisiana we *dine*!

Louisiana's extraordinary cooking styles are a wonderful mixture of French, Spanish, African, American Indian, and Italian culinary traditions all carefully blended together to form a truly American cuisine. Its sumptuous flavors make for a gourmet experience unlike anything tasted anywhere else in the world, and its delectable dishes have become legendary. Our culture and our heritage are different from anywhere else in the South. Our cuisine is a reflection of our unique lifestyle and the special history that we share as a courageous people.

It is not difficult to cook in the Cajun/Creole style, but to do so one must be able to "think" about food and about living as we do. People in Louisiana are very laid back and believe that life is to be enjoyed and lived to its fullest. Sharing good times with family and friends is what is most important to us. We have a saying in Louisiana: "You're not here for a long time, you're here for a *good* time!" Good food is part of our *joie de vivre* and goes hand in hand with family, friends, music, and good times. It is a blessing to be shared with others and savored for the subtle nuances of flavor that it tantalizes us with.

Food appreciation is a part of our enjoyment of living, and so food preparation is an art that is handed down in families from generation to generation. The family meal and Southern hospitality are time-honored traditions that are an important part of our way of life. The family meal is a sacred institution to us, a time when the family comes together every day to connect and bond over food. No TV show, sporting event, or social function is more important to us than this. We use our cuisine to bring people together to celebrate living and to share the happiness that we feel from each other's company. Visitors to Louisiana are often quite taken by the genuine warmth and hospitality that they are shown. This is perhaps the most delightful aspect of our culture, which believes strongly in sharing our celebration of life with others.

Our philosophy of life and our wonderful cuisine are both products of our truly unique history. When you are preparing a gumbo or a jambalaya you are not just cooking a recipe, you are resurrecting a piece of Louisiana history and experiencing a true culinary moment in time. Many of these recipes and cooking techniques are actually centuries old and are a reflection not only of our Cajun and Creole heritage but also of the numerous and diverse ethnic groups that came together to create them.

As you read through our book you will learn about the various ingredients found in our cuisine and acquire the tools necessary to prepare dishes in the Louisiana style. We will also teach you certain tips and techniques about cooking in general and share with you some wonderful recipes so that you, too, can prepare our food just like a Louisiana native. But you will also be learning about the history and lifestyle of a remarkable people—a people who through necessity overcame adversity, took from the bounty of the land they were given, and came together to contribute something to our common gumbo pot, creating one of the world's truly great culinary traditions.

Cooking in the Cajun/Creole Manner

In Louisiana we say that to cook in the Cajun/Creole style one must have *"la bouche Creole"*—the Creole mouth. That is to say, you must understand a particular taste that we are looking for in our cuisine. Taste and flavor are everything in this style of cooking, and we are known to do *anything* to make our food more delectable to the palate. It is not difficult to learn; once you have studied the various elements that make up our cuisine and the different cooking techniques that are involved in preparing it, you too will be able to "Cajunize" any dish that you like.

First, you have to approach each dish in a Louisiana manner. Now anybody can cook a piece of chicken or fish simply by putting it into a microwave and zapping it for a few minutes until it is done. Boring. In Louisiana the first thing that we think of is "how can I make this taste the most wonderful way possible?" Well, you could fry it, bake it, or broil it; you could stuff it, cover it with herbs and spices, or make a wonderfully tasty sauce to cover it with. You could cook certain vegetables along with it and place it over a bed of fluffy rice. There are numerous things that you could do to turn a very simple dish into something epicurean. And *that* is what Louisiana cooking is all about.

There are seven basic elements that make up Cajun/Creole-style cuisine, and the more you learn about them the more you will be able to "think" about preparing food as we do in Louisiana. These elements are roux, rice, spice, stock, trinity, wines & liquors, and sauces. Each of these will be discussed in greater detail in the following chapters, but these elements in various combinations are what make our cuisine so truly unique. They have all evolved over the years as different ethnic groups have immigrated to the state and added their own unique culinary influences into our collective gumbo pot. By learning about each of these you will be able to master the art of preparing wonderful dishes with both subtle and complex flavors that will make each meal a truly delectable dining experience.

It is *not* difficult to do this. Honestly. It merely takes a little knowledge about the background of our cuisine and a good understanding about each of these elements and how they can be used together in various combinations. Each one of these has evolved especially for the sole purpose of adding a unique flavor to whatever it is that you are cooking. And to acquire a good *"bouche Creole"* you must always be thinking about how you can make your dish more flavorful and interesting to the palate. To us, that is what cooking is all about . . . mastering the art of preparing truly delicious food that will make your family enjoy coming together to appreciate each other's company and share a special family bond over the fabulous meals that you prepare.

Food preparation is a family experience in Louisiana. These various cooking techniques are taught by parents to their children at a very early age and passed down through the generations. Once mastered, people pride themselves on the delicious meals they are able to prepare, and families love to share their food and this knowledge with others. Every meal is approached as a unique dining experience to be savored and enjoyed for all of the delectable flavors that the cook is able to give it. So the more you learn about these elements and techniques, the more accomplished at cooking you will become.

All it takes is a little study and some practice to master this. Don't be afraid to experiment in the kitchen when you are there; it is through trial and error that we learn. Once you understand how we like to prepare dishes and give them more flavor, you can apply these techniques to any recipe, and soon you will find yourself thinking about food preparation just like we do in Louisiana. Just keep thinking about how you can make each dish more flavorful and you will understand the true key to cooking in the Cajun/Creole style.

You will notice that many of these various techniques are fattening. Since flavor is the most important thing to us, it is very easy to make a dish *very* tasty by preparing it in a fattening manner. This does not mean that your food *has* to be that way, however, if you do not wish it to be so. Certainly one can steam or poach a piece of fish with some delicious herbs and spices that can taste very Cajun/Creole and still not be fattening. The choice of how to prepare the dish is up to you. That is why we want to teach you about how to think about our cuisine in the manner that we do, so that you will understand the basic concepts involved and develop your own culinary style.

Cajun/Creole cooking is the perfect cooking style to use for fancy dinner parties when you really want to impress others with your culinary ability. It can be rich and flavorful and sumptuous to taste. But once you have learned about the many ways that we like to prepare our food, you will find that there are many different techniques one can use to make food flavorful yet still healthy. How to prepare it is up to you. By studying the various elements that make up our cuisine and our different cooking techniques, you learn to create wonderfully delicious meals that you can share with your family and friends for years to come. *Bon appetit!*

The Joy of Cast-Iron Cookware

Cast-iron cookware holds a very revered place in the heart of the Louisiana cook. To us it is much more than just something to cook food in. Cast iron is seen as something magical which not only produces wonderfully delicious dishes, but also wonderfully memorable times shared with those we love. In addition to its practical advantages, there is a certain mystique about cooking with cast iron, and in Louisiana it is preferred to all other types of cookware.

The use of cast iron in cooking is centuries old, going all the way back to biblical times. The great advantage that cast iron has over all other forms of cookware is in the nature of the iron itself. Iron retains heat better than most other metals and also disperses it evenly. Thus when you are cooking a chicken in a cast-iron skillet, the sides of the skillet will be just as hot as the bottom, which is on top of the stove. As a result your food is cooked evenly all around and without the fear of burning or scorching. Iron also holds heat longer than other metals, which makes cast-iron pots the best slow-cooking pots of all. These qualities of uniform heat dispersion and heat retention are the reasons that cast-iron cookware has survived down through the centuries and still is the cookware preferred by so many.

Cast iron has been used in Louisiana since the very beginnings of the colony itself back in 1699. It was the French who first brought cast-iron pots into Louisiana to both cook and trade with the Indians. As our cuisine began to evolve, it was cast iron that we used to prepare our meals with. When African slaves brought with them the recipe for gumbo, it was cooked in a cast-iron pot. Indeed it was the African slow-cooking method utilizing a cast-iron pot that made for gumbo's delicious taste. Cast-iron cookware is at the very heart of our cuisine, and we are very sentimentally attached to it. A traditional wedding gift in Louisiana is a cast-iron pot and skillet along with a wire whisk as these are the three tools necessary to cook meals in the Cajun/Creole style. Well-seasoned cast-iron cookware is also treasured as a family heirloom and handed down in families from one generation to the next. So as you can see, people in Louisiana have a very *serious* romance with cast-iron cookware and truly value it *most* highly!

If you have never cooked with cast iron before, there are some things that you need to be aware of. Though cast iron is wonderful to cook with, it is also very heavy. Cast iron's heavy quality gives it incredible durability. In fact, with proper care, cast-iron cookware can last for *hundreds* of years. Talk about good value for your money! Also, brand new cast iron needs to be seasoned before use. This is done by baking oil onto and into the surface of the iron all over, which will help protect it from rust and also give it a non-stick finish. Over time, a very well-seasoned and used pot will have a surface just as non-stick as one covered in Teflon. The procedure for seasoning a cast-iron pot is not difficult, but does require some care.

Seasoning Your Cast Iron

First you will need to line the lower rack of your oven with aluminum foil to catch any drippings. Place the top rack in the middle position of the oven, and then preheat the oven to 350 degrees.

While the oven is preheating you need to wash your cast-iron pot, skillet, or whatever with a mild soap and a stiff brush. Be sure to scour out the pot and the lid very well to remove any dirt that might still be on it. This will be the last time that you ever use soap on the iron because iron is a porous metal and the soap can get into it, which can cause problems when cooking. We will get to cleaning and care of your iron in just a minute.

After you have washed the iron you need to rinse it off *very* well. Rinse and rinse and rinse again. I like to use a squirt bottle with vinegar in it to help to rinse off all the soap or put some vinegar in the rinse water. You have to make sure that there is *no* soap left in the iron at all.

Once your iron is thoroughly rinsed you need to coat the metal *all* over (including the lid) with some type of shortening or vegetable oil. Many people like to use lard, others vegetable oil or a vegetable oil spray. Just be sure to give the iron a good coating of the oil all over the metal.

When all of this is done and your oven is ready, place the pot on the middle rack of the oven face down and heat for one hour. After one hour, turn the heat off and let the oven cool down to room temperature. Once the oven has cooled down you can remove the iron. You will notice that it has a slight brown finish to it. If you would like to season the iron even further and give it an even darker appearance, repeat this process. It is now ready to use and enjoy for the rest of your lifetime!

Caring for Your Cast Iron

With proper care, your cast iron will honestly outlive you and your children and your children's, children's, children's children! Here are some tips on the proper care for your cast-iron cookware.

- After cooking with your cast iron let it cool down before washing it. Never put a hot pot into cold water. Wash your iron in hot water *only*. No soap or detergent at all. If you need something abrasive, use a stiff brush or sprinkle some salt onto it and wipe out with a damp towel. Remember, you do not want to use soap as that can remove some of the finish and may get into the iron, causing you some problems the next time that you cook. Do not worry. The pot will still get clean. I like to spray my iron with a squirt bottle filled with vinegar and rinse off very well, which will kill a lot of germs.

- When you have finished washing your iron, dry thoroughly with a towel and then recoat the surface of the metal with a light coating of oil. This will help to protect the finish and also help protect the surface of the metal from rust.

- Store your cookware in a cool dry place. If you have a lid for a pot you can place a paper towel between it and the pot to help air circulation.

- If you do find any rust on your pots, wash off with a mild detergent and scour off the rust thoroughly. Then reseason the pot as you did before.

Using Your Cast Iron

Cooking in cast iron is a true joy. There is something magical about the look of a well-seasoned, black cast-iron pot ready to use. Nothing cooks better, and when you are cooking with cast iron you are continuing a centuries-old tradition. You can feel the history as you prepare a meal using the same implements that our colonial ancestors used. And over time, your pot will take on a personal history of its own as its surface becomes more and more seasoned with use. There is nothing you will use that is more historic in your kitchen, and it will soon become a part of your own family's personal culinary history as well.

It is so easy to cook with cast iron; you do not have to worry about what type of utensils to use with it for fear of scratching its surface. It's tough! (After all, it *is* made of iron. . . .) Before using, make sure that your skillet or pot has a nice light coating of oil on the surface, then heat it to your desired temperature for cooking. It is better to put food into a pan that has already been heated up than to put it into a cold pan and then heat it up. This will allow for quicker and more even cooking overall. The real strength of cast iron lies in its durability and in its unique ability to retain heat, allowing for even cooking and also making it perfect for slow cooking. However, since cast iron does retain heat so well, you must allow for that. If a pan is on high and you turn the heat down to low, the pan will still be hot and take a little while before it cools down, for such is the nature of iron.

There are several different types of cast-iron cookware that are recommended for you to have in your kitchen. First off one needs to purchase a couple of good cast-iron skillets about 10 inches in diameter—one about 2 inches deep and another one about 3 inches deep. A cast-iron chicken fryer is a real joy to have and chicken cooked in cast iron has an incredible flavor. In addition, one should have a couple of cast-iron Dutch ovens or pots for making soups, stews, and gumbos; a 5-quart and a 7-quart are recommended. A little 3-quart Dutch oven is a real nice size if you live alone and do not need to cook for a large number of people all the time. Once you get into cast-iron cooking and learn about how wonderful it is you will want to increase the size of your collection with numerous other types of pots, pans, and griddles.

The most popular brand of cast iron used in Louisiana is made by the Lodge Company out of South Pittsburg, Tennessee. This company has been manufacturing superior quality cast-iron cookware since 1898. It is relatively easy to find in grocery stores or restaurant supply outlets around the country or you can go to their website and buy it online at: www.lodgemfg.com. Their address and phone number are:

Lodge Manufacturing Company
P.O. Box 380
South Pittsburg, Tennessee 37380
(423) 837-7181

Give them a call with any questions that you might have about their product, and they will be most happy to help you.

Essential Utensils

To cook in the Louisiana style, several types of utensils and cookware are essential. If you take the time to acquire these items, you will find it makes your cooking much easier and the final product more tasty.

Cast-Iron Cookware

As previously mentioned, we love to use cast iron to cook with in Louisiana. Be sure to get good-quality cast iron. We feel that Lodge cast iron is the best to use (see above for more information).

Basically you will need a good cast-iron skillet and one or two cast-iron pots. A good 10-inch cast-iron skillet is the perfect skillet to use for making a roux; and if you want to blacken anything, there really isn't anything else that you can use. Also get at least one cast-iron pot, either 5 or 7 quarts. You will find that a good pot like this will take on a magical quality and the meals that you prepare in them will become very special.

Stainless Steel Cookware

Although we *do* love our cast-iron pots to cook in, it is also advisable that you get some good-quality 18/10 stainless steel cookware as well. Copper cookware lined with stainless steel is actually the best to use next to cast iron, since copper is also an excellent conductor of heat. Copper is wonderful to cook with and also looks very pretty hanging up in your kitchen. However, copper cookware is very expensive and also requires a lot of polishing after use to keep it looking shiny and nice. Therefore stainless steel is more recommended for overall general use (unless you happen to be independently wealthy and have lots of time to spend in your kitchen taking care of your copper cookware).

A good stainless steel chef's skillet about 10 inches is wonderful to sauté vegetables in, and can make the job very easy. You will want to make certain desserts, such as Bananas Foster, in a stainless steel pan as well. Some nice small steel saucepans are necessary for cooking rice and are also good for boiling or steaming vegetables or even heating up a can of soup. You can now find stainless steel cookware that has a glass lid so that you can see what is going on inside of the saucepan while you are cooking. In addition, you will want a good-quality steel stock pot, about 8 or 10 quarts, for making stock and boiling pasta.

Chef's Knives

A good set of professional chef's knives are an indispensable tool to have in your kitchen. The biggest problem that most people have with cooking is that they do not know how to chop; thus it takes a long time for them to do their prep work. A really good set of knives will make this task *much* easier indeed. Most chefs like to use Henckel brand knives made in Germany. They are *wonderfully* made knives that with care can last you a lifetime. However, if you do not wish to invest in these, then any professional, good-quality, heavy knives will do. Keep them sharp! A sharp knife is much safer than a dull one because you can let the knife do all of the work and will not have to force it when using it, thus increasing the possibility that you might cut yourself. Wash them by hand. Do not put them in the dishwasher as that can ruin them. If you cannot afford a good set of knives and have to pick only one, go for a good chef's knife (also known as a French knife). This is the largest, big-blade knife in a set and is designed for chopping vegetables. It will make cutting very quick and easy, and with practice will cut your prep time in half.

Cutting Board

Use a good-quality thick cutting board when you do your chopping. A wooden board looks very pretty but is not completely safe to use since wood is porous and bacteria can get caught in it. Get one made of some of the newer thick plastics or polymers instead. They are easier to clean and are safer to use than wood.

Wire Whisk

A good, well-made stainless steel wire whisk is the right tool to use when making a roux. Nothing makes one better and trust me, if you get into this kind of cooking you are going to make a *lot* of rouxs! Get one with a good thick handle. It will make your roux-making much easier.

Wooden Spoons

There is a certain romance about using a good set of wooden spoons. Our ancestors used them for centuries and they still work really well, particularly if you are cooking with cast iron. Keep them clean and oiled to protect the wood. They are the perfect implement to use to scrape the little charred bits of food from the bottom of your cast iron pot without scratching it. They also look very nostalgic in your kitchen.

Salad Tongs

Most chefs use salad tongs *not* for mixing salad but for stirring food in the pan. They are very handy to use and can make stirring and mixing in a pan very easy. Once you get the hang of them you will prefer to use them instead of a spoon when you are cooking.

Colander

A nice big colander is good to have to strain your pasta. You will find other uses for it as well once you have one and will be glad to know that it is there when you need it.

Mixing Bowls

It is recommended that you obtain a good set of both metal and glass mixing bowls. They are very useful to have both for mixing ingredients for desserts and other dishes as well.

Casserole Dishes

Several nice-sized casserole dishes are also recommended to have to bake in. They can be made of CorningWare or Pyrex or whatever you prefer. They will work very well for baking Louisiana-style casseroles and making some desserts.

Tupperware

A good set of nice Tupperware-type plastic containers will be very useful. Cajun/Creole cuisine is the perfect cuisine for leftovers, and plastic containers such as these will prove invaluable to you for storing both chopped and pre-prepared food as well as leftovers in your refrigerator.

Cake and Pie Pans

If you have a sweet tooth and plan to prepare any of the numerous Louisiana-style cakes and pies, you will need to purchase some nice cake and pie pans.

Electric Mixer

The primary electrical device that is recommended for you to have is a good, professional electric mixer. It is *so* much easier to blend ingredients for desserts if you have one of these. It will save you a lot of time in the kitchen and will beat and blend your ingredients so much better than you will be able to do by hand. We recommend that you spend a little extra money on one of these to get a really nice one. The better the mixer, the better your desserts will come out and the easier it will be for you to make them.

Basic Cooking Tips

1. Always remember that when you are in the kitchen *you* are the chef so what you say goes. Don't be afraid to experiment. That is how you learn. Be creative! Try different things and see how they go. It is not difficult to learn how to cook; it just takes patience and practice.

2. *Pay attention* to what you are doing and don't get distracted. Take your time and be careful. Don't get in a big hurry. You will find that you can prepare meals just as good as anyone else if you focus on what you are doing.

3. Do *all* of your prep work *before* you start to cook. One of the biggest reasons why people overcook or burn something is because they start to cook before they have finished chopping up everything. Then the pot is cooking on the stove while you are not paying attention to it and doing something else. So make sure that you have chopped up everything first and gotten all of your ingredients ready before you start to cook. That way you can focus all of your attention on the cooking process.

4. *Be careful!* Take proper safety precautions. Accidents can happen to the best of us. Have a good-quality fire extinguisher handy at easy reach. Remember, most fires in the kitchen are grease fires and water will *not* put them out—only spread them. So have a fire extinguisher on hand just in case you need it. Small fires can also be smothered by dousing them with salt or a damp cloth.

5. Always use the freshest ingredients that you can find. The flavor and consistency of them will be superior and will make your dishes taste *so* much better.

6. Hand chopping of ingredients in most cases is better than using a food processor because the food processor has a tendency to grind everything up into a mush, which can ruin the texture of the ingredients. Chopping by hand leaves the food much more intact, thereby retaining more of its texture and natural juices.

7. For more flavor, season everything every step of the way during the cooking process. Herbs and spices will add a tremendous amount of flavor to your dish and can make even an average dish taste phenomenal! Be careful, however, not to overseason. You don't want to overpower the dish, only enhance the food's natural flavor.

8. Remember, the first 5 to 10 minutes of cooking time in any dish are the most important. That is when your base flavor will be built.

9. Heat up your skillets and the oil before you put the food in them. Otherwise your food can get overcooked or cooked unevenly. By heating up the oil first it will allow for much more even cooking and quicker cooking time as well.

10. When boiling water for vegetables or other food, bring the water to a good boil without anything in it. Then put in the food and turn the heat down to a simmer and cook for just a few minutes. This way you can avoid overboiling your food, which will break it down and make it soft and mushy, losing most of its nutrients.

11. Steaming vegetables retains more of the vitamins than does boiling. Ideally, vegetables should still be a bit crisp when cooked.

12. Remember, the longer that you cook food on a lower heat, the more flavorful it will become and the more juicy and tender it will be as well.

13. Throwing pasta up against the wall to see if it will stick will *not* tell you whether it is done. It will only make a mess on your wall that you now have to clean. It is better to remove a piece of pasta from the pot and run it under cold water and then taste it to see if it is a consistency that you like. The classical way to cook pasta is to boil it until it is what the Italians call *al dente,* which literally means "to the tooth." That is where the pasta is not soft and mushy but has a little give or firmness to it. Most Americans tend to cook their pasta until it is very soft. Try cooking it to this consistency instead and see if you like it.

14. If you place a few marbles in the bottom of a pot of water when you are steaming something, they will let you know when the water is getting low; they will start to bounce about and clatter when the water is almost gone, thus alerting you to this fact.

15. Do not use a garlic press to peel your garlic as it will crush the bud and make it bitter. To peel, simply use the flat of a chef's knife to smush the bud lightly, which will separate it from the peel and then you can chop it fine.

16. Marinating your meats in oil and vinegar will make them much more tender and juicy. It is also a wonderful way for you to give them much more flavor. Most wet marinades such as this use equal parts of oil and a wine vinegar (such as olive oil and white wine vinegar for chicken and fish and red wine vinegar for red meats). You can also sprinkle Cajun/Creole seasonings into the marinade and the meat will absorb all of these wonderful flavors, which will make for a succulent taste when it is cooked. Place the meat in the marinade and put it in the refrigerator, turning the meat every hour or so. Leave it in there for at least four hours, or overnight if you can. You will love the outcome, I guarantee!

17. Measure your hand! You will find that when most people cup their hand they can hold about ½ cup of ingredients. By doing this you will learn what your hand can hold and thus begin to learn to cook by "feel." Take a little flour or cornmeal or salt and pour it into your hand and see just how much it can hold. Try pouring a tablespoon and a teaspoon of salt in your hand to give you an idea of what it looks like in your hand as well. This can help you to measure when you cannot find measuring spoons or cups.

18. Be sure to clean as you go when you cook. This will avoid having a *big* mess when you are finished and make your wife feel *much* more comfortable with you piddling around in the kitchen, thus making for a much happier marriage.

19. Be sure to clean everything *very* thoroughly before, during, and after you cook. Bacteria is always a concern when doing your prep work, and raw foods such as chicken can carry dangerous bacteria such as E. coli. To properly clean your surface area use clean water with dishwashing liquid in it and pour into it a small capful of Clorox bleach to wipe everything down with. This is a powerful cleaner that can kill dangerous bacteria and keep your cutting board and surface area clean. Also have a squirt bottle filled with distilled white vinegar in it to spray around the kitchen. This will kill many forms of bacteria and is not as harsh as Clorox (although Clorox is the best way to kill most bacteria). Distilled white vinegar is also nice to use in the rinse water when you wash your dishes as it will clean off soap scum and leave your dishes smelling very fresh and

clean. Rosewater will also do this, as will a little fresh lemon juice. Just add some into your rinse water and everything you rinse will come out lemony fresh and smelling like a rose.

20. If you want to learn how to "flip" the food in the pan when you are sautéing just like the fancy chefs do, you can practice by putting a slice of toast in a small skillet and flipping it over until you can do it with relative ease.

21. Finally, *have fun!* Cooking should be fun and enjoyable. Play some music while you cook, dance about and savor the whole experience. It can be a wonderful time to both create and share the meal that you are preparing. So really get into it and enjoy yourself!

The 7 Elements of Louisiana Cooking

There are seven elements that make up Louisiana cooking. Virtually all of our traditional dishes (with the exception of our desserts) have some or all of these elements in them. These seven elements are roux, rice, spice, stock, trinity, wines and liquors, and sauces. Master each of these elements and you will know how to prepare virtually any Cajun/Creole dish with relative ease.

1. Roux

Roux (pronounced *roo*) is a base sauce made by cooking equal parts flour and oil (or some other shortening such as butter or lard) in a heavy skillet over a medium heat, stirring constantly with a wire whisk. The use of roux in our cuisine dates back to the French colonial period and is the basis for many of our traditional dishes such as gumbo, étouffée, sauce piquant, and others. It is so commonly used that, when describing a recipe to someone, Louisiana cooks usually start by saying, "First you make a roux." And indeed, once you have made a roux you can literally make scores of different dishes.

Roux is used both for thickening dishes and as a sauce for flavoring them. When roux is put into a sauce or a soup it will act as a thickening agent much like cornstarch. It has a marvelous nutlike flavor it will add to any dish it is put into. Roux is cooked until it reaches the desired color that the cook wants it to be. The longer that you cook it the darker it will become and the nuttier the flavor will be. However, the longer that you cook it the less of a thickening agent it also will be. What you are actually doing as you cook your roux is to cook out all of the glutens from the flour in it. So whatever color you make your roux is extremely important and will directly affect the color, flavor, and thickness of your dish.

In general, white roux is made with butter and used for white sauces, while medium brown, dark brown, or black roux is made with oil or lard. Medium brown roux is usually used for beef and game dishes and thicker gravies, while dark brown roux is used more for pork, rabbit, fowl, and seafood dishes. Many Cajun cooks have been known to make a black roux for their gumbos, but most people tend to use a dark brown roux instead. Again, this is all very general and just depends upon the desires of the cook. As you become more experienced at making roux you will learn more about its characteristics, and can then make a better decision as to what color you think is appropriate for a particular dish.

Safety Precautions

There are certain things that you need to be aware of before you start to make your roux. First, you want to use a good heavy dry skillet to cook your roux in. Cast iron works best, but if you do not have that a good heavy-gauge stainless steel skillet will work just fine. It needs to be clean and free from any moisture. Next, you want to use a professional wire whisk with a big handle to hold on to. This works much better than using just a wooden spoon and will make your roux much more fluffy.

Roux can take a good twenty minutes or so to cook, depending on how high you have your heat, so make sure you have plenty of time to devote to making it with *no* distractions at all. Take your phone off of the hook. Once you start to cook your roux you *cannot* stop it for anything. You have to continue until it is completed so don't even *think* about doing *anything* else at this time. If your roux should burn then you have to start all over again so *pay attention* to what you are doing.

You also need to be *very* careful as you are cooking it. Roux is usually made on a medium to high heat and is very hot. Should any of it splash up on you while you are making it, it will stick to your skin and burn just like hot candy. In the New Orleans restaurant industry roux is referred to as "Cajun Napalm" because of this characteristic, so you want to pay attention to what you are doing and wear a long-sleeved shirt while you cook it. If you do get some on your hand or arm, run it under cold water immediately.

It is recommended that you heat your oil over a medium heat and have the air vent on over your stove. Making a roux can produce a fair amount of smoke and you do not want to set off your smoke detectors. Also, have a fire extinguisher handy. Some oils such as olive oil have a very low burning point, and if the heat is too high it could catch on fire. If the oil in the skillet does catch on fire don't panic. You can put it out very easily. Simply take the skillet off of the burner and put the fire out with your fire extinguisher or dowse the pan with a generous amount of salt (which will smother the fire and also put it out). *Do not try to put the fire out with water.* Water will only spread the fire and make the situation much worse. And do *not* try to pour it into the sink either because you could set yourself on fire!

Cooking Your Roux

The dimensions for making a roux are usually half flour and half oil or shortening. It may be in tablespoons or cups, depending on the size of the dish that you are preparing. To cook your roux, heat up the oil in the skillet over a medium heat (this usually does not take more than 4 to 5 minutes). When the oil is hot enough add in your flour a little bit at a time and begin to stir it up with your wire whisk. You need to stir this continuously for the entire time that you are making it. *Do not stop stirring* for anything. As long as you keep stirring the roux it will not burn. So keep it moving. You can whistle Dixie if you like while you are making it. That would be a nice Southern touch.

After a few minutes of stirring (which may seem like hours), you will begin to notice a wonderful nutlike smell starting to emanate from the skillet. This is the glutens beginning to cook out of the flour. Very shortly now you will notice the roux start to change color and get a darker brown. At this point many first-time roux makers get scared and even panic as they feel that now they have got a tiger by the tail and are not sure what to do next. *Just keep on stirring.* Remember, as long as you keep the mixture moving in the pan it will not burn. If you are a tad bit concerned you can turn your heat down to low and keep on stirring. That will slow down the cooking process. With a modern stove we have an advantage that our culinary ancestors did not have: we can raise and lower our heat very quickly. So if you feel that the roux is starting to cook a bit fast for you then just reduce the heat a bit to slow down its cooking. *Just keep on stirring.* If you like you can even take the skillet off of the heat entirely until you regain your courage and then put it back on. *Just keep on stirring.*

Once the roux begins to change color it will start to darken very quickly; at this point you have to make a decision as to just how dark you want your roux to be. This will depend on what you are cooking the roux for and just how brave you truly are if you are a first-time roux maker. When your roux has reached the color that you want it to be you are ready to stop it. To stop the roux from cooking take the skillet off of the heat, put your whisk down and pick up a spoon, and then stir into it your chopped vegetables. Be sure to stir the vegetables in very well. It will produce a bit of steam when you pour them in, but don't worry. That is alright. We use a specific vegetable combination in Louisiana called trinity, which consists of chopped onions, bell peppers, and celery. These vegetables are water based and the water in them will stop the roux from cooking and at the same time begin to cook them as well.

C'est voilà! Now you have done it! Aren't you proud? At this point both the roux and the vegetables will start to impart flavors that will smell heavenly. You can now add this to your dish if you like; however, many chefs at this point will put the skillet back onto the stove on a lower heat and continue to cook the vegetables for a short time while they season the roux with herbs and spices. Once your roux is completed, you can literally make hundreds of different dishes, depending on what you have in your fridge.

2 ✐ Rice

Rice is an integral part of Louisiana cooking. Rice production began in the Louisiana colony as early as 1716 under the French, and so many of our traditional dishes are prepared and then served over rice. Rice usually comes in two forms: brown and white. Once harvested, the grains are separated from the stalks by threshing, and the inedible hulls are removed by pounding, grinding, or cracking the grain. This produces brown rice, the type most eaten in Asia. It is rich in vitamins. However, it takes a bit longer to cook and can become rancid if stored for a long time. In the West, rice is further processed by rubbing the grain to remove the outer layer or bran and then "polishing" it with an abrasive such as talc, chalk, or glucose. This produces white rice, which takes less time to cook and can be stored for longer periods of time but has no vitamins, since they are all contained in the bran that was removed.

Louisiana is the third largest producer of rice in the United States. In addition to the standard "Louisiana rice," which is grown in the state, there are two delicious varieties of rice that are produced here as well. The first of these is called "popcorn rice." Popcorn rice is a hybrid of Basmati rice (grown in India) with Louisiana rice. This cross produces a rice that has a rich nut-like flavor reminiscent of popcorn that is simply heavenly! The other strain is called Wild Pecan Rice and is produced by Conrad Rice Mill in New Iberia, Louisiana. This variety of rice has a rich pecan flavor to it that is truly delicious. Both of these varieties of rice will add a wonderful nutty flavor to your dishes.

Cooking Your Rice

It is not difficult to cook rice, and you can find recipes for rice in the recipe section of this book. Basically the proportions for white rice are one cup of rice to two cups of water. You bring the water to a boil and then put in the rice. Next you bring the water back to a good rolling boil and then put the lid on the pot and turn the heat down to simmer, cooking the rice for 20 minutes. After 20 minutes you lift off the lid and voilà! Your rice is done. Brown rice is cooked in a similar manner but the proportions are a bit different. Instead of two cups of water you use 2¼ cups of water to 1 cup of brown rice and cook for 45 minutes.

Now this is all well and good, but there are some ways that you can add *much* more flavor to your rice when you cook it should you wish. First, instead of using just plain water you can use a good chicken stock, which will give the rice a wonderful chicken flavor. (If you are a vegetarian or don't like chicken you can use a vegetable stock or some other type of stock instead.) You can also add in a small pat of butter, a teaspoon of Worcestershire sauce, and a little Cajun/Creole seasoning and when you take the lid off of the pot you will have what we call "tasty rice," a *deliciously* flavorful rice that is just out of this world!

3 ∞ Spices, Herbs, and Seasonings

If you had to sum up Cajun/Creole cuisine in one word, it would be *flavor!* People in Louisiana will do *anything* and *everything* to get more flavor into their dishes. Bland food just doesn't cut it with us. Period. And this is where the true art of cooking comes into play. It is not difficult to get more flavor into your cooking. By playing around in the kitchen and experimenting you can learn to become very creative and adept at producing *very* flavorful dishes when you cook.

One of the principal keys to flavoring your food is to use herbs and spices in your dishes. Now people in Louisiana tend to use *a lot* of different herbs and spices in their cooking (something that continues to baffle our French cousins, who tend to use only one or two herbs in preparing their food). Because of the French and Spanish influences on our cooking, we like to use not only several herbs but also several hot spices as well. We like for our food to excite your mouth with wonderful flavors that will enhance the natural flavor of the dish and make you crave each and every bite.

Herbs

Using herbal combinations in our food dates back to the French colonial period in Louisiana. It was the French who brought with them their own knowledge of using flavorful herbs to make their food much more appetizing. Traditionally, we like to use bay leaf, garlic, sweet basil, thyme, marjoram, parsley, and filé for our herbs. The use of oregano in Creole cuisine increased with the coming of the great Italian immigration in the late nineteenth and early twentieth centuries. The extensive use of oregano in Italian cooking had an influence on Creole cuisine; however, this "Italian connection" in Creole cooking did not make its way out into the Cajun country as a whole, and as a result, this is one of the main differences between Creole and Cajun culinary styles.

Bay leaf (*Laurus Nobili*)—Comes from the bay laurel tree native to the Mediterranean. In ancient Greece and Rome a wreath of laurel leaves was made to crown the winners of the Olympics, scholars, poets, and famous people—hence its name in Latin, which means "to praise the famous." Bay leaf is an essential herb in both French and Cajun/Creole cooking. It is used in soups and stews and goes well with fish, meat and poultry. Bay has a very strong flavor and should be used sparingly. One or two leaves will do for a pot of gumbo.

Garlic (*Allium Sativum*)—A perennial plant native to Asia but grown in the Mediterranean for centuries. Garlic gets its common name from the Anglo-Saxon *gar* (lance) and *leac* (pot herb). In ancient times it was prescribed as medicine. It does have the medicinal quality of discouraging many forms of bacteria (and let's not forget vampires either). Its strong, sensuous flavor is indispensable in Latin and Creole cuisine and goes very well with any savory dish.

Sweet basil (*Osimum Basilicum*)—A small bushy herb native to India but grown in the Mediterranean for thousands of years. The ancient Romans considered the herb to be an aphrodisiac sacred to the goddess Venus and used it extensively in their cuisine. The herb was introduced into French cooking in 1533, when Catherine de Medici of Florence married King Henry II and brought with her court several Italian chefs (this was also the beginning of what we today consider French cuisine as well). The French refer to sweet basil as the *herbe royale* and use it extensively in their cuisine. In Louisiana the herb is considered a favorite with most cooks because of its rich, buttery flavor that is especially wonderful on tomato dishes as well as meats, seafood, poultry, and vegetables.

Thyme (*Thymus Vulgaris*)—A small perennial plant with tiny leaves and little purple flowers native to the southwestern Mediterranean and southern Italy. Thyme was used extensively in Ancient Greece medicinally as well as in the kitchen, and even today thyme oil (thymol) is used in mouthwash and as a treatment for coughs. The word *thymus* comes from the Latin meaning "energy" and it is believed in aromatherapy to increase one's strength and energy. Thyme has a savory-sweet flavor that is truly wonderful and is used throughout France and Louisiana in virtually all of our dishes.

Marjoram (*Origanum Marjorana*)—A small bushy herb with small white flowers native to Asia and naturalized to southern Europe. In ancient Rome wreaths of marjoram were worn by the bride and groom to symbolize love, honor, and happiness. In Medieval Europe it was thought to be an antidote for poisons and convulsions as well as a culinary seasoning. During the Elizabethan era in England, marjoram was eaten in salads. The herb goes very well in tomato, bean, and vegetable dishes.

Parsley (*Petroselinum Sativum*)—Grows as a soft, rounded, leafy mound. It is native to northern and central Europe. In ancient times parsley was thought to be a remedy for poisons and was supposed to have been one of the ingredients in the poison antidote of Mithridates the King of Pontus (132 B.C. –63 B.C.). In Medieval Europe it was used in many herbal "cure-all" remedies. While most Americans prefer the curly leaf parsley in Louisiana we prefer the European flat leaf parsley, which has a stronger flavor. It is a wonderful garnish to any dish and is particularly tasty when used with tomatoes, potatoes, and peas. Parsley is also an indispensable ingredient in a bouquet garni. In Cajun/Creole cuisine parsley and green onions (which we call shallots) are always chopped up and sprinkled liberally on top of a finished dish to give it a little raw crunch.

Oregano (*Origanum Vulgare*)— A perennial that grows in busy mounds with white-pink flowers. It is native to Europe, central Asia, and the Middle East. Medicinally, oregano has been used as an expectorate, an antiseptic, and to relieve indigestion. The herb has been used as a culinary flavoring since ancient Roman times in Italy and is often coupled with marjoram. It adds a delightful flavor to all tomato dishes as well as bean, egg, and cheese ones. In Louisiana its use crept into the Creole cuisine of New Orleans with the arrival of Italian immigrants in the late nineteenth and early twentieth centuries.

Filé (*Sassafras Albidum*)— It is actually not an herb but a deciduous tree native to North America. Native Americans boiled the roots of the tree to make sassafras tea, which was used as a remedy for fevers. Sassafras is still used in American folk medicine as a blood thinner. In Louisiana, however, the leaves are clipped off and dried and ground fine to make filé powder. Filé is used as a thickener like cornstarch. When the powder is put into a hot liquid it will start to make the liquid very thick. However, you do not want to put filé into a liquid that is boiling because the heat will be too much and will make the liquid look "stringy." The word *filé* comes from the French meaning "to make threads" because of this characteristic. Therefore filé is usually put into a hot soup at the table and the heat from the bowl will be enough to make the soup thick but not stringy. Filé is used primarily in gumbo. It has a delightful light, sassafras flavor that is absolutely delicious. Filé gumbo usually refers to a gumbo that is thickened with filé instead of okra.

Bouquet garni—A bouquet garni is a small bunch of fresh herbs that are tied together with a string and put into a soup or stew to add an herbal flavor to it. Sometimes the herbs are placed in a small cheesecloth bag tied with string and then lowered into the pot of soup. It is similar in nature to the *"fines herbs"* (a blend of chives, parsley, tarragon, and chervil) used in French cooking; however, in Louisiana the herbs that we use for a bouquet garni are usually bay leaf, thyme, sweet basil, and parsley (although they could consist of any herb that the cook wishes to use).

Historically, the Creoles of New Orleans tended to use more herbs in their cooking than did the Cajuns 200 years ago. This was based primarily on the fact that the Creole "city dwellers" had greater access to markets of produce available to them than did the Cajuns, who for the most part lived off of the land in the country working as hunters, trappers, farmers, and fishermen. Today, however, both styles of cooking have begun to merge together, making it difficult to distinguish subtle differences between them, which is why the term "Cajun/Creole" is used.

As far as herbs are concerned, you will find that dried herbs have a much stronger flavor than fresh ones. This is because dried herbs contain not only the ground-up tops of the herb but also the stem, which has much more concentrated flavor than the leaves of the plant. However, using fresh herbs in your cooking rather than dried can add a delightful light, "fresh" flavor to your cooking which is very subtle. Prior to the twentieth century people tended to use fresh herbs more than dried. This is because dried herbs were not marketed commercially back then to the extent that they are today, and people tended to cook with the seasons, using only those herbs that were available to them at the time.

Choosing which herbs to use in your cooking is purely up to you. Our Louisiana garlic/thyme/sweet basil/parsley herb combination is an incredible Cajun/Creole taste sensation that goes well with all foods. Poultry, meat, seafood, vegetables, eggs, you name it. It is a very Louisiana flavor that everyone who tastes it thoroughly enjoys! And if you like oregano, just add that in as well and your cooking will take on a more New Orleans Italian Creole flavor that just can't be beat!

Peppers and Spices

All peppers, with the exception of black pepper, are native to Central America. Prior to the discovery of America by Columbus, the only pepper that was available in the rest of the world was black pepper, which came from Asia. If you look at ancient cookbooks such as the book *De Re Coquinaria* on Roman cookery written by Apicius in the late fourth century A.D., you will see that the only pepper used in their recipes is ground black pepper because that was the only pepper that was available to them at the time. Pepper was highly valued as a spice for cooking. During the Middle Ages in Europe, pepper sold for the same price as gold. It was even used as currency at times with pepper being accepted as a dowry and even partial payment in some areas for one's rent or taxes!

Indeed, the quest for pepper and spices was one of the very reasons that Columbus was sailing west in the first place back in 1492. During the Late Middle Ages, as a result of the Crusades, Europeans had been reintroduced to pepper and spices and had developed an insatiable desire for them. To acquire them, spices had to be brought overland to Europe by caravans traveling from Asia. As these spice caravans traveled through the Middle East Arab merchants would place high tariffs and taxes upon them which raised the price for spices considerably by the time they finally reached European markets. By sailing west, Columbus was attempting to sail directly to Asia to buy pepper and spices and thus, break the stranglehold that Arab merchants had on the spice caravans traveling through the Middle East and by so doing obtain cheaper prices. With his discovery of America, however, Columbus and the Spanish were introduced to new varieties of numerous other peppers (known collectively as chili peppers) that were far hotter and more flavorful than mere black pepper. These new peppers soon became all the rage in Europe, and within just a few decades of the discovery of the New World these peppers spread through trade throughout the rest of the Old World.

Peppers and Spices in Louisiana

The use of peppers in our cooking is generally believed to go back to the Spanish colonial period in Louisiana. It is possible, however, that peppers could have been introduced even earlier than that, given the illicit trade that existed between Louisiana and the Caribbean Islands and Spanish Florida prior to Spain receiving the colony in 1762. Africans as well are believed by many to have also introduced spicy peppers into Louisiana's cuisine, particularly after the slave insurrection on Saint-Domingue in the 1790s, when large numbers of Frenchmen and their slaves swarmed into New Orleans fleeing the revolt and bringing with them an Afro-Caribbean influence into Louisiana's cuisine.

Today we primarily use black, white, and cayenne peppers as well as sweet paprika in our food. Cayenne pepper is the hottest of these peppers, but it is by no means the hottest pepper out there and many people are fond of using banana, cherry, tabasco, and other hotter varieties of peppers. Up until the twentieth century it was common to use whole fresh peppers in our dishes which were sliced and cooked in with the recipe. Cooking them would have brought out the natural sweetness as well as the heat, which would give them a slightly different flavor from that of ground pepper. By the mid-twentieth century, however, the availability and convenience of using dried ground pepper had become so widespread that its use began to replace that of fresh peppers. If you read old Creole cookbooks from the nineteenth century you will also see that the Creoles at that time liked to use more spices such as mace, allspice, and cloves in their cooking, even in their savory dishes, which would have given their food a much sweeter flavor than ours today.

Black Pepper—Indigenous to India but now grown also in Indonesia and Brazil. The plant grows as a vine and the unripe green berries are picked, fermented, and dried to produce black pepper. Whole peppercorns can last indefinitely but the flavor begins to diminish quickly after they are ground so it is best to use whole peppercorns in a mill and grind them at the time you want to use them.

White Pepper—Comes from the same green berries as does black pepper, only the berries are left on the vine to ripen and turn red. After they have ripened they are picked, skinned, and then dried to produce white pepper. White pepper has a more intense burn and a slightly different flavor from black pepper.

Cayenne Pepper—A native of Central America and Mexico originally, now very widely grown around the world. It is also known as a guinea pepper. The pepper is a thin-fleshed, elongated red pepper with a very pungent heat and an acidic, tart flavor. It is mostly dried and ground into cayenne powder, which is sold commercially around the world as a seasoning. Many brands of cayenne powder, however, are actually made with a blend of several different peppers, and it can be difficult to find "pure" cayenne powder.

Sweet Paprika—Originally from Mexico, paprika has a light, sweet, pungent flavor to it that can be either very mild or fairly hot. Be sure to read the label when you are purchasing to make sure which it is. Originally brought to Spain by Columbus, today it is grown primarily in Spain, the United States, and Hungary. Hungarian paprika is considered by gourmets to be the finest variety. Paprika is used extensively in both Spanish and Hungarian cuisine and is known for adding a wonderful flavor and bright red color to your dishes.

Some people believe that Cajun food is spicier than Creole food, but actually *both* styles of cooking like their food to have a good "bite." This pepper/spice combination of black, white, cayenne, and sweet paprika used in varying quantities can really excite a dish with a spiciness that will enrich the bland quality of your food and stimulate your taste buds to where your tongue will really dance around in your mouth! Peppers are good for you (especially chili peppers). They are rich in vitamins A and C and are also a good source of potassium, folic acid, and vitamin E. Peppers contain the chemical capsaicin, which increases blood circulation and causes the brain to release chemicals known as endorphins, which are natural painkillers that promote a sense of well-being and make the body feel good. So in theory, the more peppers you eat the better you will feel. Your body can easily build up a tolerance for peppers and even develop a craving for them as well.

You will find that the more pepper you eat, the more pepper you *can* eat, and then the more you will *want* your food to have a bit of spiciness to it. If you are a bit squeamish about eating spicy food, then start out small and watch how you will be able to build up your tolerance and your enjoyment of it very quickly.

Now Louisiana food does tend to be spicy but not necessarily hot. It need only be as hot as whoever is cooking it wants it to be. There are plenty of other cuisines in the world that like their food *much* hotter than we do (just travel to India sometime and see how hot they like their food!). We like for our food to be a bit spicy, but it doesn't have to burn your mouth. It should have a bit of "zip" to it, however, to make the food more interesting. So try a little spice in your diet. You will soon learn to appreciate the fun of spicing up your food!

Cajun/Creole Seasoning Blends

There are a myriad of different seasoning blends produced in Louisiana. These are usually marketed as "Cajun seasoning," or "Creole seasoning," or "Cajun/Creole seasoning," or "Louisiana seasoning," but essentially they are all the same thing—that is, a blend of herbs and spices mixed with salt that you can conveniently use to sprinkle on your food to add a Louisiana flavor to your cooking. Just like the French in the South of France use herbes de provence to flavor their cuisine (a mixture of fresh herbs including oregano, savory, thyme, marjoram, and rosemary), we in the south of Louisiana use Cajun/Creole seasoning to flavor ours.

Seasoning blends are very easy to use because everything you need is in one jar. You merely have to sprinkle some on your food during or after the cooking process and it will add that flavor to it. It is very simple, so the key to using seasoning blends is finding one that has a flavor you particularly enjoy. Now, these blends are very popular in Louisiana, however, many Cajun/Creole "purists" look down their nose at them and do not like to use them because in their mind you are adding nothing more than a prepackaged flavor to your food. To them, the real "art" of Louisiana cooking is in knowing the right combinations and amounts of herbs and spices to use in your dishes to show off your own culinary skills in the kitchen. It is hard to argue with this line of reasoning, so if you happen to fall into this category, then practice using individual amounts of herbs and spices in your cooking to develop your own culinary style for flavoring your food. Learning about the qualities of different herbs and spices as well as what amounts you are comfortable with in seasoning your dishes is indeed a true art and one that should be encouraged. It is not difficult to learn but does take a little trial and error at first.

If, however, you are a bit unsure of yourself and feel more comfortable using the convenience of a manufactured seasoning blend, there is nothing wrong with this. Simply find a blend that you really enjoy and use it. If you like you can even make your own blend that you can use which can be a great way to learn about the various qualities that different herbs and spices possess. Try mixing 1 teaspoon each of salt, garlic powder, and onion powder in a bowl. To this, add in ¼ teaspoon each of black pepper, white pepper, cayenne pepper, and sweet paprika. Then, blend in 1 tablespoon of two or three of your favorite herbs, such as sweet basil and thyme. Now you have a seasoning blend that will give your food lots of wonderful flavor.

To test your new blend, go cook a piece of chicken or some fish, sprinkle on your new blend and taste the results. You may find that you like it or that it might need a bit more salt or more/less pepper or some other type of herbs. It all depends on your own individual taste. This is all part of the fun of learning how to season your food, so get creative! Experiment with different amounts. Once you have hit upon a blend that you particularly like you can store it in a jar and keep in a cool, dark place. If kept cool, a good seasoning blend can last up to five years. *Never* keep your jar of seasoning blend on the shelf over the stove. Although I know it is handy to have it there, the heat from the stove will very quickly dry it out and sap it of its flavor.

Colonel Paul's Authentic Louisiana Cajun/Creole Seasonings

The Colonel has developed his own blend of Cajun and Creole seasonings that are made in Opelousas, Louisiana, in the heart of the Cajun country. They are called Colonel Paul's Cajun Seasoning and Colonel Paul's Old New Orleans Creole Spice. The Colonel's Cajun Seasoning is unique to most other blends in that it comes in Mild, Medium, or Hot n' Spicy so that you can enjoy authentic Cajun flavor at whatever heat level is right for you. It is all natural with no MSG or preservatives and uses only those herbs and spices that are traditionally used in Cajun cooking, so you can have a very authentic flavor. The Colonel's Seasonings also have less salt, so they don't have an overpoweringly salty taste. It comes in a 5.6 oz (159g) container and is delicious when sprinkled on chicken, seafood, meats, vegetables, eggs, or anything that you like.

The Colonel's Old New Orleans Creole Spice is similar to his Cajun seasoning but is more finely ground so that you can also use it right at the table instead of salt and pepper. It is made using only those herbs and spices that are traditionally used in the Creole cuisine of New Orleans. It is also wonderful on all kinds of different foods but is particularly good on pizza, French fries, seafood, chicken, eggs, or right at the table on whatever mom has put in front of you to eat. It comes in a 2.25 oz (63.84g) container and is also all natural with no MSG or preservatives (see page 281 for more information).

4 ✺ Basic Stock

Stock is a basic ingredient in making your soups, stews, and gumbos much more flavorful. Stock is a very important ingredient in these dishes and should be made with great loving care. It is very easy to make, although a bit time consuming (I usually take about a day to make my stock and a day to then make the soup), but it is *much* more delicious than just using plain water or bouillon cubes and well worth the effort!

To begin with, get a large stock pot (anywhere from 8- to 20-quart capacity) and put into it the bones, heads, fins, claws, or other animal parts that you are going to use in your dish. For chicken stock use chicken bones and carcass. For a seafood stock use fish heads, crab claws, shrimp heads and shells, and bones (if using only shrimp heads and shells you need about 1½ to 2 pounds). The fish and shrimp heads are very important because there is a lot of flavor in them, so go the extra mile to try and find them. For a ham stock use one large meaty ham bone or pork necks, pigs feet, or other pork parts. The whole idea is to use as much of the bones and parts as you can to extract the most flavor out of them for your stock. **Note:** Do not use the liver, gizzard, kidney, heart, or tripe of an animal and wash everything *very* well to remove all traces of blood as these things will make your stock taste strong and bitter.

To this pot add one large onion quartered with the skin still on, two unpeeled large carrots cut up, 2 or 3 ribs of celery with the green leaves still on, and one large garlic bud broken apart and crushed. If you are making a seafood stock you will also want to quarter a lemon and add it into the pot. You do not need to worry about peeling any of these since you are going to strain the stock after it is completed and every little bit of this has flavor in it that you want to add to your stock. Just be sure to wash everything very well before using them.

If you wish to give your stock even *more* flavor, place the bones and vegetables into a large roasting pan and roast them in an oven at about 350 degrees, turning them over often until they have all browned and have a brown crust on them. This will take about 2 hours. This crust is basically caramelized sugar, which will dissolve in the water of your stock and give it a very rich and full flavor. Be careful not to burn them as this will make the stock very bitter.

Once your pot is filled with all of your ingredients, cover all of this completely with very *cold* water, put the heat on high, and bring to a good rolling boil. You can use any-where from 2 to 4 quarts of water. (I find that using about 3 to 4 quarts will net you a lit-tle over 2 quarts of stock.) As the stock begins to boil you may notice a film arise on the surface of the water. This is fat and oils from the bones. You can take a spoon and skim this off while the pot is boiling, which will make the final soup much less oily.

After you have brought the pot to a good rolling boil and skimmed off as much of the oil as you wish, add a couple of bay leaves and several sprigs of fresh herbs. Traditionally in Louisiana we use bay leaf, thyme, sweet basil, oregano, and parsley to flavor our dishes. I recommend a small bunch of at least three of these fresh herbs. (For a Cajun dish you could leave out the oregano, for a Creole dish you could include it.) Be sure to add the stems of the herbs as well, since there is more flavor in them than in the leaves.

Stock made without herbs will smell bad and will make your whole kitchen smell bad as well! Many chefs in New Orleans actually make their stock just like that, however, pre-ferring to put the herbs into the final dish while it is cooking. We have a saying in the New Orleans restaurant industry, "Smells like hell, but tastes like heaven." I personally prefer to use fresh herbs in my stocks and then season the final dish with dried herbs. This will make the stock smell wonderful while it is simmering and give the final dish *incredible* flavor that will taste even better the longer that it sits out. However, you do not want to use salt or spices in making your stock as they will increase in their potency as the final dish is cooked and you will be unable to regulate their flavor in the final dish.

Once your stock has come to a good rolling boil and you have skimmed off the ex-cess oil and put in your fresh herbs, cover the pot and reduce the heat to a simmer. Be-cause you have put into it the herbs it will smell heavenly and I recommend coming by every so often and stirring the pot. The longer that you simmer this pot, the more flavor-ful it will become and the more it will reduce in size. At the very least you need to sim-mer this pot for a minimum of 4 hours. The preferred cooking time is 8 hours. Remember, the longer that you simmer this pot the more flavorful it will become.

When your stock has cooked for the desired length of time, take it off of the heat and strain it into a smaller container. I like to strain mine twice, once in a colander and then a second time in a large strainer. Be sure to squeeze the bones/vegetables in the stock to extract every bit of flavorful juice from them. After you have strained your stock you will need to cool it down very slowly—you do *not* want to put hot stock in the refrigerator. The best way to cool it down is to place the container of stock in the sink and fill the sink with cold water, replacing the water after it warms up. When the stock has cooled down to at least room temperature, *then* put it into the refrigerator. Stock should not stay in the refrigerator for more than two days. All of these precautions will prevent the growth of bacteria. After the stock has chilled for a while, the fat that is left in it will solidify and rise to the top. This should be skimmed off as it will cause the soup to be a bit oily and could possibly go rancid very quickly, adversely affecting the taste of your dish.

Completed stock can be frozen for up to six months to be used in your soups or stews. A neat way to freeze some is to fill ice cube trays with stock and freeze them. Then when you are heating up a can of soup, you can melt one or two of the cubes in the soup to add in a touch of flavor. When your stock is finished, you are ready to take it out and cook your soup/stew/gumbo. I generally take one day to make my stock, cooking it with a lot of tender, loving care, and then the next day make the soup. By doing such you will be able to prepare an incredibly flavorful dish as fine as any restaurant in the Crescent City!

5. Trinity

Trinity refers to the three vegetables that are most commonly used in our traditional dishes: onions, bell peppers, and celery. This combination is a Louisiana version of what the French call a *mirepoix*, which consists of onions, carrots, and celery. It is called "trinity" because it is the holy trinity of vegetables used in our cooking. The usual proportions are two parts chopped onions, to one part chopped bell peppers, to one-half part chopped celery. These vegetables are usually sautéed in a skillet and seasoned and then added to the dish. Trinity is used in just about every Cajun/Creole dish and adds a wonderful base flavor for that fabulous Louisiana taste.

In addition to the trinity that we use, people in Louisiana also use two more vegetables in their food that should be mentioned: green onions and parsley. Green onions (which are called "shallots" in Louisiana even though they are technically not shallots at all) and parsley are usually chopped up and sprinkled onto a completed dish raw as a garnish. They will add an additional last minute flavor and a bit of "crunch" to the completed recipe that will complete the Louisiana taste that we strive for. No recipe in Cajun/Creole cuisine is complete without a little sprinkling of fresh chopped green onions and parsley on it.

6. Wines and Liquors

Creole cuisine, like its French forebears, is especially noted for its copious use of wines and liquors in its dishes. In the early nineteenth century clarets and sherries were particularly favored as an ingredient in many Creole recipes. The use of wine in Creole cooking typifies the fancy "citified" nature of this cuisine as opposed to the more "countrified" nature of Cajun cooking, which does not tend to use wines extensively in its cuisine (although again this is just a tendency and you can find many exceptions to this since the two have begun to merge over time).

As a rule of thumb, red wines are used more with red meat dishes while white wines are used more in white meat and seafood dishes. Wine can add a distinct "elegance" to your cooking and will provide a very refined flavor to whatever you are cooking. One can pretty much use whatever wine one likes although historically in Louisiana French wines were preferred over all others. What one does *not* want to use is ordinary "cooking wine," which is not very good and will not add a particularly nice flavor to your dish. Use instead a good quality wine that you would enjoy to drink. This will have much more flavor and add a much more refined taste to whatever you are cooking. If you are concerned about putting alcohol in your food, you will find that the longer the dish cooks the more the alcohol will evaporate, leaving only the distinct flavor of the grape. Turtle soup with sherry and bread pudding with rum or bourbon sauce are particular favorite dishes made with wine and liquor that people especially enjoy when visiting the Creole capital of New Orleans.

7 ⚜ Sauces

The use of rich sauces in our cooking dates back to the French colonial period in our history and is a reflection of France's significant culinary contribution. As far as sauces are concerned, Louisiana cuisine has three traditional *Sauces Mere* or "Mother Sauces" from which most other sauces descend. They are Sauce Espagnole or brown sauce, Sauce Allemande or German sauce (which is actually a basic white sauce), and Glace or glaze. The Sauce Espagnole and Sauce Allemande are actually variations of what we today call roux in Louisiana, which is cooked by heating up flour and oil or shortening in a skillet and stirring it constantly with a wire whisk until it reaches the desired color. The basic roux sauce is the foundation for numerous Creole and Cajun dishes and a good knowledge of how to properly prepare one is fundamental in learning how to prepare food in the Louisiana Cajun/Creole manner.

In addition to these three "Mother sauces," however, Louisiana cooking follows in the French tradition and uses a number of different sauces to enrich our food. By utilizing a rich, flavorful sauce a simple piece of meat can be transformed into a very elegant and sumptuous dish indeed. Classic French sauces such as Bordelaise, Hollandaise, and Béchamel are used on numerous Louisiana dishes, as well as sauces of our own creation such as remoulade and Creole sauce. Sauces are relatively easy to prepare, and a good background in their composition will enhance your culinary ability. Impress your friends anytime by "dressing up" a simple dish and turning the ordinary into something extraordinary!

Cajun/Creole Cooking Techniques

In addition to the seven elements of Louisiana Cooking there are five primary cooking techniques that are most commonly used in this style of cuisine. If you understand these techniques you will be able to add considerable flavor to your cooking.

Slow Cooking

This is a method of cooking brought to our cuisine from the Africans. It is a method used most frequently in "pot foods", (i.e., anything cooked in a large pot, such as a soup, stew, gumbo, or any kind of dish that has a sauce or is semi-liquid, such as an étouffée or red beans and rice).

Basically, in slow cooking, food is put into a large pot and brought to a boil at which time the lid is placed on the pot and the heat is reduced to a simmer. In doing this, great amounts of flavor are extracted from the herbs, meat, vegetables, or anything else in the pot. The longer you simmer the pot, the more flavorful the dish will become. This is particularly wonderful when you use lots of different herbs and spices.

Individual Cooking

Just like in Oriental cooking, Louisiana cooking sometimes uses the technique of cooking certain ingredients individually in a separate skillet to season them with different flavors, and then adding these cooked ingredients back into a common pot to cook everything together. In doing so we can "bring out" the flavors of the individual ingredients and also add different seasonings to them to enhance the overall flavor of the dish. For example, in a particular dish the meat can be cooked in one type of seasoning, the vegetables can be cooked separately in a different kind of seasoning, and they can both be added to a pot in a third type of seasoning to influence the overall flavor of the dish.

Flavor Building

Flavor building is a technique taught by Chef Paul Prudhomme in which particular ingredients are cooked in stages so as to bring out different flavors and consistencies in them. Thus you are literally able to build flavor upon flavor in your dish so that each bite you take will be different from the first. For example, one could start out by cooking trinity (onions, bell peppers, and celery) in a skillet with a little oil until the vegetables turn a dark brown color. This brings out the sugars and natural sweetness in the vegetables. Then, you could add more trinity into the pan to sauté them until they are just lightly cooked. Finally, you could add in the same vegetables raw so that you have three different types of flavor and consistency in the vegetables in the same dish. (Pretty cool, huh?) You could also use different seasonings at different stages in the preparation of the dish.

Blackening

This is another cooking technique developed by Cajun Chef Paul Prudhomme and is used to "fast cook" a piece of meat, fish, or vegetable in a spicy seasoning blend to give it a seasoned crust. It is a very delicious cooking technique as long as you use a seasoning blend that you like. This technique is best done outside on a gas grill because it tends to produce a mountain of smoke! First you take a dry cast-iron skillet with nothing in it and place it on the gas grill, heating it up until it is white hot (white hot is a step above red, and remember, it is dry, with nothing in it). Then, you take your meat or vegetable and dip it into a pan of already melted butter. After this you take it out of the butter and cover it completely with your seasoning blend. The rest is simple. Merely place the food into the hot skillet and cook it for one minute on one side and turn it over and cook it for 1½ minutes on the other side. If your skillet is hot enough the butter on the outside of the meat will burn and the flavors from the seasonings will be sucked into the center of the meat. Everything comes out very juicy and succulent and tender and with an incredible flavor (depending upon your choice of seasoning blend). It is a wonderful technique to use for steaks, particularly if you like your steaks rare or medium rare.

Deep-Fat Frying

This is another cooking technique brought to Louisiana (and the South as a whole) from Africa. Anyone who has traveled anywhere in the South knows that we all like fried *anything*! In the old days food would have been battered with cornmeal or flour and completely submerged in bacon grease or lard and fried until it was juicy on the inside and crispy on the outside. Most people today use oil instead to do this with. Peanut oil works very well with this because it can be heated up to a very high heat without burning or catching on fire. A recent dish that has become very popular throughout the South is deep fried turkey: a whole turkey is completely submerged in hot peanut oil and fried until it is done. If done right it has a wonderful texture and taste and is perfect for a Thanksgiving dinner.

Cajun/Creole Culinary Terms

Sauté—from the French *sauter*, meaning "jump," refers to a cooking method in which food is put into a pan with a little bit of oil on medium to high heat and cooked very quickly while stirring or flipping it in the pan until it is done.

Panée—In Louisiana food that is "panéed" is pan fried in a skillet with enough oil to come up the sides of the food but not completely cover it. In this respect it is different from deep frying, in which the food is completely covered in oil. Panéed foods can have a really nice crispy crust to them, and this method of cooking is very popular.

Flambé—To flambé something is to pour a small amount of an alcoholic beverage into your cooking pan of food and then set it on fire. It is a very impressive spectacle to witness and can make for a very elegant presentation. One should never pour the alcohol directly from the bottle as the flame could shoot up into the bottle and explode! It is better to pour the alcohol into a small cup or ladle and then pour it into the dish to light. As long as you stir the food in the pan the flame will continue to burn (use a long-handled spoon for this). To stop the flaming, merely stop stirring and the flame will go out. Dishes such as bananas foster and café brulot are flamed and can make an exciting finish to a great meal when done at the table for your guests.

Étouffée—Means "smothered" in Louisiana French and refers to a dish that is literally smothered in a sauce. The sauce that we most often use to make étouffée with is a roux.

Bisque—A thick cream soup usually made with shellfish or seafood. While you can find bisques that are not made with cream, the classical bisque is a cream soup. The king of bisques is crawfish bisque, which is absolutely heavenly. Another favorite is oyster and artichoke bisque.

Gumbo—Gumbo is a soup that originally comes from West Africa. In Louisiana gumbos are considered to be in a class all their own and thus different from soups and stews. The two most common types of gumbo are okra gumbo, made with the vegetable okra, which is used as a thickener, and filé gumbo, which has filé powder put into it as a thickener. The word *gumbo* is used both as a noun and also as an adjective to mean a different mixture of things or people.

Jambalaya—Jambalaya is a rice dish in which different types of meat, seafood, and vegetables are cooked together in a pot with rice so that the rice takes on the flavor of everything in the pot. Like gumbo, the word *jambalaya* also is used as both a noun and an adjective to mean a different mixture of things or people.

Sauce Piquant—Literally means "spicy sauce," and that is exactly what it is. The sauce is usually made with roux, tomato sauce, and various herbs and spices and served with meat, fish, chicken, or game recipes. Many people make sauce piquant like a stew, while others make the sauce and pour it over some meat or fish. It is usually *very* spicy and has a wonderful flavor.

Lagniappe (pronounced *lan-yap*)—A running together of three old French words, *pour la niappe*, which means "for the other." Today it is translated to mean "a little something extra." It is a custom that we have in Louisiana and is similar to a "baker's dozen," in which you go to the baker to buy a dozen rolls and he gives you thirteen instead of twelve. It is a delightfully charming custom in which people give you a little bit more than what you ask for. People get and give Lagniappes all the time in Louisiana, and it is a big part of our culture of hospitality.

Pirogue—A long, low, flat-bottomed boat which is used by people to pole along in the shallow bayous and swamps of southern Louisiana. In culinary terms it refers to a vegetable carved in the shape of a boat and then cooked and stuffed with different kinds of meat or seafood. Mirlitons, zucchini, and eggplants are most commonly carved, cooked, and stuffed in this manner, and they are a delicious way to prepare a creative-looking dish.

Louisiana Ingredients

Many different ingredients are used in Louisiana cooking to give our food its unique quality. Many of these are locally made. People in Louisiana are very proud of their local products and prefer to use them instead of something made elsewhere. If you cannot find any of these in your area, information on ordering them from Louisiana is in the Resources Guide in the Appendix.

Cajun/Creole Seasonings—There are numerous locally made brands of Louisiana-style seasoning blends. The Colonel even has his own brand, made in Opelousas, Louisiana. Basically, these are mixtures of different herbs and spices blended together in a jar with salt, which you can use to season your food either during or after cooking. They are very convenient to use, and the trick to them is finding a blend that you particularly enjoy. They are all similar, yet all different and have a wonderful flavor that you can add to all foods when you are cooking. Popular brands include Tony Chachere's Cajun/Creole Seasoning, Konriko Creole Seasoning, Zatarain's Cajun Seasoning, Rex Creole Seasoning, Paul Prudhomme's Louisiana Magic Seasonings, and Chef John Folse's Louisiana Seasonings, to name just a few.

Crab Boil—Also known as seafood boil. Crab boil is a small perforated bag of *very* spicy seasonings and herbs that is used when we boil shrimp, crabs, crawfish, or whatever. It is very hot and *very* delicious and will spice up a big stock pot of boiling seafood in a most delicious way. People in Louisiana would never *think* of boiling seafood without a bag of crab boil thrown in to flavor the pot.

Louisiana Hot Sauce—Just as there are numerous types of Cajun/Creole seasonings, so, too, are there numerous brands of Louisiana hot sauce. In fact, hot sauce was invented in Louisiana back in the mid-nineteenth century, and you can tell that you're in Louisiana when you notice that the bottles of hot sauce on the restaurant table are bigger than you've ever seen! We *love* it! (Tabasco sauce can even be bought in a Gallon jug here!) All hot sauces basically fall into three categories: blended, aged, and cooked. Your choice in using them all depends upon the flavor that they have and what your personal preference is.

Blended hot sauce is made by taking fresh peppers and mixing them with salt and vinegar and grinding them up. You can even make one yourself by taking fresh peppers and putting them into a blender with a little salt and covering them all up with vinegar and then grinding this all up into a mash. When you are finished merely strain the juice from the mash and you have hot sauce! These hot sauces are very simple to make, and most hot sauces produced in Louisiana are of the blended type. Popular brands include Trappey's, Crystal, Rex, and Louisiana (which is very popular in New Orleans and is distinguished by a large red dot on the label). But again, this is just the tip of the iceberg, as there are hundreds of brands made in Louisiana!

Aged hot sauce is made by aging the mash mixed with the vinegar for a long period of time before straining it. Aged hot sauce is considered to be gourmet hot sauce and the king of these types of hot sauces is Tabasco Sauce which is made on Avery Island near New Iberia, Louisiana. The McIlhenny family has been making Tabasco sauce since the end of the Civil War and was probably the first company to commercially market hot sauce in Louisiana. Tabasco sauce gets its name from the fact that they actually use Tabasco peppers to make their sauce. This sauce is aged in oak barrels covered in salt for up to four years before it is ready to hit the stores. It is considered by many people worldwide to be the finest hot sauce ever made in Louisiana and can literally be found *anywhere* on the planet!

Cooked hot sauce is just what the name implies. A hot sauce in which the ingredients are cooked before bottling. Cooked hot sauces can have a particularly wonderful flavor to them and a smoothness that other hot sauces do not. They also have the advantage that different types of herbs or other flavoring ingredients can be cooked into the sauce along with the peppers and vinegar. Panola brand hot sauce, made in Lake Providence, Louisiana, and Tiger Sauce, made in New Orleans (the official hot sauce of the Louisiana State University Tigers in Baton Rouge), are two good examples of cooked hot sauces. They have a smooth, sweet, and hot flavor that is very delicious and is great on all types of food. They are especially nice when used as a spicy steak sauce.

Hot sauce can be put into your food either while you are cooking or right at the table. And just as in the case of Cajun/Creole seasonings, they are all similar yet different, so your choice in which hot sauce to use depends on how hot you want it to be and the type of flavor that it has. But all of them can add a nice bite and a wonderfully exciting taste to your food.

Pepper Sauce—Pepper sauce is similar to hot sauce in that it too is made with peppers and vinegar. However, in pepper sauce the peppers are not ground up but merely marinated in the vinegar. People in Louisiana like to sprinkle the vinegar from pepper sauce on their spinach and turnip greens at the table to give it a spicy vinegary flavor. Many people also like to eat the peppers right out of the jar. With pepper sauce once the vinegar is all gone you can pour more vinegar back into the bottle to replenish it and let it soak up the flavor of the peppers still in it. So a bottle of pepper sauce can last you a fairly long time. The Trappey's company in New Iberia, Louisiana, makes a real nice pepper sauce with tabasco peppers in it that will add a great spicy flavor to your greens.

Worcestershire Sauce—This is one of the few ingredients widely used in Cajun/Creole cooking that is not made in Louisiana. Worcestershire sauce is put into almost all of our dishes for the rich flavor that it adds to our cooking. Some people probably even put it in their ice cream! Lea and Perrins is one of the most popular brands used in the state.

Creole Mustard—This is a Louisiana-made type of spicy mustard that is very coarsely ground and has a great flavor. It is believed to be a good example of the German influence on our cuisine and is very popular throughout Louisiana. Many people like to take Creole mustard and spread it on fish before they batter it and fry it for a very unique taste. Popular brands include Rex and Zatarain's Creole mustard made in New Orleans.

Crawfish—Crawfish are called *ecrivisse* in French and are affectionately known as "mudbugs" locally. They are considered to be a *real* delicacy in Louisiana and we eat them up by the *ton!* The French were first introduced to crawfish by the local Indians in the eighteenth century, and we have been eating them ever since. The Cajuns have a story that says that the crawfish actually descend from lobsters who were so saddened by the Acadians being exiled from Acadia by the British that they followed the Acadians down to Louisiana. However, the trip was so long and hard that, by the time they had gotten to Louisiana, they had shrunk in size and now are forever small.

Crawfish are crustaceans that inhabit the swamps and bayous of the state and are a very fierce little critter indeed! The most common way to eat them is to boil them in what is called "crab boil" or "seafood boil," a *very* spicy blend of seasonings used to boil the little fellas up in a large stock pot usually along with corn and potatoes. The tail is the most commonly eaten part. We have a saying at crawfish boils to "pinch the tail and suck da head." To do this, one breaks the boiled crawfish in half and pinches the tail meat out, popping it into the mouth. Then one takes the body of the crawfish and sucks out all of the spicy juices that it has been boiled in. To the true connoisseur of crawfish this is a pure delight and is absolutely *delectable*! (It's a Louisiana thing. . . .)

Crawfish tails are very succulent, with a flavor slightly reminiscent of shrimp, only a bit sweeter. We like them fried, boiled, broiled, baked, stuffed, sautéed, and any other kind of way that you can possibly think of. We absolutely *cannot* get enough of them! One can buy crawfish tails already peeled in Louisiana and use them for such dishes as crawfish étouffée, a dish of crawfish tails sautéed with trinity and served over rice with a spicy roux smothered on top.

Andouille Sausage—Andouille sausage is a spicy Cajun sausage that is used in numerous Cajun dishes. Andouille is a smoked sausage with chunks of pork and spices in it that make it truly delectable. Prior to the twentieth century, chaurice sausage, a French version of the Spanish chorizo sausage, was used extensively in Creole cuisine. However, in recent years Andouille has become the most popular sausage to use in Cajun/Creole cooking.

Tasso—Tasso is a very spicy seasoned pork ham used as a flavoring meat to season dishes. In Southern cooking plain pork meat is typically used to flavor greens or bean dishes, but in Louisiana we like to highly season our pork to make tasso to use instead for such dishes.

Okra—This small, green pod-like vegetable is native to West Africa and was brought to the South along with the transatlantic slave trade. Okra is commonly used in our gumbos for its flavor and its thickening quality. However, we also love to slice the pods, batter them, and then fry them in a little oil or shortening. Okra has a delicious flavor and is now quite common throughout the South.

Mirliton—Known as chayotes or vegetable pears, mirliton is a small pear-shaped vegetable originally from the West Indies. It has a *great* flavor and is easy to cook. In Louisiana we like to carve little "pirogues" or small boats out of them and stuff them with seafood.

Creole Tomatoes—These are vine-ripened tomatoes grown in the Mississippi Delta region of south Louisiana. Because of the richness of the Delta soil, these tomatoes are the biggest, juiciest, most *beautiful* tomatoes that you have ever seen with a *great* flavor and texture to them. They are the absolute best tomato to use for any sort of dish that requires tomatoes in it. If you cannot get them in your area, it is recommended that you use the freshest type of vine-ripened tomato that you can find.

Wild Pecan Rice—This hybrid strain of white rice has a strong nutlike flavor. Its nutty flavor is purely wonderful to use in rice dishes or simply on its own as a side dish. Another variety of rice grown in Louisiana is "popcorn rice," which is a hybrid cross of Louisiana rice with Basmati rice from India. It too has a strong popcorn flavor that is absolutely delicious! The Conrad Rice Mill in New Iberia, Louisiana, produces Wild Pecan Rice, which is sold throughout the state.

Chicory Coffee—Chicory coffee is a real staple in New Orleans for breakfast. The Creoles historically are famous for making a very strong drip coffee to drink in the morning. In today's New Orleans, however, we additionally take coffee and mix chicory in with it. Chicory is the ground-up, dry-roasted root of the endive lettuce plant. We began using chicory in our coffee during the Civil War, when the blockade placed on the city by Union forces caused severe shortages of coffee and other food products. The taste is very unique and adds a wonderfully strong flavor to your coffee. People in New Orleans feel that it is the perfect coffee to use for Café au lait—brewed coffee mixed half and half with boiled milk. Community brand coffee and chicory is very popular in New Orleans.

Filé Powder—Filé is the ground-up leaves of the sassafras plant, which is used in our soups and gumbos as a thickener like cornstarch. When filé is put into a pot of hot soup, it starts to get thick and adds a wonderful sassafras flavor to it. The word derives from the French and means "to make threads," because if filé is put into a pot of boiling liquid it tends to clump up and get stringy. Therefore, most people do not cook with it but instead will sprinkle a tablespoon or two in their bowl of gumbo at the table; the heat from the bowl will be enough for the filé to make the soup thick but not get stringy.

Ribbon Cane Syrup—A strong-flavored syrup made from sugar cane in Louisiana. The sugar cane industry in Louisiana dates back to the mid-eighteenth century with the beginning of the first plantations in the state. Sugar cane syrup has a deep, dark color with a flavor similar to molasses only lighter. It is rich in iron and vitamins and is very sweet and tasty on pancakes and "lost bread" (a Creole version of French toast). Steen's Ribbon Cane Syrup, made in Abbeville, Louisiana, is an excellent brand of cane syrup used throughout Louisiana. The Steen family has been making ribbon cane syrup at the family mill since 1910 and still uses the traditional open-kettle boiling process that our Creole ancestors used 200 years ago. Their syrup is *wonderfully* delicious and is an authentic part of Louisiana history.

Pralines (pronounced *prah-leen*, not *pray-leen*)—In Louisiana, pralines are a candy made with brown and white sugar, pecans, butter, and cream (although there are many variations to this). They are named for Comte Cesar Du Plessis-Praslin, Duc de Choiseul, et Marshal de France (1598–1675). Count Praslin (who was also made the Duke of Choiseul in 1665) was a famous military leader and diplomat in France during the reigns of Louis XIII and Louis XIV. He participated in almost all military actions that went on during this period, including the siege of La Rochelle against the Huguenots (1628), and also commanded an army in Lombardy during the Thirty Years War (1618–48). He was made a Marshal of France in 1645 and supported Cardinal Mazarin during the second phase of the *Fronde* uprising by the nobility against the crown (1649–53). After a very distinguished military career, Marshal Praslin later served as Minister of State for Louis XIV.

Now in addition to all of this, the count was known for having a bit of a sweet tooth and also suffered occasionally from indigestion. The story goes that it was his personal chef who gave him almonds covered in sugar to help him with his digestive problems. These little sugar-covered nuts became all the rage in France and were named "pralines" in honor of Marshal Praslin (how very French, to be a famous, successful general but then be remembered down through history for a sugar-covered nut!). In fact, the name "praline" is still used in France today to refer to any sort of sugary confection with nuts.

When the first French settlers came to Louisiana they brought with them their love of this candy, but unfortunately could not find any almonds native to the area. Instead they found pecans (pronounced *pe-cons*, not *pee-cans*), which they used as a substitute. It is possible that the first Pralines were actually made with cane syrup since the French Creoles did not learn how to effectively crystallize sugar until the late eighteenth century. If one boils cane syrup for a very long time it will indeed solidify, and with a little butter and some pecans added in you could make pralines (undoubtedly with varying degrees of success). Given the very distinctive molasses flavor that cane syrup has, pralines made like this would have had a much different flavor to them from what we are used to today.

By 1793 when Etienne Bore first successfully crystallized sugar in New Orleans, it became possible to make the modern Louisiana praline as we now know it made with crystallized brown and white sugar, butter, and pecans. During the nineteenth century, black Creole ladies wearing their distinctive "tignon" headdress (a bright, multi-colored scarf tied around their head in the West African fashion) could be seen all over the streets of the French Quarter in New Orleans selling fresh homemade pralines. By the twentieth century, pralines were sold in a decorative, colored cylindrical tin which looked very charming; however, the pralines tended to break inside of them. Today, pralines are made in many different ways and sold in boxes all over the city of New Orleans and around the state.

Creole Cream Cheese—A farmer's-style cheese similar to a Neufchatel with a rich flavor sort of like a cross between a ricotta and crème fraîche. In New Orleans it is served fresh with a little sugar or fruit on top or frozen and covered with a sweet dessert topping for a wonderfully delicious dessert.

Part II

The Evolution of Cajun and Creole Cuisines

The Land of Louisiana

Louisiana is the child of Canada. It began as a dream: a desire on the part of the French to link up all of the land east and west of the Mississippi River stretching from the Gulf of Mexico all the way to Hudson's Bay and thereby dominate the entire interior of North America in the name of France. The territory was claimed by France in 1682 when the French explorer René Robert Cavalier, Sieur de la Salle sailed down the Mississippi River with a small band of Canadians and Indians erecting a post at the mouth of the river, and naming it *Louisiane* in honor of King Louis XIV. La Salle's dream was to found a city at the mouth of the Mississippi that would dominate trade on the great river the Indians called "the Father of Waters." This city would eventually be known as New Orleans and would give birth to Louisiana's world-famous Cajun/Creole cuisine.

It was an *immense* expanse of territory comprising the better part of ten modern-day U.S. states east of the Mississippi and fifteen states west of the great river. Indeed the western boundaries of Louisiana were not even known! When Napoleon sold the Louisiana Purchase to the United States in 1803 he was asked what the territories' westernmost boundaries were and he was quoted as saying "I am sure that you will make the most it." One could more accurately describe this territory as "Greater Louisiana" as opposed to the modern-day state of Louisiana, the boundaries of which were set after it was purchased in 1803.

You cannot imagine the extraordinary beauty that was greater Louisiana at the time it was first seen by Europeans. If one reads some of the original accounts of the very first Europeans who beheld the Continent, you can see how truly awestruck they were at the wonders they found. Ancient forests of trees literally hundreds of years old, some trees so large that twenty men linked hand in hand could still not reach completely around them! All of North America at that time was one gigantic forest so thick that it was said that a squirrel could travel from the Atlantic Ocean to the Mississippi River jumping from tree to tree and never once have to touch the ground!

It is believed by many that the Native Americans who lived here at that time did not change the land that they lived on, but this is incorrect. What the Indians did was to burn off all of the scrub growth between the trees. This allowed for more grass to grow for grazing. The result of their efforts was to create an overpopulation of game animals. The entire Continent was a hunter's paradise, with a proliferation of game the likes of which had not been seen in Europe since the Neolithic Age!

The southernmost extension of Louisiana where the Mississippi River flows into the Gulf of Mexico is an alluvial flood plain. As the river flows south it carries with it mud and sediment from the north with which it periodically floods the area, creating the Louisiana wetlands. This area is rich and fertile, filled with swamps and bayous all teeming with game such as crawfish, alligators, muskrats, nutria, deer, rabbits, possums, raccoons, fish, and birds of all species. It provides a veritable bounty for those who live there and it is from this bounty that we draw to make our *wonderful* Cajun and Creole cuisines.

The modern-day boundaries of Louisiana range from the marshes and wetlands in the south to the prairies in the west and the forests and hills of the north. Between the Mississippi River and the prairies lies the great Atchafalaya Basin, the largest swamp in North America. The inhabitants of the state include the Creoles of southern Louisiana, the Cajuns who live predominately in the southwestern prairies, and the Anglo-Americans who reside in the north with countless other immigrant groups scattered about the state. It is a real gumbo pot of people including African-Americans, French, Spanish, Anglos, Irish, Italians, Germans, Yugoslavians, Vietnamese, Mexicans, and scores of other peoples all joined together by their love of Louisiana and the unique culture and lifestyle that we have created here. And it is from the history of the countless numbers of these immigrants who have settled here that our cuisine has evolved and is continuing to evolve to this day.

Outline of Louisiana Culinary History

with Historic High Points

1682

René Robert Cavalier, Sieur de la Salle, claims the entire Mississippi River basin from the Gulf of Mexico northward to Canada for France and names it *Louisiane* in honor of French King Louis XIV.

1699

Pierre Le Moyne, Sieur d'Iberville and his younger brother Jean Baptiste Le Moyne, Sieur de Bienville land in Mobile Bay on the ships *Badine* and *Marin* with two companies of French Marines and about 200 colonists (mostly French Canadians) to found the first permanent settlements in Louisiana. The first permanent French settlement established in Louisiana is called Ft. Maurepas, near present-day Ocean Springs, Mississippi.

1701

Jean Baptiste Le Moyne, Sieur de Bienville takes over as commander of the Louisiana colony.

1702

City of Mobile founded and made capital of Louisiana. Extensive trade exists between Canadians and local Indian tribes for local foodstuffs, particularly corn. French begin to blend local Indian cuisine with that of France due to food shortages.

Queen Anne's War (the War of the Spanish Succession) fought between England, France, and Spain begins with fighting centered mainly in New England and the French Canadian colony of Acadie (Acadia—modern-day Nova Scotia).

1704

Bishop of Quebec sends 23 young ladies to the colony to become wives for the colonists. Upon their arrival the women revolt, threatening to leave the colony because of the lack of proper "French" food . . . particularly French bread. Bienville's housekeeper Madame Langlois conducts very first cooking class for colonial women in Louisiana, teaching them how to adapt Indian cooking techniques and food with French cuisine. (Begrudgingly, the ladies stayed. . . .)

1713

Peace of Utrecht ends Queen Anne's War (the War of the Spanish Succession). As a result, Great Britain is given control of the French colony of Acadie (Acadia). The French colony is the original homeland of the Louisiana Cajuns.

1717–22

First large number of German immigrants begin to come to Louisiana. Most of these people come from the Rhineland and are farming families. They are given land concessions along the Mississippi River between New Orleans and Baton Rouge, an area later called the German Coast. It is these farmers who will feed the colony during times of privation. German immigration dies down by 1722 and German immigrants adopt French customs, language, and culture. It is believed by some that German-style sausages and Creole mustard come into Louisiana's cuisine as a result of these first German immigrants.

1718

New Orleans founded by Bienville on a crescent bend in the Mississippi River. The capital is moved from Mobile to New Orleans. Over time, New Orleans will grow to become the largest city in Louisiana and the largest port for the colony. The city will become the dominant influence on Creole cuisine in Louisiana.

1719

First large shipment of African slaves arrives in Louisiana, bringing with it the first African culinary influence to the existing French and Indian cuisine in the colony. Over the course of the next 100 years more and more African slaves will be brought into Louisiana, directly influencing and changing the local French cuisine.

1720

Rice begins to compete with corn as main staple crop in Louisiana. Supply ships from France arrive infrequently, forcing colonists to eat Indian style foods as well as their native French cuisine. First large plantations begin to be established in the colony.

1727

The Order of the Ursuline Nuns arrives in New Orleans to establish a convent, administer to the sick, and educate the women of the colony. It is believed by many that the Nuns also introduce the recipe for "beignets," a square, fried donut without a hole that has since become a Louisiana staple for breakfast along with a strong cup of café au lait.

1754–63

The French and Indian War (Seven Years War) is fought between France and Great Britain over possession of the Ohio Valley in upper Louisiana. The war becomes a contest for domination of North America that the English will win. Louisiana becomes isolated and abandoned by France during this war, receiving very few supply ships, and as a result has to fend for itself.

1755

Le Grand Derangement ("The Great Trouble"). French Acadians in Canada are forcibly exiled from Nova Scotia by the British who had occupied the colony in 1713. Over 7,000 Acadians are rounded up by British troops, who burn down their homes and force them onto ships with little more than the clothes on their back. The ships disperse the Acadians to some of the English colonies, France, various islands in the Caribbean, and parts unknown where they will languish in refugee camps or be forced into slavery. Over the course of the next thirty years Acadians on their own will begin to migrate to Louisiana to resettle and start a new life for themselves. The majority of these immigrants will be given land grants in the southwestern part of southern Louisiana. Eventually these Acadian settlers will come to be known as "Cajuns."

1762

Treaty of Fontainbleau, a secret treaty made between France and Spain which cedes all of Louisiana west of the Mississippi River plus the city of New Orleans to Spain to keep the colony out of British hands as a result of France's imminent defeat in the French and Indian War (Seven Years War). This Treaty will guarantee a Spanish culinary influence upon the colony.

1763

Treaty of Paris signed between France, Spain, and England ending the French and Indian War (Seven Years War). As a result of the treaty, England is ceded all of Louisiana east of the Mississippi River (except for New Orleans) and Spain is forced to give up all of the Floridas to the British.

1766

Antonio de Ulloa, first Spanish governor of Louisiana, arrives in New Orleans to take possession of the colony in the name of the King of Spain. The French colonists soon become resentful of his administration and the restrictions placed on French trade.

1768

"The Revolution of 1768." Angry mobs of French colonists upset over inept Spanish rule chase Governor Ulloa onto the ship *El Volante* bound for Cuba. Local legend claims that the French colonists became infuriated after shipments of bad Spanish rioja wine arrived in New Orleans instead of French bordeaux or burgundy. After expulsing the governor, the colonists attempt to no avail to have Louisiana returned to France.

1769

Alexander O'Reilly, Irish general in the Spanish army, arrives with a large Spanish army to occupy Louisiana after Governor Ulloa was run out. He formally establishes Spanish law & order and ushers in Spanish rule of the colony. Spanish culinary influences begin to filter into the local French cuisine.

1779

Spanish immigrants from the Canary Islands arrive in Louisiana and settle in St. Bernard Parish. Called Los Islenos or "the Islander's," these people continue to reside in St. Bernard Parish to this day and speak an old dialect of Castilian Spanish. They are a living example of Spain's colonial and cultural influence on the state.

Reluctantly, Spain declares war on England as an ally of France in supporting the American Revolution against Great Britain. Spain's efforts will be to supply the American rebels with arms out of New Orleans and to reconquer West Florida from the British.

1779–80

Spanish Governor Bernardo de Galvez leads an expedition of French Creole, Mexican, and Spanish troops that attacks and conquers Baton Rouge, Mobile, and Pensacola in British West Florida, bringing it under Spanish control until the War of 1812.

1782

Spanish authorities establish a formal marketplace in New Orleans out of an Indian trade market on the edge of the city. This marketplace will come to be called the French Market and will be an open-air farmers market with fixed stalls where farmers, Indians, and others can sell their produce. The French Market is still in existence in the modern French Quarter of New Orleans.

1788

First of two great fires in New Orleans starts on Good Friday in a house on Chartres Street and sweeps through the city, destroying 856 buildings.

1789

French Revolution sweeps through France. It is believed by some that refugee aristocrats and some French chefs immigrate to New Orleans to escape "Madame Guillotine," and as a result the city's restaurant industry is significantly influenced.

1791–94

Massive slave insurrection occurs on the island of Saint Domingue (modern-day Haiti). The result is a large immigration of French planters and slaves to Louisiana, bringing an Afro-Caribbean culinary influence into Louisiana's local cuisine. It is the last large immigration by a French population into Louisiana.

1793

The cocktail is invented at 727 Toulouse St. in New Orleans by a local pharmacist. It was originally called a coquetier or a "cock's tail" because it was served in a special double-ended cup. The name is soon changed by the Americans to "cocktail," which they found easier to pronounce.

Etienne de Boré, a French plantation owner, first successfully granulates sugar in Louisiana, making sugar cane production profitable. The sugar cane industry begins to take off, with sugar plantations being built all over the southern part of Louisiana.

1794

The second great fire hits New Orleans, started by children who are playing with fire on the Feast of Immaculate Conception. The fire sweeps through the city in about three hours, destroying 212 houses. Although it destroyed less of the city than the first fire, it did much more in terms of property damage. The Spanish governor, Francisco Luis Hector, Baron de Carondelet, orders that the city be rebuilt of brick to protect it from further fire. The result is the birth of the modern French Quarter in New Orleans, with its beautiful Spanish-style architecture epitomized by overhanging balconies with ornate iron lace and charming interior courtyards.

1799

Napoleon Bonaparte instigates a coup d'etat of the French Directory in Paris and sets himself up as First Consul of the French Republic.

1800

The secret treaty of San Ildefonso signed between Spain and Napoleon returns Louisiana to France in exchange for the province of Tuscany in Italy and recognition of the King of Etruria. Spanish rule however still continues in Louisiana throughout this period. Napoleon entertains the idea of having a renewed French colonial empire in North America centered around reestablishing French dominance over the island of Saint Domingue.

1801

President Thomas Jefferson sends Robert Livingston to Paris to negotiate with Napoleon for the purchase of the city of New Orleans.

Napoleon sends a large French army to Saint Domingue to reconquer the island from the former slaves, which it easily does. However, the army soon becomes decimated by a severe yellow fever epidemic and constant guerrilla warfare, thus ending his dream of a French colonial empire in North America.

1803

Louisiana Purchase. With Napoleon's realization that he is unable to secure Saint Domingue as a base for his colonial empire he decides to sell all of Louisiana to the United States for $15 million dollars (.03 cents an acre!). Legend has it that Napoleon made up his mind to sell Louisiana while taking a bath. William C. C. Claiborne named first American territorial governor.

1812

Louisiana enters the Union as the eighteenth state. By this time Americans have begun to pour into the territory, eventually outpopulating the French and Spanish Creoles. They bring with them their own Southern-style Anglo-American culinary influences, which will blend with those of the French Creoles in Louisiana.

1812–14

The War of 1812. The United States goes to war with Great Britain for a second time since the Revolutionary War. The war is fought over British impressment of American sailors on the high seas by the Royal Navy and an attempt on the part of the Americans to invade and conquer Canada.

1815

The Battle of New Orleans. The British send a major expeditionary force to capture the city toward the end of the War of 1812. The battle is actually fought after the peace treaty was signed. British forces under General Sir Edward Pakenham are soundly defeated by the American and Creole troops under General Andrew Jackson.

1815–60

La Belle Epoque: Golden Era for New Orleans. The city becomes the largest and richest port in the United States. Creole culture and cuisine blossom in the city under American rule. New Orleans Creole cuisine becomes sophisticated and refined and Creole style restaurants thrive as the city becomes a very popular tourist attraction.

1845

Large numbers of Irish immigrants fleeing the Potato Famine in Ireland begin to settle in New Orleans. The Irish will make up a large percentage of the labor force in the city and over time will grow to become one third of the population in New Orleans.

1861–65

The American Civil War. Southern states secede from the Union in an attempt to establish their own country. The war will result in the destruction of the plantation system in the South and freedom for the South's black slave population. It will also cause a severe economic depression throughout the South, which will transform the region from the richest part of the country to the poorest.

1861

Louisiana secedes from the Union and joins the Confederacy. The Union Navy institutes a naval blockade of Southern ports, resulting in major food shortages. Creole chicory coffee develops at this time in an attempt to stretch limited supplies of coffee.

1862

New Orleans falls to Union forces invading the city. Federal troops will occupy New Orleans until 1877, ruling the city as a military district.

1870–1910

Italian and Sicilian immigrants swarm into New Orleans, affecting the city's Creole cuisine and grocery industry. They bring with them Italian culinary influences and foods that directly affect the Creole cuisine of New Orleans. However, their influence does not reach as far as the Cajun country of southwest Louisiana. In time their influence will become so strong that Italian Americans will come to dominate the New Orleans grocery industry.

1906

The famous muffuletta sandwich is created by Central Grocery in the French Quarter of New Orleans. It is a *huge* sandwich served on round, crusty Italian bread and made with ham, Genoa salami, and slices of provolone cheese all drenched in a special "olive salad" dressing made with olives, pimentos, garlic, capers, cocktail onions, red wine vinegar, olive oil, celery, parsley, and oregano. The sandwich is legendary in New Orleans and can easily feed two people.

1929

The brothers Benny and Clovis Martin come up with the idea of the po' boy sandwich in an attempt to feed striking streetcar employees. The sandwich is made on French bread and can consist of any type of meat or fish. They are usually served "dressed," meaning with lettuce and tomatoes. Po' boys become the standard Louisiana sandwich, catching on everywhere in the state.

1980–1990

Cajun cuisine becomes popular throughout the United States due to celebrities such as television cooking show host Justin Wilson and Cajun Chef Paul Prudhomme, who popularize Cajun cooking around the country.

Both Cajun and Creole cuisines are what the French call a mélange, a mixture. They incorporate the culinary influences of the French, Spanish, West African, Caribbean, Native American, and Italian cooking traditions (with a little German, Irish, and Anglo-American thrown in for good measure). If you really want to understand the differences between Cajun and Creole cuisines, you must first examine how these two cooking styles evolved. The story of their evolution as well as their similarities and differences is a fascinating tale interwoven in the very fabric of our history. And it is because of this historic blending of several diverse culinary traditions that our Louisiana cooking has become *so* very tasty indeed!

The French Colonial Period

The French

Louisiana was originally settled by the French starting in January 1699. It was named *Louisiane* after King Louis XIV of France (who had a *giant* ego and liked having this land named for him, but didn't really care to do much with it except to admire it on his map). The territory was an immense expanse of land which included the entire Mississippi River system stretching from the Gulf of Mexico all the way to Canada and included the better part of twenty-five modern-day American states. The very first colonial settlers were primarily Canadian *Quebecois* and a few native Frenchmen who established the first settlements at Ft. Maurepas (modern-day Ocean Springs, Mississippi) in 1699 and in Mobile (modern-day Alabama) in 1702. The colonists brought with them their own knowledge of eighteenth-century French cooking and thereby introduced the very first ingredient into the Cajun/Creole culinary pot.

Throughout the French colonial period Louisiana suffered terribly from both governmental mismanagement and royal disinterest on the part of the French crown. The colony was actually transferred several times during the French colonial period between the Crown and private individuals in an attempt to make it a profitable enterprise but to no avail. Louisiana was situated in the middle of a Spanish sea inhabited by Indians, infested with malarial swamps, and plagued by annual hurricanes. Living conditions were harsh, food shortages were common, and the death rate for colonials was very high. Deportation to Louisiana was considered to be a death sentence, and the people of France on the whole were not that interested in immigrating to the colony; thus, the colony's growth proceeded very slowly.

Between 1718 and 1720 the Company of the Indies (which owned the Louisiana colony at the time) in its infinite wisdom, tried to alleviate this problem by emptying

French prisons and shipping convicted criminals and prostitutes to the colony in an ill-conceived attempt to bolster its population, with disastrous results. The French attempted to start up several different industries growing sugar cane, rice, indigo, tobacco, and trading furs, but none of these efforts produced any substantial revenues for either the colony or the mother country. As a result, the Louisiana colony was viewed in France as an expensive colonial failure.

But the colony did indeed grow as more and more settlers arrived to build a new life taken from the rich bounty of the land. A French presence was firmly planted in Louisiana and it would not go away. New Orleans was founded in 1718 and made the capital of the colony. In time it grew to become the largest city in Louisiana and the center of French commerce and culture in the South. It would be the queen city on the Mississippi River and the mother that would give birth to our legendary Louisiana Creole cuisine.

The Indians

Shortly after Louisiana was founded, the colonists discovered that supply ships from France arrived irregularly at best. Out of necessity they turned to the Indians during such periods to trade with them for food. At this time there were numerous Indian tribes in southern Louisiana such as the Houma, Chitimacha, Attakapa, Natchez, Acolapissa, Bayougoula, Coushatta, Biloxi, Mobilia, Apalache, Taensa, Caddo, Tunica, Cawasha, Pascagoula, Alibamu, Chickasaw, and Choctaw (to name but a few). The initial contact between the French and Indian peoples was made with the Bayougoula and Biloxi tribes. The largest and oldest of the tribes in the area were the Chitimacha Confederacy, whose origins date back about 6,000 years and may even go back as far as 12,000 B.C.

Although the French initially had good relations with the various Indians in Louisiana, the early history of the colony was marked by several terrible wars between the French and shifting alliances of Indian tribes, which, along with outbreaks of European diseases, greatly decreased the population and power of the native peoples in the area. These wars included most notably the Chitimacha War (1706–18), the Natchez Revolt (1729–31), and the Chickasaw War (1736–40). It is believed by some that the Chickasaws had an influence upon French culture and cuisine however this is highly unlikely since the Chickasaws were ardent enemies of the French. They preferred English trade goods to those of the French, and as a result were major trading partners and allies to Britain instead of France.

The tribes that had the greatest influence on the French in terms of cultural exchange were the Chitimacha and the Choctaw. In the first days of the colony the colonists traded extensively with the Chitimacha, and the Choctaw were close trading partners and allies with the French. Even though relations with the Chitimacha eventually broke down into war in 1706, one result of the Chitimacha War was that large numbers of this tribe were made slaves in the French colony. Indeed, in the early years of the colony's development the majority of Indian slaves came from the Chitimacha tribe. Many Indian ladies were taken on as housekeepers by the male bachelors of the colony, which undoubtedly had an affect on French Louisiana society and the culinary influences that these particular tribes shared with them.

The Indians introduced the French to locally grown foods and herbs such as corn, beans, squash, pumpkins, melons, shellfish, and wild game, which they bartered with the colonists in exchange for European trade goods. This trade not only kept the colony alive at times but also resulted in the introduction of the first significant culinary influence that would transform French cuisine in Louisiana. However, though Indian food was welcomed by the French out of necessity, Native American cuisine was not totally accepted by everyone in the colony at first, particularly by the women who immigrated to Louisiana from France.

In 1704 the bishop of Quebec sent 27 young ladies from Paris to Louisiana aboard the ship *Le Pelican* to provide wives for the colonists. Four of the ladies died en route before the ship docked in Mobile. The ladies were enthusiastically greeted by the men of the colony and were all married off very quickly. But after living in the settlements for only a short while, the ladies became disheartened by the lack of proper "French" food—in particular, French bread. In an effort to remedy the situation, the ladies got together and staged what has become known as "the Petticoat Rebellion," in which they marched up to the governor's house and demanded either proper French food or the next boat back to France. To appease the ladies, Governor Bienville turned them over to his housekeeper, a Madame Langlois, who proceeded to conduct the first recorded cooking class in North American history.

Photo by Christi Key

Madame Langlois instructed the ladies how to make cornbread from cornmeal and how to prepare many of the meats and vegetables that the Indians had introduced to the colonists. Although the French never did like corn very much and always preferred French bread over cornbread, her class appears to have been a success, as the ladies did indeed stay in the colony and learned how to prepare local Indian foods and incorporate them into their own style of French cooking. This blending of European and Indian culinary styles was the first step in the transformation of classical French cooking into a more Louisiana cuisine.

Photo by Christi Key

The Germans

Between 1717 and 1722 a fairly successful ad campaign was run in the Rhineland of the German states to attract German immigration to the colony. Large numbers of hard-working German farm families were given free land to come and settle in Louisiana along the Mississippi River between New Orleans and Baton Rouge. Several small farming settlements were established in this area that came to be known as the *Cote des Allemands*, or the German Coast; and it was these German farmers who provided most of the locally grown produce for the colonists to live on during the times when French supply ships did not arrive. Though they brought with them a German culinary influence, they quickly became absorbed by the dominant French culture in the area even to the extent of changing some of their names (such as the German surname *Zvieg*, which was changed to the French *Labranche*—both meaning "twig" in English). Over the course of the next two hundred years, more Germans would immigrate to Louisiana in successive waves and establish residence in the city of New Orleans. Their presence would have a definite and long-lasting influence on shaping the future culture of the city as they intermarried with Italian and Irish immigrants and grew to outnumber the original French inhabitants of New Orleans.

The Africans

In 1719 the first boatload of African slaves were introduced into Louisiana. These African peoples had been purchased by the French from various African tribes as the result of numerous intertribal wars that were being fought throughout West Africa at the time. Whole villages were attacked and captured by warring African tribes fighting against each other and then sold to the French in exchange for European trade goods. The French Company of the Indies, which owned Louisiana from 1717 to 1731, also owned a land concession on the African coast specifically for the purpose of purchasing African slaves. The resulting wars ravished the African countryside as different tribes vied for greater power and influence and got rich off of making war on their enemies. The majority of the African peoples shipped to Louisiana during the French colonial period came from the Wolof, Mandinka, and Bambara tribes of the Senegambia region of West Africa. This subtropical region in Africa has its own distinctive culture and traditions that are unique to that area.

The voyage over from Africa to Louisiana took about three months, and the conditions with which these poor people were forced to endure were deplorable to say the least. Shackled together in cramped spaces in the hulls of slave ships with poor food and little water many died en route during the voyage. Upon arrival in Louisiana the Africans were purchased by colonial planters to work the plantations harvesting rice, tobacco, indigo, and sugar cane. In addition, many of these people were purchased to be used as housekeepers, particularly working in the kitchens of the French colonists. Unforeseen at the time, the forced infusion of this African society into the mainstream French colonial cultural mix was to prove to be tremendously influential in the further transformation of Louisiana French cooking.

As the colony grew, more and more slaves from this particular region of Africa were shipped to Louisiana to be sold as cheap labor. Over time, it became common practice for wealthier French colonists to own African slave cooks to assist in preparing their meals. Drawing from their own culinary expertise, these cooks applied African cooking techniques and even added recipes to the French cuisine that they were taught to cook. By the end of the French colonial period, half of the population of the city of New Orleans consisted of African slaves, and their cultural and culinary influence had already become part of the Louisiana colonial establishment. This African culinary influence would prove to be quite extensive and would forever change Louisiana's French culinary tradition, transforming it with additional cooking techniques and recipes that still influence Louisiana cuisine to this day.

The Legacy of the French Colonial Period

France would rule Louisiana for sixty-three years after planting its first permanent settlements in the gulf. In that time French culture in the area would begin to transform its cuisine by blending it with the numerous ethnic groups that immigrated to the colony. Overall, however, Louisiana produced nothing of any substantial worth for the mother country and the colony existed for the most part not much beyond the subsistence level, dependent upon supply ships from France throughout this period. As a result, Louisiana was viewed by the French crown as a white elephant and a continual drain on the Royal treasury. But in spite of all of this, a permanent French presence had indeed been established in the gulf and the foundations for a wonderfully new, exciting cuisine combining elements of French, African, and American Indian influences had been created.

The Spanish Colonial Period

In 1762 France signed a secret agreement with Spain known as the Treaty of Fontainbleau, by which the colony of Louisiana west of the Mississippi River plus the city of New Orleans (which is on the east bank of the Mississippi) was given by France to Spain as a reward for aiding France during the French and Indian War (known in Europe as the Seven Years' War). The French crown was quite frankly glad to be rid of Louisiana, since it had not been a profitable colonial enterprise. Just to compare, the tiny little French island of Martinique in the Caribbean produced more revenue from its annual sugar cane harvest than did all of the Louisiana territory combined!

When word reached Louisiana that their colony had been given to Spain, the colonists were appalled! Being loyal Frenchmen, they lodged official protests to the king to have the colony returned to France, but to no avail. The deal was done. Spain was not overly thrilled about being given Louisiana either, since they knew that the colony did not produce much to make it a profitable venture. However, with the end of the French and Indian War, England received all land in North America up to the Mississippi River, which placed the British ominously close to Mexico, Spain's most important colony in the New World. Therefore, Spain began to view Louisiana as a buffer zone between the British and Mexico. If war were to break out with Britain, then Spain could defend Mexico by fighting in Louisiana. As a result, Spain took on the expense of administrating Louisiana and began to build a series of forts up the Mississippi River with which to defend the colony and thus protect Mexico.

The Spanish

Louisiana was to prosper much better under Spain than it did under France; however, it got off to a very rocky start. The first Spanish governor, Don Antonio de Ulloa, did not arrive in the colony to take formal possession until 1766. He brought with him only one company of Spanish soldiers to help keep order and thus had to rely on French colonial marines to assist him with keeping order. Governor Ulloa tried his best to implement Spanish laws and customs into the colony, but without proper police authority his efforts proved all in vain and merely rubbed the French the wrong way. After two years of his administration the colonists had had enough.

The straw that broke the camel's back came in 1768. Governor Ulloa had ordered the standard European mercantilist policy of requiring the colony to trade only with the mother country (in this case Spain and all Spanish possessions in the New World). The Louisiana colonists who had been used to trading with France resented this action very much. The story goes that one day a ship sailed into the port of New Orleans loaded with good Spanish Rioja wine, a delicious Spanish red wine that unfortunately does not travel well. When the casks of wine were opened on the dock it was discovered that the wine had gone bad during the voyage. The French became incensed that they were now to be reduced to drinking bad Spanish wine instead of their beloved bordeaux and burgundy. An infuriated mob descended on the governor's house, chasing him onto the ship *El Volante* bound for Cuba, which set sail immediately. He was never seen again.

Now the real truth of the matter actually is that Governor Ulloa did not have the proper means at his disposal to effectively assert Spanish authority over Louisiana. The issuing of Spanish laws over the colony without any real police power emboldened the colonists to believe that they could run off the governor and then appeal to the French crown to have the colony returned to France. In New Orleans, though, we *love* to tell this story. In Boston, they had a tea party, but in New Orleans, we had a wine party!

Louisiana, however, was not to be returned to France, in 1769 General Alexander O'Reilly (a famous Irish general in the Spanish army) landed in New Orleans with a major Spanish army to avenge the colonists' insult to Spanish honor. O'Reilly again took formal possession of the colony in the name of Spain, executed the ringleaders of the revolt of 1768, and reasserted Spanish authority in Louisiana, which Spain effectively held until 1806. Spanish colonial administration proved to be far more efficient and beneficial for all parties concerned than that of the French, and it was during the Spanish colonial period that Louisiana's cuisine began to come together in its modern form to take on its distinctive taste and flavor.

Spanish rule for the most part was very benevolent and Louisiana prospered under Spain like it had never done under France. Spain financed the rebuilding of New Orleans after the city burned down in two disastrous fires in 1788 and 1794, the legacy of which can still be seen in the magnificent Spanish-style architecture of the French Quarter. The Louisiana colony was granted certain leniency that other Spanish colonies did not have. Merchants in Louisiana had the privilege to trade not only with Spain and her possessions but also France and French possessions in the Caribbean. This trade opened up the colony to Spanish and Caribbean foods and culinary influences that would affect Louisiana's own developing culinary traditions.

The Caribbean influence was particularly felt in New Orleans between 1791 and 1794, when thousands of French refugees and their slaves flocked into the city from St. Domingue (Haiti) fleeing the slave insurrection there. These French refugees and their slaves brought with them an Afro/Franco/Spanish culinary tradition that was injected into the French Creole cuisine of New Orleans. Though this immigration seemed large at the time, it proved to be the last major cultural surge of a sizeable French population into Louisiana.

In governing Louisiana, Spain encountered the same problems that France had with the colony—namely, that few people from Spain wanted to immigrate to Louisiana either. The one exception to this was a group of Spanish settlers from the Canary Islands that are known locally as Los Isleños or "the Islanders." These hard-working, industrious farmers and fishermen were given land grants to settle the land south of New Orleans in St. Bernard Parish where their descendants live to this day, speaking a dialect of Castilian Spanish and echoing their proud Spanish heritage from a bygone era.

The Creoles

It was during Spain's rule that the local population and their cooking began to be known as Creole. The word "Creole" is the French derivation of the Spanish word *criollo*, which literally means "a child born in the colonies," or in other words a colonial. It refers to someone or something that was born in or comes from a colonial area, and has absolutely *nothing* to do with race or mixing of races or anything like that whatsoever. In Louisiana history the Creoles were the descendants of the original colonial settlers who immigrated to the colony. They could be French, Spanish, German, African, or any other nationality—or yes, even a mix of nationalities—as long as they were born in the colony. It is not what makes up your pedigree that makes you a Creole but rather where your pedigree was born that does. The best way to understand the true meaning of the word is to substitute the word "colonial" when you see the word "Creole" and you will know exactly how the word was originally intended to be used.

The confusion as to what constituted a Creole started after the American Civil War, when the word began to change in usage as many people wrongfully believed that to be "Creole" someone had to be part black or Indian or Spanish or French or whatever. This is actually *not* true to the original definition of the word, as anyone who has done any serious historical research in this area can tell you. However, you will find *many* people today who still believe that a Creole is a mixture of this or that, and therefore that definition cannot be entirely disregarded, even though these people are wrong. It is a continual argument within Louisiana itself and *everyone* there has a *very* decided opinion on the subject. The historical data, however, supports the original definition of the word; therefore, the word "Creole" has absolutely nothing at all to do with race and merely refers to someone or something that comes from a colonial area.

Today in Louisiana you can find Creole *anything* from Creole tomatoes to Creole ponies, all of them referring to something that is made in or comes from Louisiana. The center for Creole culture and cuisine in Louisiana was then, and still is today, the city of New Orleans. Creole cuisine therefore is merely the cuisine developed in New Orleans by the colonials who inhabited the city. It has become world renowned for its fancy dishes with rich sauces and fantastic flavors and, in our opinion, to this day the city of New Orleans still has the finest restaurants in North America.

The Cajuns

The Acadian people began to arrive in Louisiana during the Spanish regime. The Acadians (known as Cajuns in Louisiana) are Frenchmen originally coming from Nova Scotia in

Canada (which at one time was a French colony known as "Acadie," or Acadia). The French colony of Acadia had been founded as early as 1605 and settled by hardworking farmers and fishermen. The French presence was strong there and the people lived a hard but good life in the colony. But like all colonies in North America in the eighteenth century, Acadia was caught up in the European struggle for dominance of the New World. The British were given Acadia by the French according to the terms of the Treaty of Utrecht in 1713, which ended Queen Anne's War (known in Europe as the War of the Spanish Succession 1702–13). Great Britain at that time made no immediate plans to settle the colony and instead chose to rule Acadia as a subjugated state.

In 1755 the British decided to exile the Acadians from Acadia—because the people refused to swear an oath of allegiance to the British crown—and then to resettle the colony with Scottish settlers (hence the renaming of Acadia into "Nova Scotia," which means "New Scotland" in Latin). Therefore, British troops began to round up Acadians, put them on boats, and ship them to parts unknown. Some of these people were sent to the thirteen British colonies on the Atlantic seacoast. Some were sent to the Caribbean, where they were made slaves. Many people were sent to refugee camps in France, where even the French refused to accept them; others were shipped to wherever the boat that they got on took them! To this day, because France refused to accept the Acadians back into the country, the Cajuns use the French word *drapeau*, which means "flag," to refer to a baby's diaper.

You cannot imagine how shockingly terrible this was for the Acadian people. Entire communities were forcibly uprooted by British troops with nothing more than the clothes on their back. Homes were burned down. Families were split up. People were literally driven at bayonet point onto ships, herded like cattle, and sent to destinations unknown. They were scattered to the four winds to live an uncertain future like the Romans did to the Hebrews centuries before. This exile is known by the Cajuns as *Le Grande Derangement* (the Great Trouble). But like the Jews of old, the Acadians refused to die, and as a testament to their strength and courage they retained their cultural identity in the face of adversity. Slowly, one by one, family by family, group by group, they began an incredible migration from Europe, the English colonies, and the Caribbean to Spanish Louisiana, which had the next largest French population in North America outside of Canada. Between 1755 and the 1790s the Acadians filtered into Spanish-held Louisiana, where they were given free land and tools and a chance to make a fresh start.

The Acadians originally received land grants along the Mississippi upriver from New Orleans, down Bayou Lafourche, and on the prairies in southwestern Louisiana. After receiving their land, the Acadians moved off into the bayous and prairies of the state and settled small farming and ranching homesteads. Being country people, these Cajuns, as they came to be called, were very thrifty hunters, farmers, and fishermen that lived off the land. Within about ten years of their arrival they had begun to rebuild their lives and establish new homes in this new land, creating a "New Acadia," where they would thrive and prosper like they never had before.

The Legacy of the Spanish Colonial Period

Spain's legacy in Louisiana can be seen almost everywhere. Under Spanish rule the colony continued to grow and became much more prosperous. Local industries such as rice and sugar cane became much more developed and the port of New Orleans grew in size to handle more shipping. The city itself was rebuilt in the Spanish architectural style and the people became more refined and wealthier. Louisiana's Creole cuisine began to incorporate a Spanish flavor, which transformed it from a bland French style into a unique, spicy culinary tradition as delicious as any of the world's great cuisines. Louisiana was nurtured by Spain and, because of that, it thrived and blended the best of all of the immigrant cultures that came to settle there. The state and its remarkable cuisine would not be what it is today had it not been for the care and nurturing that the Spanish bestowed upon it.

The American Period

In 1800 the secret Treaty of San Ildefonso was made between the king of Spain and Napoleon Bonaparte. The terms of this treaty returned Louisiana to France in exchange for the province of Tuscany in Italy and recognition of the king of Etruria. Though it was technically now a French colony once again, the administration of Louisiana was still in Spanish hands and would remain so up until 1806. Napoleon had a grand design for Louisiana, hoping to re-create the great French colonial empire that had existed in North America only thirty-eight years before. His great colonial scheme depended upon one thing: a powerful naval base in the Caribbean to protect the colony from the British royal navy.

To this end, Napoleon dispatched a major French army to the island of St. Domingue, in an effort to recapture the island from the slaves who had overthrown their French masters in 1794 and made St. Domingue an independent state. Napoleon's army easily retook the island, but soon became decimated by a yellow fever epidemic and constant guerrilla warfare. France was unable to effectively secure St. Domingue to use as a naval base to defend Louisiana, and so Napoleon realized that his grand designs for the colony could never materialize.

Now while all of this was going on, U.S. President Thomas Jefferson had sent Robert Livingston to Paris to negotiate with Napoleon for the sale of the city of New Orleans. Jefferson realized that whoever owned New Orleans would control all trade on the Mississippi River, and therefore wanted to purchase the city to have a place to ship out American goods from up north.

In 1803 Livingston (who was now joined by James Monroe) met with Napoleon's brother Joseph and was shocked to hear that Napoleon was willing to sell *all* of Louisiana to the United States if they wanted it. Napoleon had realized that if he could not secure a proper naval base in the Caribbean he would be unable to protect Louisiana from the British and thus it became pointless to try and do anything else with the colony. In addition, relations with Great Britain were once again going sour, and Napoleon needed money to raise another army to fight an impending war with the British. So after a little bargaining back and forth, the price was finally set at $15 million for the entire Louisiana Territory which came out to about 0.3 cents an acre! It was a tremendous land deal, one that doubled the size of the United States.

The terms of the Treaty of San Ildefonso stipulated that France could not give or sell Louisiana back to anyone else except to Spain, so the Louisiana Purchase was an illegal sale to begin with. Of course, Napoleon was not known for being one to keep his word when it came to treaties; and even though this sale was illegal and infuriated both Spain and Great Britain, he needed the money and therefore was more than happy to sell the colony to the Americans no matter what the British, the Spanish, or even the Louisiana colonists themselves felt about it. In addition, Jefferson was a strict constitutionalist who believed very strongly that the president could not do anything that was not specifically spelled out in the U.S. Constitution. And nowhere in the Constitution does it give the president the authority to buy or sell land. But it was such a *sweet* deal that he just *had* to overlook his principles on this occasion for the sake of the country.

And so in 1803 the United States purchased the Louisiana Territory from France and it officially became American. The really interesting part to this story is this: Jefferson was easily able to get the bill for the purchase of Louisiana passed in the Congress. However, there was not enough money in the U.S. Treasury at the time to afford to buy Louisiana. Therefore, to raise the capital for the purchase, the United States borrowed money from the banking firms of Hope & Company in Amsterdam and Baring & Company in London to pay Napoleon for Louisiana, so that he could then raise an army to fight Great Britain. So in essence the British actually financed the French army to fight the very next war that Great Britain fought against Napoleon!

The Americans

In November of 1803 Louisiana was officially transferred from Spain to France. The following month, it was again officially transferred from France to the United States, with William C. C. Claiborne named as the first territorial governor. Spanish colonial administrators; however, continued to rule in the territory jointly with the Americans for another two years, until finally leaving Louisiana in 1806. Quite frankly, it was all a bit much for the French Creoles who lived there. The Creoles had never liked the Americans very much and considered them to be uncouth country bumpkins with very few qualities of refinement or grace about them. But American the colony now was and would so remain forever and a day.

With the American acquisition of the territory Louisiana entered into a golden age. Americans (and in particular American money) poured into the territory and Louisiana prospered as never before. The dream that La Salle had way back in 1682 was finally coming true and being realized beyond anyone's wildest imagination. Creole society became elegant and refined and the restaurant industry flourished in New Orleans, featuring Creole dishes that had evolved over the past hundred years. The substantial American trade coming down the Mississippi River made New Orleans *rich* and it soon became the largest port in the country. Louisiana became a state in 1812 and continued to prosper and grow under American control up until the Civil War.

As the Americans poured into the state so did their Anglo-American culinary influence. Dishes commonly eaten in the South were soon being seen on Louisiana tables—particularly in the northern part of the state, where many Anglo-Americans settled. Louisiana soon became integrated into the South as a southern state, but it was a southern state different from all others. Unlike the rest of the South, whose heritage was primarily Anglo, Scots-Irish, and African, Louisiana was French, Spanish, and African (but with increasing numbers of Anglo-Americans coming every day). It was a bastion of Franco/Spanish culture in an Anglo sea, and despite ever-increasing American cultural influences on the area, it retained its European uniqueness and merely absorbed elements of Anglo-American culture without being overwhelmed by it. This is still reflected in its cuisine, which retains its European roots while at the same time sharing American dishes and culinary ideas.

The Italians
During the mid-nineteenth century large numbers of European immigrants from Italy, Sicily, Ireland, and the German states began to arrive in the city of New Orleans, forever influencing its Creole cuisine. As their populations grew they began to intermingle with each other, and soon a new culture made from their union became dominant in the city as the descendants of the original French Creoles shrank in number.

In New Orleans these people are referred to as the "Yats" because of the greeting that they give when they meet one another: "Where y'at?" Interestingly, the typical "Yat" accent, which is now considered to be the native New Orleanian accent, sounds very similar to the Brooklyn accent of New York City, whose population is also made up of a cross between German, Italian, and Irish people. Apparently, when these three immigrant groups intermingle with each other, the result is a sort of Brooklyn-type accent. It is quite fascinating indeed when one considers that this phenomenon occurred in two different cities thousands of miles apart!

By the mid-twentieth century these people had absorbed the existing Creole culture that existed in the city and added their own unique cultural twist to it based on their mixed Euro-American heritage. Of these three different immigrant groups that came to the city, the Italians and Sicilians would influence Creole cuisine the most and contribute what would become the major difference between Creole and Cajun cooking.

This Italian connection is the primary difference between Cajun and Creole cuisines today. This Old World Mediterranean culture from southern Italy and Sicily transformed the Creole cuisine of New Orleans with the addition of their ancient culinary heritage. Within 100 years of their arrival, Italian culinary influences became incorporated into the mainstream local Creole cuisine. Their influence in New Orleans was considerable and extended particularly into the grocery industry. Italian Americans still dominate the grocery industry in the city.

Very soon, Italian restaurants began to spring up all over New Orleans serving both Italian and Creole dishes, while Creole restaurants began to offer Italian dishes on their menus as well. It was a marriage made in Heaven that left an indelible stamp onto Creole cuisine forever. However, this influence never extended very far beyond the boundaries of Orleans Parish and never made it out to the Cajun country in Southwest Louisiana. As a result, Cajun cooking techniques remained predominantly the same as they had been in the previous century.

In Louisiana, we believe our cooking—both Cajun and Creole—is the finest cuisine in all of North America, one that has tremendous flavor and is perfect for parties and celebrations. Our cuisine has evolved just as we have because of our history. And everyone in Louisiana—Cajun, Creole, and everybody else—love to celebrate life with good food, good friends, good music, and good family. It is all part of our wonderful cultural heritage and a reflection of our history as a truly unique people.

The Difference Between Cajun and Creole Cuisines

So what *is* the real difference between Cajun and Creole cooking? Well, in a nutshell it is downhome country cooking (Cajun) versus fancy city cooking (Creole). Creole comes from the Greater New Orleans Area and tends to be rich and "highbrow" with many fancy dishes, some of which are cooked with wines and rich sauces. A Creole meal tends to have numerous different dishes as well and can be very extravagant. Being a port city, New Orleans was the center for receiving numerous immigrants and additional culinary influences that over time would greatly affect the city's Creole cuisine.

Basically, Cajun cooking is eighteenth-century Creole cooking—but with a country twist. Cajun cooking comes from the southwestern prairies of Louisiana centered around the town of Lafayette, their unofficial capital. Cajun tends to be more plain and simple fare and less fancy than its Creole cousin. A Cajun meal tends to be less extravagant and consists of a lot of one-pot dishes. Cajuns tend to cook a lot more game recipes, given the fact that they have a tradition of being hunters and fishermen, and their food is considered to emphasize more herbs and spices than fancier, rich sauces.

Both styles are a blending of French, Spanish, African, and American Indian culinary traditions, but Creole goes one step further and has an Italian component to it that Cajun does not tend to have. There are those who believe that Cajun cuisine is actually hotter than Creole cuisine, but that really is up to individual taste. Cajuns *do* tend to like their food spicy, but then so do the Creoles of New Orleans. Both styles have the same roots and both styles cook pretty much the same recipes. Once the Cajuns moved out into southwestern Louisiana their cooking tended to remain fairly unchanged while the Creole cuisine of New Orleans continued to evolve. We both cook the same things. . . . we just tend to cook them a little differently from each other, that's all.

Take jambalaya, for example, a rice dish with different meat, seafood, and vegetables in it that is cooked all together so that the rice will take on the flavor of everything in the pot. It is believed by many to be a Louisiana version of a Spanish paella, although some people believe that the dish is actually African in origin and was first developed by African slaves in Louisiana during the Spanish colonial period. (The debate still goes on to this day.)

In New Orleans we will cook a jambalaya with chicken, sausage, shrimp, ham, and then tomatoes, tomato sauce, and different herbs and spices, including oregano added in, which gives it a rich tomato flavor and colors it red. All of this is a result of our Italian Creole heritage. But out in Lafayette, the Cajuns will make it with the same ingredients but without the tomatoes and tomato sauce and possibly oregano because to them that would ruin it and it will not have a red color or a tomato flavor. Instead, Cajuns will tend to leave all of that out and some may even add a dark brown roux to the pot, which gives the jambalaya a brown color and a nutlike flavor. So here you can see an example of both peoples cooking the same dish, but because of their different historical culinary background will prepare it in just a little different manner and with their own unique cultural twist.

By the late twentieth century both styles of cooking began to merge together as a result of public education, television, and the Internet, and therefore have now come to be referred to as "Cajun/Creole" cuisine. However, there are still subtle differences between them that can be seen primarily in individual homes across the state. Both are absolutely *delicious* and reflect the history of the state that created them. They have evolved over the years and continue to evolve as Louisiana enters the twenty-first century and adds additional culinary influences into our collective gumbo pot. They are a uniquely American culinary creation and are the special gift that Louisiana has given to the world.

Though every ethnic culinary influence has been important in shaping Cajun/Creole cuisine, it was France that laid out the first building blocks of our culinary style to which all others would be added. In essence, the French tradition was the roux that Louisiana's cooking evolved from. Without the French influence in the first place, there would be no Cajun/Creole culinary style at all.

One can trace the roots of French cooking all the way back to Julius Caesar's conquest of Gaul in 51 B.C. and the resulting mix of Roman and Celtic culinary traditions. However, most people generally agree that the beginnings of modern French cuisine started during the Renaissance around 1533 when Catherine de Medici of Florence married Henry the Duke of Orleans (who later became King Henry II of France) and brought with her several Italian chefs who influenced French cooking in the royal court.

When the first French settlers arrived in the Mississippi Valley 167 years later, they brought with them their own knowledge of eighteenth-century classical French cooking. This included preparing rich sauces, using fresh culinary herbs, cooking with wines and liquors, making pastries and confections, and French bread. These culinary characteristics were to become the foundation for Louisiana's Cajun/Creole cuisine upon which all other ethnic culinary influences that were introduced would build.

Two of the most important features that the French introduced in this area were French bread and rice. The French people have always loved their crusty wheat bread and cannot bear to eat a meal without it. They tried to grow wheat in Louisiana to make their bread but unfortunately were unsuccessful in their efforts. As a result, the colonists were dependent upon supply ships from France to bring them the wheat flour they needed to make their bread. When the supply ships did not arrive, they were forced to eat bread made from cornmeal, which they never did really like and ate only out of necessity.

Bread was very important to the French diet. It was extremely versatile. When freshly baked it was eaten either as the main course (if one was too poor to afford anything else to eat) or as a side accompaniment to the main dish. When it went hard and stale it could be sliced and mixed with milk and eggs to make either a dessert such as bread pudding, served with a whiskey or rum sauce, or a delightful breakfast dish called pain perdu (lost bread), served with cane syrup. French bread was literally the staff of life, and to this day French bread is still eaten in enormous quantities by both the Creoles and the Cajuns.

Rice was introduced in Louisiana around 1712 by way of the Carolinas, originally to be sold as a cash crop grown on plantations in the area. Indeed rice was shipped to the colony both from the West Indies and on slave ships from Africa to be sold along with African slaves who were knowledgeable in growing and harvesting it. Though rice is not thought of as a traditional element of French cuisine, it became one in Louisiana out of necessity. Given the infrequency in which supply ships from France landed in the colony, rice was turned to as a staple food to supplement the colonists' diet. Over time rice became a very important element of Louisiana French cuisine and accepted by the French colonists as part of their culinary tradition.

French knowledge of using fresh herbs in their cooking was an important seasoning technique that they brought with them. Herbs such as garlic, thyme, sweet basil, marjoram, and bay leaves were used to give their dishes an herbal flavor that would enhance the natural flavor of the food that they cooked and could thus turn an otherwise average dish into something extremely flavorful indeed. Cooking with herbs was a learned skill that French cooks also used to make foods that they might not normally like more agreeable to their Gallic palate.

Cooking with wine and liquors was a particular culinary art used extensively in French cuisine. The French were known for drinking a prodigious amount of wine, and loved the flavor of the grape to be added to the food that they prepared. Indeed, early on after the founding of New Orleans in 1718 the city earned a reputation for being a hard-drinking town. Fabulous French wines were imported into Louisiana by the shipload from Bordeaux, Burgundy, and all over France. Wine was both consumed and poured into dishes that were baked, broiled, stewed, and sautéed, and the skillful cook learned the subtle art of matching the right wine with particular foods to further enhance its flavor.

It was in sauces that the French made one of their most significant contributions to Louisiana cooking. As mentioned before, there were three sauce mere or "mother sauces" that were primarily used in Louisiana French cuisine. They were sauce espagnole (Spanish sauce, a brown sauce), sauce allemande (German sauce, being a white sauce), and glace or glaze. However, in addition to these numerous other sauces were used and created to complement a prepared dish. The French learned that by making a rich, flavorful sauce they could create a new dimension to any ordinary dish and a good sauce could even dress up an old or poor cut of meat and make it sumptuous and elegant.

But of all the sauces used by the French, it was the common roux that would have the most effect on Louisiana's cuisine. This very basic sauce made by browning flour and oil together in a skillet was put into virtually *everything* that the Louisiana colonists prepared. It was used to enhance both the texture and the flavor of a dish, and its use became widespread in Louisiana as cooks used it as a base to literally scores of different dishes to which additional ingredients were then added. This one French culinary technique was to become the very cornerstone for an entirely new cuisine, founded upon the culinary traditions of France but expanded with the addition of other culinary influences to become something truly unique to the world.

One cannot overemphasize the importance that France brought to the development of Louisiana's culinary heritage. Braving harsh elements and dealing with colonial administrative ineptitude, France hacked out its settlements in the Mississippi Valley and through dogged persistence planted a firm French presence in Louisiana that simply refused to go away. Their culinary ingenuity absorbed other cooking styles and transformed traditional French cooking into a distinctive "Franco-American" style that became world renowned for its inventive blending of flavors and cooking techniques as only a Frenchman could have developed.

The Native American Influence

Were it not for the American Indians, Louisiana's Cajun/Creole cooking might never have taken off in the first place and would certainly not resemble its present form at all. The Southern Indians taught the first French settlers how to survive in the Louisiana wilderness and kept the colony alive with the food staples that they traded with the colonists. Indeed one of the primary reasons that the city of New Orleans was established at its present location is that the area was used by the Indians as a trading market to trade produce and other commodities with each other. The various Indian tribes traded locally grown foods and herbs with the French upon their arrival, which soon became incorporated into the French cuisine of the day.

The foundation of Indian cuisine centered around what is known as the "three sisters": corn, beans, and squash (including pumpkins). These three crops were grown together in Native American gardens. Unlike the Europeans who planted their crops in furrows, an Indian garden consisted of small mounds. Corn would be planed in the center of the mound with beans planted around the corn and squash and pumpkins planted around the beans. As the corn grew tall the bean vine would wind itself up around the corn stalks and the squash and pumpkins would sprout up at the base of the mound. These three vegetables, supplemented with fish, shellfish, and wild game, were the mainstays of the Native American diet.

The Indians lived in towns for the most part along rivers and streams which they used for transportation. Houses were built around a central courtyard with a large campfire that was used for cooking. It was common for these people to have as many as three or four houses situated around the courtyard. One house was an open-air hut with no walls, known as a chickee, that was used in the summertime. Another was a walled hut with no windows that was used as a winter "hot house" with a constant fire kept burning inside. Another hut with no windows was used as a storehouse. Cooking was usually done outside in the courtyard except during inclement weather. Meals were prepared over the campfire, usually by boiling or roasting. The Indians had no set mealtime and instead merely ate whenever they were hungry. Some of their more popular foods that would become incorporated into Louisiana's cuisine were corn, filé powder, crawfish, and alligator.

Corn in various forms—cornmeal, hominy, and corn dishes—was the main staple used by the Indians and eventually became very commonly used in Louisiana cooking (even though the French had to develop a taste for them at first). During times of severe food shortages the colonists relied heavily upon locally grown corn and the numerous dishes that one could make from it. This very versatile plant slowly began to be accepted by the French colonials, who learned the various ways that it could be prepared and then added their own culinary techniques to it to give it a flavor that they would find more pleasing to their Gallic palate. The most famous Indian corn dish to make its way into Louisiana cuisine is called maque choux (stewed corn and tomatoes). This is made by sautéing corn kernels with onions, bell peppers, and tomatoes then adding in some chicken stock and a little bit of cream to stew the dish until it is done. Though considered today to be a traditional Cajun dish, its roots most definitely spring from the Southeastern Indians.

Perhaps the most important and influential herb that the Indians introduced to the French was filé powder. Not actually an herb at all, filé powder is the ground-up leaves of the sassafras plant. It is used in our gumbos and soups as a thickening agent much like cornstarch but with a delightful sassafras flavor. The French colonials loved the flavor of filé and were intrigued by its ability to thicken a soup or stew. Even in the late nineteenth century, Choctaw Indians could still be found at the French Market in New Orleans selling freshly ground filé to Creole cooks to use in their evening meals.

The Native Americans ate a prodigious amount of game, which usually was roasted over an open fire on a spit or boiled in soups and stews. The most important of these was venison, which was eaten as commonly as we do steak today. Numerous other game animals were eaten such as rabbit, turtle, possum, and a variety of fowl. Interestingly, the Indians had their own version of keeping "kosher" in which they believed that animals that could fly should not be cooked together with animals that walked, thus keeping the world of the sky separate from the world on the ground. As a result they would never cook fowl with non-flying game in the same pot.

Alligator was considered to be a great delicacy. Being a reptile, alligator meat is very high in protein and is lean with very little fat. The most commonly eaten parts are the tail and the meat along the legs and backbone, which are cut up into little nuggets. The first French governor, Pierre le Moyne, Sieur d'Iberville, recorded in his journal about hunting alligators and said, "I killed a small one eight feet long, which is very good to eat, the flesh being very white and delicate but smelling of musk, which is a scent that the flesh must be rid of before one can eat it." Alligator is still considered to be quite a delicacy in Louisiana. The meat is usually either breaded and fried or sautéed and smothered with a sauce and served over rice such as in the dish alligator sauce piquant.

Of all of the foods introduced to the French by the Indians, though, it was the Louisiana crawfish they loved the most. Boiled crawfish, first eaten by the Indians centuries ago, has become a Louisiana delicacy that is *very* popular throughout the state. The Indians showed the French numerous ways to cook the crustaceans, and as French cuisine evolved so to did the ways that they prepared them. Crawfish are used in numerous Louisiana dishes either singularly or mixed in with other foods, such as in a seafood gumbo or a jambalaya. Just like the Indians, we love to eat our crawfish *any* kind of way!

Relations with the Indians were not always good. Several wars were fought with various tribes, such as the Chitimacha and the Natchez, which virtually wiped them out. After the first 100 years of French settlement the Indian population in the colony was substantially reduced in numbers from war, disease, and European encroachment on Indian lands. However, many of these tribes continue to live in the state to this day, such as the Houma, the Coushatta, the Chitimacha, and the Choctaw, and still enrich our culture just as their ancestors did with their ancient civilization. Louisiana cuisine benefited very much from the culinary exchange it received from the Indians, and their influence can still be seen (and particularly enjoyed) in numerous dishes that continue to be a part of our wonderful Louisiana culinary heritage.

The African Connection

Perhaps one of the most significant influences upon Louisiana cooking has come from the African culture first introduced into the colony in 1719. African slaves were used extensively throughout the Louisiana colony, particularly in home kitchens, and they had a definite "hands-on" influence which left an indelible stamp on Cajun/Creole cuisine that can easily be seen (and tasted) to this day. Their significant contributions came in the form of various different foods and recipes imported with them and, most significantly of all, two very important cooking techniques that are used in our food preparation.

Various foods that we think of today as "Southern" actually originated in Africa: such as black-eyed peas, yams, peanuts, rice, and okra all were brought to Louisiana (and the rest of the South as well) with the African people as part of the transatlantic slave trade. Their introduction enriched our cuisine as these foods soon took root in the colony and became part of the staple diet that the colonists ate. And along with these foods came specific African recipes for preparing them which have since become incorporated into our cuisine. In Louisiana the most famous of these foods is okra, which came along with the recipe for gumbo that it is so lavishly used in.

The word *gumbo* actually comes from the African name for okra, *gombo*, and refers both to the vegetable okra and the soup that is made with it. In Louisiana we generally feel that gumbo is not a soup or a stew but is in a class all its own. Originally, gumbo was made with okra used both for its flavor and as a thickener to make the gumbo rich and thick. Though many people mistakenly believe that gumbo originated in Louisiana, the actual dish most definitely comes from West Africa, where it has been cooked for hundreds of years. This truly wonderful dish was introduced into Louisiana most probably as early as the first Africans were. As more and more Africans were brought into Louisiana to work on the plantations, gumbos became more common and popular with all who tasted their delectable flavor.

There are many different types of gumbo. In West Africa, gumbo is basically an okra stew that, like its Louisiana cousin, is made with many different sorts of meats and vegetables in it. Louisiana gumbos are very similar to African gumbos, the difference between them being mainly in the types of different meats and vegetables and herbs that are used to prepare them. To the gumbo "purist" (or snob if you prefer), a good Louisiana gumbo should have at least one of two different ingredients in it to make it thick: either okra or filé (which the Creoles picked up from the Indians) but *never* both. Personally, the authors of this book feel that such attitudes are absolutely ridiculous and if you like using both at the same time then go right ahead. It's *your* gumbo, so you can make it any way that you like.

Literally *anything* can go into a gumbo, and one can find gumbos made with chicken, sausage, duck, squirrel, seafood, alligator, or whatever! It all depends on how creative you are and what you have on hand in your kitchen. To the Creoles, the king of gumbo is considered to be gumbo z'herbes, which is a vegetarian gumbo made with lots of herbs and greens and usually served during Lent. Along with the recipe for gumbo came the special African cooking technique to prepare it.

African slaves were commonly used in Louisiana kitchens, where they learned French colonial styles of cooking and then blended these techniques with their own African culinary expertise. Principal among these special cooking techniques was that of simmering or slow cooking of soups and gumbos to extract more and more flavor from whatever was put into the pot to cook. This technique will make the most delicious and flavorful soups that you have ever tasted, particularly when combined with the French knowledge of using fresh herbs to impart additional wonderful flavors into the magic pot.

Another African culinary technique that was soon incorporated into Louisiana cooking was that of deep fat frying for meats and vegetables. This simple and very tasty technique was introduced throughout the South by Africans who used it extensively for cooking practically anything. Various foods were coated in a batter made with flour or cornmeal (which was also picked up from the Indians) and then deep fried in fat, shortening, or oil until it was nice and crispy and brown. It soon became extremely popular because of the delectable flavor and crunchy texture that it gave to food and came to be considered a distinctly Southern method of cooking that spread throughout the Southeast.

By the end of the French colonial period in 1762, almost half of the population of the Louisiana colony consisted of African Americans, who made a very considerable contribution to the early development of Louisiana's French Creole cuisine. Their extensive influence left an indelible stamp that is still felt to this day in numerous dishes and cooking techniques that transformed French cooking into a new and wonderfully delicious culinary style that is now unique to the world.

With the transfer of Louisiana from France to Spain in 1762 came a uniquely Spanish twist that would forever change the overall form and identity of French Creole cuisine. Throughout the Spanish colonial period new ports were opened up to the French colonists, which introduced them to new cooking styles based on Spain's own culinary development after the discovery of the New World. The Spanish love of spicy peppers and their practice of mixing meats and fish together in dishes and serving them over rice became increasingly popular with the Louisiana colonists. These culinary influences crept into Louisiana's cuisine and blended with that of the French to create new dishes filled with exciting and wonderful new flavors.

The Louisiana colony prospered much more under Spanish rule. Spain nurtured the colony, exposing it to new foods and culinary ideas that became readily accepted by the local population at large. Louisiana was unique among all Spanish colonies in that it was allowed to trade both with Spain and her colonial possessions *and* France and French colonial possessions in the Caribbean. Thus, the Louisiana colonists had access to more ports and Spanish culinary influences than they had when they were ruled by France. Soon new dishes began to appear with exotic-sounding names such as jambalaya and congri, both influenced by Spanish traditions and prepared by African cooks utilizing their own unique culinary expertise.

Jambalaya is a rice dish similar to a Spanish paella, with rice cooked in a pot with different meats, vegetables, and seafood so that the rice takes on the flavor of everything in the pot instead of just being flavorfully cooked food served over bland rice. The origins of the word *jambalaya* are shrouded in mystery. Some believe that the dish comes from the French word *jambon*, for ham, which is used in the dish, while others feel that it is African in origin, coming from the African word *jamba*, meaning "gift," and another African word, *ya*, meaning "rice," thus making the whole word to mean "gift with the rice." Rice was used as a daily ration for the slaves in Louisiana at this time (just like cornmeal was used as a ration for them in the rest of the South) and anytime the master gave them some additional meat or vegetables to go along with it, that would have been a gift for them indeed. Though we are not sure how this delicious dish actually evolved, we do know that it has both Spanish and African influences, and that it became popular during the Spanish regime in Louisiana.

Congri, another Spanish-style dish with both Spanish and African influences, is basically black beans and rice, a staple in Louisiana. The beans are cooked in a pot separately and then served over cooked rice, sometimes with a bit of ham or sausage. Beans and rice dishes were very common in the Spanish colonies and most probably were introduced into Louisiana through the increased trade that went on with Spain's colonial possessions in Florida and the Caribbean. These dishes were very inexpensive to make and very filling, with lots of both protein and carbohydrates in them. Of all of these types of dishes, the most famous of them has become red beans and rice, which is still commonly eaten throughout Louisiana, particularly in New Orleans.

Traditionally, red beans and rice was eaten in New Orleans on Mondays because Monday was considered to be wash day (which was an all-day chore) and the women who did most of the cooking in the colony (both black and white) did not have time to both wash clothes *and* cook a meal. So the beans could be put in a pot and slow simmered in the African method all day long while the clothes were being washed and at the end of a very hard day a delicious meal would be ready to eat.

Red kidney beans are the most commonly used bean for making this dish today; however, there is a small, round red bean called a "red bean" that is believed by many to be the original bean used in this dish. The beans are usually soaked overnight in water to make them swell up and then they are slow cooked over a low heat for hours on end with flavorful herbs and spices until they are soft and incredibly delicious! To this day, restaurants in New Orleans will offer specials on red beans and rice every Monday.

Perhaps the most exciting of Spain's culinary influences introduced into Louisiana's cuisine was that of adding hot peppers to their food. Peppers were discovered in the New World on Columbus's very first voyage and introduced into Spain, where they became very popular and spread very quickly around the world through trade. Spaniards had a great love of spicy food and brought that love with them when they took over the French colony. With greater access to trade with Spanish colonial possessions, new markets opened up for the sale of peppers and very soon numerous types of peppers began to appear in Louisiana and be used in the colonists' food preparation. This introduction of spicy peppers into the French cuisine was to have a permanent effect as people began to use more and more peppers in their dishes to make their food more interesting and exciting.

The results of Spain's culinary influence in Louisiana were to help shape the transformation of the cuisine from a more bland French style to that of a more spicy Caribbean style of food. It was to be a permanent influence that would take hold and become a wonderful part of Louisiana's evolving culinary tradition that we enjoy to this very day!

The Acadian Migrations

The Acadians began their migration from French Canada into Louisiana very soon after their expulsion from Acadia (Nova Scotia) by the British in 1755. This expulsion scattered these people all over the Atlantic Seaboard, France, and the Caribbean. Over the course of the next forty years the Acadians slowly began to migrate to Louisiana. The majority of these people arrived in the colony after it had been transferred to Spain in 1762. The Spanish crown offered Acadian refugees free land and tools to come and settle in Louisiana in an effort to bolster the colony's small population. Once in Louisiana they were exposed to a new and foreign culture that was similar to yet still quite different from their French homeland back in Canada.

Their homeland in Acadia was part of the Canadian Maritime Provinces, and the cuisine these people were used to was basically meat and potato–type dishes and chowders. Their primary culinary influences had been France and England, and their palate simply had nothing in common with what was transforming in Spanish Louisiana at that time. For the most part the Acadians ate bland food seasoned only with an occasional herb or two and cooked very plainly by boiling or lightly frying. The Acadian national dish was

known as *poutine rapure* or "Rappie pie," basically a meat pie with potatoes and cheese cooked together in a pie-type crust: very filling, but very bland and not spicy at all. French bread made from wheat was a staple of their diet as were turnips and cabbages. Salt pork was the primary meat that they ate. Many of the Acadians, who were hunters and fishermen, also had a taste for Atlantic seafood and Canadian game, but this, too, was cooked in a very bland and unexciting manner.

The Acadians were a hardy bunch—good people with a strong sense of family and community. They were used to hard work and living off of the land and knew how to be thrifty and how to survive. They also knew how to cook, and could be very inventive and creative in the kitchen when they had to. Settling in the Louisiana colony opened up their eyes to a whole new culinary experience that was fasci-

Photo by Christi Key

nating, delicious, and exciting. Their immigration into Louisiana occurred at the same time that the French Creole cuisine in the colony was beginning to transform itself from a strictly French culinary style into that of a more Caribbean-influenced cuisine blended with elements of French, Spanish, African, and American Indian traditions. This new cuisine was foreign to the Acadian palate and must have appeared exotic and fascinating to them indeed.

Upon their arrival in Louisiana the Acadians were first deposited in the city of New Orleans, where they waited to receive land grants to relocate them to other parts of the colony. It was here that they were first exposed to the Creole cuisine that was developing in the city at that time. This exposure would leave a lasting impression: an entirely new cooking style, with intriguing new dishes, made with ingredients that some of them had never seen before. It was a cuisine filled with exciting new flavors and exotic-sounding names. And the taste was unbelievable! The Acadian people were greatly influenced by what they learned from the Creoles in the colony and definitely took it to heart.

In the short time that the Acadians were in New Orleans, they learned how to prepare this new cuisine, and quickly forgot all about the bland French-style cooking of their homeland back in Canada. But they themselves would also very soon influence the Creole cuisine of Louisiana, adding their own distinctive culinary expertise to the preparation of this new food, one that emphasized thrift and economy of market and a knowledge of using what was on hand taken from the bounty of the land. In time they were to develop their own culinary style, which drew from what they had learned from the Creoles but utilized their own unique culinary touches added in. It was to begin a transformation of their own culture and change who they were from the Acadians to that of the Louisiana Cajuns.

La Belle Epoque

With the acquisition of Louisiana by the United States in 1803, New Orleans entered a golden age of development that lasted up through the American Civil War. It was an era in which Creole society blossomed, becoming elegant and refined, an era in which the city grew to become the richest port in the country and saw the development of a sophisticated restaurant industry featuring its newly evolved Creole cuisine.

As New Orleans became more prosperous, the French Creoles took on an almost aristocratic air and considered their society to be more cultured and European than that of the Americans who immigrated into the city. They developed a genteel society that emphasized enjoying life to its fullest, and in particular appreciating the finer things in life, especially fine dining. This tradition of fine dining coupled with the new wealth of the city created an environment in which restaurants and restaurant appreciation flourished.

During this era numerous restaurants opened, each trying to outdo the other in serving fabulous meals in the new Creole style. Many of them would create new and exciting dishes that would become famous parts of Louisiana's culinary experience. Dishes such as pampano en papillote (fish cooked in a parchment paper bag), turtle soup, and shrimp and crab meat au gratin began to appear on the city's menus as chefs tried to show off their culinary skill and create sumptuous dishes that reflected the many different ethnic influences that had come together in Creole cuisine.

With the coming of the Civil War, the golden age of New Orleans came to an end;

the city lost much of its wealth due to its occupation by Federal troops and the general decline of the South's economy. Over time the city of New York overtook New Orleans as the country's most important port. The French Creoles began to dwindle in number as more and more European immigrants from Italy, Ireland, and Germany poured into the city and simply outpopulated them, creating a new Creole society. However, with the end of the Reconstruction period in Southern history, New Orleans again took its place as the South's most important port city. Through it all, the tradition of fine dining and fine eating establishments continued to flourish in the city.

One restaurant actually remains from this period of history, and stands as a testament to the elegance of this bygone era: Antoine's. Originally opened in 1840, Antoine's has been serving phenomenal meals to people in New Orleans ever since. When one eats in this great restaurant they are literally experiencing a moment in time from the golden age of Creole society. Though it is renowned for its fabulous meals, Antoine's is most famous for the dish Oysters Rockefeller which it created and named for the oil magnate John D. Rockefeller, because the dish was considered to be so rich and elegant it was worthy of the likes of a wealthy man such as Rockefeller.

The tradition of fine dining in New Orleans has given birth to many restaurant families in the city who have influenced the development of the city's restaurant industry. Most notable among these is the Brennan family. Dick and Ella Brennan, the owners of Commander's Palace, Brennan's, and Mr. B's Bistro, set the standard for elegant dining and exceptional service in their restaurants, and a visit to any of their establishments is a true connoisseur's delight and an experience worthy of any of the finest restaurants in the world. The environment for elegant dining in the city is such that it is even possible to find establishments where the waiters are sons and grandsons of waiters who have worked there providing absolutely outstanding service to their customers.

The number of fine restaurants in New Orleans is numerous indeed and many "old line" restaurants have operated for decades. Restaurants such as Galatoire's, Arnaud's, Commander's Palace, Pascal's Manale, and Tujacque's (to name but a few), have been serving up sumptuously elegant meals to customers who appreciate fine dining at its best. In addition, "newer" restaurants (in New Orleans a restaurant can be thirty years old and still considered to be new) featuring incredible meals and dishes are appearing all the time, such as K-Paul's Louisiana Kitchen, owned by Chef Paul Prudhomme and featuring his internationally famous dish Blackened Redfish, and Chef Emeril Lagasse's restaurants Nola, Emeril's, and Delmonico's.

The restaurant industry in New Orleans today is truly magnificent. People come here from all over the world just to take a "culinary tour" of the city, dining at a different fine restaurant for each meal that they eat during their stay. It is truly a *wonderful* way to experience one of the finest features of Louisiana culture, and will give one a gastronomic experience they will remember for a lifetime!

The Italian Influx

With the end of the Napoleonic empire in Europe in 1815, the Italian peninsula was divided between France, Austria, and Spain, with the Hapsburg dynasty being the dominant influence among the Italian States. Over the course of the next 56 years a series of wars were fought between the European powers in Italy, which eventually led to full unification of the country in 1871 under King Victor Emmanuel II. It was during this period that the first Italian immigrants began to come to America. Though their arrival was slow at first it was greatly increased in the 1880s, after Italy suffered a severe economic depression. Most of those people who would immigrate to America came from southern Italy and Sicily and many of them would choose to come to New Orleans. This mass migration of Italians and Sicilians into the city would continue up until the First World War and would have a tremendous cultural effect on both Creole society and cuisine in New Orleans.

These Italian immigrants were hard-working, industrious people who brought with them their own centuries-old culinary expertise, which they naturally applied to the local cuisine as they found it. Among the many culinary innovations that Italians shared with the Creoles were pasta, increased use of tomatoes, tomato sauces (known as red gravy in New Orleans), frequent use of oregano, Italian cheeses (such as mozzarella and Parmigiano Reggiano), and dishes made with foods such as eggplant and artichoke. Wonderful Italian wines also began to be available in the city, and over time Italian Americans began to dominate the grocery industry in New Orleans, bringing with them new foods and condiments that would further enrich the city's outstanding cuisine.

The Italian influence on Louisiana Creole cuisine is indeed very strong. Like the French and Spanish coming from a Mediterranean civilization, Italian culinary influences easily took hold in New Orleans and blended with that of the local Creole population. The resulting mix forever transformed the city's cuisine and added a new dimension to it; fabulous new flavors and dishes began to appear that made Creole cuisine even fancier and more delicious than it was before the Italians arrived. Creole dishes that had once been prepared and served over rice were soon being served over pasta instead and sprinkled with a little grated Parmigiano Reggiano, adding a delightful Italian flair to them.

Newer Italian-style dishes were added to Creole menus as well, such as seafood-stuffed eggplant, stuffed artichokes, antipasto, linguine, and the list goes on and on. One of the most famous Italian Creole dishes created in New Orleans is Oysters Mosca, from Mosca's restaurant. This heavenly dish is basically baked, breaded oysters filled with subtle yet intricate flavors that will simply melt in your mouth! Another famous Italian Creole dish is the renowned muffuletta sandwich, which was created in New Orleans at Central Grocery on Decatur Street in 1906. This *huge* sandwich is made with Italian ham,

Genoa salami and provolone cheese, and drenched in a special olive oil salad dressing called "olive salad." It is served on a 10-inch round crusty Italian loaf bread. One sandwich is enough for two!

The effect that Italian culinary traditions had on New Orleans cuisine was indeed significant *and* permanent. However, this influence extended primarily only to the greater New Orleans area and at the time of its introduction did not spill over into the Cajun country of South Louisiana, and thus, one of the principal differences between Cajun and Creole cooking was born.

This difference created a new dimension to the state's exceptional cuisine by further enhancing it with the addition of an Italian flair being introduced to food prepared in the Creole area of New Orleans. Thus, the Italians are responsible not only for transforming Creole cooking, but also for enriching the state's cuisine by adding a deliciously unique variety to it in New Orleans that is relished by gastronomes the world over!

Acadian to Cajuns

By the late eighteenth century the majority of Acadians had relocated to Spanish Louisiana and had begun to rebuild their lives in this new land. They had overcome great deprivations and had migrated to the colony virtually destitute. But with hard work and perseverance, within ten years of their arrival they had created a new life for themselves equal to the one they had left in Canada. In a very short time they learned to adapt to their new environment and flourished as they had never done before. The adaptations that they made transformed them from the Acadians into the Cajuns and became most apparent in the new culinary style that they learned from the Creoles of New Orleans.

In Acadia, their cuisine had been a simple, bland French country style of cooking that was filling but unimaginative. However, in Louisiana the Cajuns learned wonderful new dishes and cooking techniques that excited their palate. Pork was still their primary meat of choice, but now they were exposed to new ways of preparing it. Corn, which had not been grown in Acadia, in Louisiana became their main staple grain. Unlike the Creoles who detested corn and preferred to eat rice instead, the Cajuns loved it in all of its various forms. Since wheat flour was scarce in the colony, cornbread would become a feature at every Cajun meal. It was commonly eaten with cane syrup, just as they had eaten wheat bread with maple syrup back in Canada.

For the most part the Cajuns set up farming homesteads in various settlements on the Mississippi River, Bayou Lafourche, and in the southwestern prairies of Louisiana. They were farmers, hunters, trappers, and fishermen. Many of them picked up cattle ranching, which they had also done in Acadia. As cowboys the Cajuns were very successful, and their herds multiplied very quickly, providing beef for the people of New Orleans and the surrounding areas. Virtually every home had a small garden where they grew their own fresh vegetables. The turnips and cabbage they had eaten in Acadia were not very common in Louisiana and were soon replaced with beans, peas, squash, and pumpkins. The Cajuns were very thrifty people and their farms grew and raised everything that they needed to sustain themselves and their community in their new homeland.

They learned to prepare new dishes utilizing fresh vegetables and emphasizing herbs and spices to give their cooking a delightful "fresh" flavor that was both simple, yet complex. Gumbo was quickly picked up and served on special occasions they would share with family and friends. The Cajuns prided themselves on their gumbos and the different ways that they could prepare them to bring out the most flavor.

Fish and game were plentiful in Louisiana, and recipes for preparing them were both learned and created utilizing the cooking techniques they had been taught. Dishes such as courtbouillon, *lapin au sauce piquant* (rabbit sauce piquant), and roast duck and venison were enjoyed by the Cajuns, who delighted in creating new ways to prepare foods that would emphasize simplicity, freshness, and above all else, flavor!

In a very short time the Cajuns adapted to their new environment and flourished through hard work and perseverance. They benefited from the bounty of the land and reveled in the new cuisine they had learned to cook so well. In a sense, they learned Creole cuisine in its purest form and practiced the art of cooking it with simplicity and economy of market, striving to prepare dishes based on freshness of flavor. The real ingenuity that they brought to this cuisine was in using the freshest ingredients that were on hand and maximizing its flavor to the fullest. The Cajuns prospered in Louisiana and, in their prosperity, helped others to prosper as well. They shared with others the bounty that they discovered and brought into the colony, a strong sense of family and community that believed in hard work, moral values, and good family fun. They rejoiced in where they lived and the food that they could savor and share with others. And these wonderful traits were brought by them to Louisiana and became a part of our cultural and culinary heritage that we all now love to share with others.

A Very Creole Breakfast

To the Creoles of New Orleans, breakfast is a very important meal and one that should be not only large but also sumptuous. Numerous breakfast dishes have evolved throughout our history that are truly unique and not only nourishing but also exquisitely flavorful! A good Creole breakfast is a dining experience that can last for a good couple of hours easy, and is an absolutely *wonderful* way to start off the day.

To begin any Creole breakfast, one is first served a good strong cup of Creole coffee. It could be café noir or café au lait, but one thing is for sure, it will be good and *strong!* The Creoles pride themselves on making the finest, richest, strongest coffee in the world and believe that no day should start without a delicious cup of it. In the old days this coffee was made in a special "Creole coffee pot," a tall, slow-drip pot that took a long time to drip the coffee, assuring that it would be rich and strong. In New Orleans, coffee is also accentuated with a little chicory added in for flavor. Chicory is the dried, roasted, ground-up root of the endive plant, which is sprinkled into our coffee to add a bittersweet flavor that is truly delectable! Chicory coffee is the perfect coffee to use in café au lait (coffee and boiled milk) and is a richly wonderful way to start off your morning.

One of the oldest and tastiest Creole breakfast dishes is called calas. This simple and delicious dish originally comes from Africa and is basically deep fried rice balls. Cooked rice is mixed with a little milk and sugar and then formed into a ball, rolled in flour, and deep fried. The resulting little balls of fried rice are usually served with a little powdered sugar sprinkled over them and/or some cane syrup. These little gems are absolutely delicious and have a long history in New Orleans. During the nineteenth century it was quite common to see African women in their distinctive dress and colorful tignon headdress selling calas on street corners in the French Quarter. These delectable little morsels are loved by all who sample them.

Another old Creole favorite is the traditional dish of Grillades and grits. Grillades are veal cutlets lightly breaded and paneed in a skillet and usually served with a little Creole sauce over them. When accompanied with a nice healthy serving of grits they become a breakfast dish fit for a king, and a most delicious way to give you plenty of fuel to get through the morning.

If one is just in the mood for a nice light breakfast (which would appall the Creoles to no end) then you might try a few beignets. These are Creole-style doughnuts that are square with no hole and lightly fried till they are nice and puffy, and sprinkled with powdered sugar. Beignets are an *old* favorite treat throughout the city and are absolutely heavenly when served alongside a nice rich cup of café au lait.

The Creole version of French toast is called pain perdu or "lost bread," so called because it is made with stale French bread before it is "lost" and has to be thrown out. (The Creoles were famous for wasting absolutely *nothing* when it came to food.) The bread is sliced and mixed with a little milk or cream, sugar, and beaten eggs and then fried in a skillet until it is nice and crispy brown and served with powdered sugar and/or cane syrup. It is a wonderfully sweet breakfast dish that is much more filling than ordinary French toast.

Of course, if you are in the mood for eggs for breakfast, then you are in for a *real* treat. There are many different Creole egg dishes that will tempt your palate with extraordinary flavors and bring a new dimension to the simple egg. You could have eggs creole, basically scrambled eggs in a Creole sauce, or a creole omelet stuffed with shrimp and crabmeat. If you want to get fancier there is Eggs Sardou or Eggs Hussarde. Even a simple poached egg will be uplifted by the addition of a little Creole seasoning and sauce. These are all absolutely mouthwatering egg dishes that can bring you to new heights of culinary ecstasy.

In today's fast-paced modern world we have gotten away from the long, large break-fast that is savored as a true dining experience. One should make the time at least once a week to sit down and enjoy a truly wonderful breakfast with someone that you love and savor the food, the company, and the moment. It is a small part of enjoying life for its own sake and appreciating one of the finer things in living. To the Creoles, *that* is what life is all about, for true!

Mardi Gras

The tradition of the Mardi Gras is an ancient holiday that stems from the ancient Roman festival honoring Bacchus, the god of wine. As the Roman Empire became Christianized, the Roman Catholic Church changed the holiday from one honoring Bacchus to a final time of feasting and partying before the austere season of Lent began. In Louisiana and the Gulf Coast Mardi Gras is a religious holiday seen as a time of celebrating life before the solemn Lenten season occurs.

To many people outside of Louisiana, Mardi Gras is still seen as some wild Bacchana-lian rite with a very seedy reputation indeed. However, nothing could be further from the truth. Though one can see some pretty off-the-wall things in the French Quarter of New Orleans on Mardi Gras day, the farther out you get from that district the more family ori-ented the holiday becomes. To the Cajuns and Creoles it is a time of celebration and a family event in which revelers dress up in fancy costumes and celebrate life as a commu-nity. Indeed, if one visits New Orleans or Mobile or anywhere else on the Gulf Coast on the day *after* Mardi Gras, they will find that the churches are all filled to the brim with de-vout worshipers beginning the season of Lent to honor Christ's forty days and nights of fasting in the wilderness.

The Mardi Gras or Carnival season officially begins on the twelfth day of Christmas with a series of parties and parades that increase in number leading up to Fat Tuesday, which is the day before Ash Wednesday, the start of Lent. In the United States the largest Mardi Gras celebration is in New Orleans; however, the city that has the honor of cele-brating the oldest Mardi Gras goes to Mobile, Alabama. The Mardi Gras is a Latin holi-day first brought to Louisiana by the French in 1699. Numerous traditions are associated with the Mardi Gras and one could write an entire book on the subject (and many people already have). It is a wonderful time, with parties and parades all leading up to Fat Tuesday or Mardi Gras Day, when the entire city will come out into the streets dressed up in fancy costumes and party together in one humongous block party. It is a *lot* of fun and one can see *all* kinds of different cute, quaint (and yes, even seedy, depending on where you are) costumes that families and individuals dress up in to celebrate the holiday.

During the Carnival season, parades are put on by special Carnival "krewes," clubs that exist only for the purpose of providing a parade for the crowd and then having a fancy Mardi Gras ball afterward where paraders can party. The parades are a particular lot of fun as fancy floats drive down the streets with costumed people riding on them, throwing strands of plastic beads and small metal doubloons to the crowd. This is perhaps one of the most fun aspects of Mardi Gras, as the crowds go wild trying to catch these souvenirs, thus making for a lot of audience participation in the event.

One of the most delightful Mardi Gras celebrations occurs in Cajun Country in Breaux Bridge, Louisiana. Here, special Cajun riders known as Courier de Mardi Gras dress up as clowns and cowboys and ride a circuit around to various farms in the area, collecting produce and foods for a gumbo that will be cooked in the heart of the city for all who attend. It is a *wonderful* family event as the crowd cheers the Mardi Gras Riders when they enter into town with their goodies and a giant gumbo is made for everyone and all of the revelers dance to Cajun music and party in the streets of Breaux Bridge.

One of the most popular traditions associated with Mardi Gras is that of the king cake party. A king cake is a sweet bread that is covered in white icing and sprinkled with colored sugar crystals in purple, green, and gold (the official colors of Mardi Gras). Hidden inside of the king cake somewhere is a tiny plastic baby (in the old days they used a bean, but that was too easy to swallow). At the party the cake is sliced and everyone gets a piece. Whoever gets the piece with the baby is crowned the king (or queen) of the party and as a result has to throw another party for everyone so that the parties will go on and on up until Ash Wednesday. (See why they stopped using the bean.) It is a delightful tradition (and a very delicious cake) that leads to numerous parties being celebrated during the Carnival season.

Mardi Gras is definitely an event that one should see at least once in their life. It is a truly unique celebration that will be fun for the whole family and an experience that you will remember for a lifetime! It is a truly special Louisiana cultural event that echoes from a bygone era and celebrates life and living and the good times that people can share both as a family and as a community.

Boucherie and Fais Do-Do

In the Louisiana Cajun country the traditions of the boucherie (*boo-share-ee*) and the fais do-do (*fay dough-dough*) are two of the most delightful and fun-loving events that one can possibly experience. They are *very* Cajun social events that everyone should experience at least once in their lifetime. And if you do, you are guaranteed to "pass a good time," as the Cajuns say, for true!

The tradition of the boucherie originated as an outdoor barbeque that occurred during hog-killing time when hogs were slaughtered and "dressed" and then the meat salted to preserve it for the winter months. To the Cajuns this was a big event in which at least one of the hogs would be roasted and served to the community at a big outdoor barbeque that everyone could enjoy. Families from all over the community would come over to help with the work and make a big party out of it all. The hogs were slow roasted on a spit and other distinctly Cajun dishes would be served such as gumbo and jambalaya that everyone would enjoy. It was an all-day community event going on into the night as people would eat and cook and dance to Cajun music played by a local band and celebrate their good fortune and their sense of community and family.

The favorite dish that could be prepared at a boucherie was cochon de lait or roast suckling pig. This was the most tender and succulent pork of them all and is still considered to be the national Cajun dish. Today cochon de lait is slow cooked in what is called a "Cajun microwave." This is a Louisiana variation of the old Hawaiian luau pit. It is basically a large box with a spit running through the middle of it and a tray for hot coals to be placed on top of the box so that the heat comes from above instead of below. Pigs roasted in a "Cajun microwave" are slow cooked for a *very* long time on a low heat which cooks the meat very slowly so that when it is finally done the meat is literally falling off of the bone, it is so juicy and tender. When seasoned with good Cajun seasonings it is a truly delectable dish that is usually eaten up *very* quickly!

As the party moves on into the night, it begins to turn into a fais do-do. The fais do-do can best be described as an adult slumber party in which the children are eventually shuffled off to bed and the adults continue to eat, drink, dance, and party on through the night. A fais do-do can last for a very long time indeed and is *so* much fun to attend as couples dance through the night to wonderfully played Cajun or zydeco music by a live, local band.

If you have never danced to Cajun music before, you have missed out on one of life's true treasures. The instruments used are guitars, fiddles, drums, and a special eight-button accordion called a "Chank a Chank," which originated in Germany in the nineteenth century. The music is sung in Cajun French and only two types of dances are played, two-steps and waltzes. In Louisiana there is nothing more wonderful than to hold a pretty young girl and gaze into her eyes and waltz her about the floor to a Cajun waltz. A Cajun dance is a family social event and, indeed, when you are on the dance floor you have to be careful not to step on a child because the mommas start teaching children as young as age two how to dance.

The traditions of the boucherie and the fais do-do are time-honored institutions in Cajun Country, and anyone who visits the state should most definitely take the time to experience them. Once you attend one you will feel the genuine warmth and sincere hospitality that these wonderful people will share with you, and you will begin to understand the *joie de vivre* that we feel from our culture, our cuisine, and from living.

Part III

Cajun and Creole Recipes

So these then are our recipes. Most of these are traditional recipes with a few exceptions. Most of them have been chosen because they represent the nature of our culinary style and utilize the various techniques that are used in preparing food in our cuisine. Some of them are fancy and some of them are plain, but all of them are delicious!

Now remember, a recipe is nothing more than a road map. And like all road maps, there are many different ways to get from point A to point B. So before you jump right in, take some time to study the recipe that you are about to prepare. Read it all the way through before you begin cooking. None of these recipes are carved in stone nor should they be. Louisiana cuisine is the perfect cuisine to use for leftovers. Whatever you have on hand in your refrigerator can be used to prepare whatever you like.

As you study these recipes, you will see the many techniques that are used and it will give you a better understanding of what is involved in preparing food in the Louisiana style. You are perfectly free to add ingredients or leave out some if doing so makes the dish more appetizing to you. This will encourage your own culinary creativity and help to develop your own personal art of cooking. So study the recipe before you begin to prepare it and think about what is going on with it. Identify the techniques that are used in its preparation so that you will feel more comfortable with how to prepare it and also know if there is something that you might like to add to it or leave out.

Once you have mastered all of the various techniques that are used in our foods preparation you will understand that there are few set rules to follow and that this cuisine allows for a lot of variation on the part of the cook. A chicken gumbo can very easily be turned into a chicken-shrimp gumbo if that is what you have on hand and wish to put into it. It is all up to you. There is absolutely nothing wrong with substituting ingredients. People in Louisiana substitute ingredients in recipes all the time based on what they like, don't like, or are allergic to. The important thing here is that you learn the cooking techniques involved in our cuisine so that you can then prepare food in a Louisiana style *your* way, to your taste. That is what is most important. Then you will enjoy cooking our cuisine more and developing your own unique culinary style just as we have done.

Many of these recipes are made with olive oil, which was traditionally used by the French, Spanish, and Italians in preparing our food. However, so also was butter and lard, and if you wish to see what a particular recipe would taste like using any of these then by all means try it. Most of these recipes are also written to use either your favorite Cajun/Creole seasoning blend (or your own if you prefer) or to use individual seasonings to prepare the dish from scratch. Our cuisine allows for a lot of leeway, so take some time and read through these recipes and see which ones you wish to try out and then get creative. And *laissez les bon temps roulez!*

Classic Sauces

<table>
<tr><td>1. Bordelaise Sauce</td><td>10. Sassy Lemon Sauce</td></tr>
<tr><td>2. Classic White Cream Sauce</td><td>11. Cajun Sauce Piquant</td></tr>
<tr><td>3. Rémoulade Sauce</td><td>12. Creole Mayonnaise</td></tr>
<tr><td>4. Creole Sauce</td><td>13. Whiskey or Rum Sauce</td></tr>
<tr><td>5. Béarnaise Sauce</td><td>14. Sauce Espagnole</td></tr>
<tr><td>6. Béchamel Sauce</td><td>15. Lemon Butter Sauce</td></tr>
<tr><td>7. Creole Hollandaise Sauce</td><td>16. Creole Cocktail Sauce</td></tr>
<tr><td>8. Creole Meuniere Sauce</td><td>17. Praline Sauce</td></tr>
<tr><td>9. Marchand de Vin Sauce</td><td>18. White Wine Sauce</td></tr>
</table>

Photo by Keith Dunn

Bordelaise Sauce

This is a classic sauce used for steaks and red meat. If you substitute white wine instead of red wine and add in 1 teaspoon of lemon juice, it can be used as a delightful dip or sauce for seafood.

1 teaspoon Seasoning Mix (see below)	2 green onions, finely chopped	1 teaspoon chopped fresh thyme
4 ounces (1 stick) unsalted butter	1 tablespoon chopped garlic	¼ teaspoon Worcestershire sauce (optional)
	1 teaspoon chopped fresh parsley	2 tablespoons dry red wine

To make the Seasoning Mix, in a mixing bowl combine all of the Seasoning Mix ingredients and mix well. You may prepare this in advance and store in an airtight jar in a cool, dry place.

In a saucepan melt the butter over a low heat. When the butter is almost melted, add the green onions, garlic, fresh herbs, and Seasoning Mix (and optional ingredients if you like) and let simmer for about 1 to 2 minutes, stirring occasionally. (Be careful to watch the garlic that it does not brown.) Add the red wine and stir everything to mix well. Serve immediately. **Makes about ¼ cup of sauce.**

Seasoning Mix

Use 1 teaspoon of your favorite Cajun/Creole seasoning blend or 1 teaspoon of the following mix:

- ¼ teaspoon salt
- ¼ teaspoon cayenne pepper
- ¼ teaspoon sweet paprika
- ¼ teaspoon garlic powder
- ¼ teaspoon ground thyme

Classic White Cream Sauce

A classic white cream sauce is made by making a blonde (or white) roux and adding milk or heavy cream. If you choose to use cream instead of milk, it will be very rich, indeed. A cream sauce can also be made very fancy by adding a splash of white wine and a sprinkling of grated Parmigiano Reggiano cheese. With the addition of a few ingredients, this fancy cream sauce is sinfully rich.

2 tablespoons unsalted butter	½ cup grated Parmigiano Reggiano cheese (optional)	¼ teaspoon garlic powder (not garlic salt)
2 tablespoons all–purpose white flour		¼ teaspoon white pepper
1½ cups milk or heavy cream	¼ teaspoon salt	¼ teaspoon onion powder
2 tablespoons dry white wine (optional)		

In a small, heavy saucepan or skillet melt the butter over low to medium heat. Add flour and begin to stir constantly with a wire whisk to make a blonde roux. You need only cook this for about 2 minutes, stirring constantly so there is no color change. Add milk or cream and continue stirring, making a smooth sauce. Add wine, cheese, and spices. Let this cook for about another 5 minutes, continuing to stir to avoid lumps. The longer you keep this on the heat, the more it will reduce in size and thicken. Taste occasionally to see if the flavor is to your liking. Remove from heat and let cool slightly. **Makes about 1½ cups of sauce.**

Cook's Note

If you wish to season your cream sauce, it is best to use only white colored spices such as salt, white pepper, garlic powder, and onion powder. These will affect the flavor but not the color of the sauce. The quantities should be to your own personal taste. For this recipe we recommend using no more than ¼ teaspoon of any or all of these spices and then taste the sauce to see if you want a little more or less of any ingredient.

Rémoulade Sauce

This is a classic Creole-type sauce used for cold seafood. Traditionally, it tends to be a bit spicy. It is often used for Shrimp Rémoulade, a classic appetizer served in most upscale Louisiana restaurants.

2 tablespoons Seasoning Mix (optional, see below)	1 cup olive oil	¼ cup chopped fresh thyme
½ cup chopped celery	½ cup horseradish	4 cloves fresh garlic, chopped
2 green onions, finely chopped	2 tablespoons Worcestershire sauce	Juice of 1 lemon
1 cup Creole mustard (or spicy, coarse-ground German mustard)	Dash Tabasco sauce	
	½ cup tomato ketchup	
	¼ cup white wine vinegar	
	¼ cup chopped fresh parsley	

To make the Seasoning Mix, combine all of the Seasoning Mix ingredients and mix very well. If you want your blend to be a bit spicier, you can increase the amount of pepper. You may prepare this in advance and store in an airtight jar in a cool, dry place.

To make the sauce, in a mixing bowl combine all of the ingredients and mix thoroughly with a whisk. Cover with plastic wrap and refrigerate for at least 4 hours to let all the flavors meld. The longer it sits in the refrigerator, the more flavorful it will become. For the best flavor, refrigerate overnight before serving.

Serve as a sauce for cold seafood; it is a perfect sauce for Shrimp Remoulade. **Makes almost 2 quarts of sauce.**

Seasoning Mix

A seasoning mix is actually optional in this recipe since there are so many different flavorful ingredients used in making it. However, if you want to have even more flavor, you can add 2 tablespoons of your favorite Cajun/ Creole Seasoning or 2 tablespoons of the following blend:

2 teaspoons sweet paprika
1 teaspoon dried thyme leaves
1 teaspoon dried sweet basil leaves
1 teaspoon dried oregano leaves
½ teaspoon garlic powder
½ teaspoon onion powder
¼ teaspoon salt
¼ teaspoon cayenne pepper
¼ teaspoon white pepper
¼ teaspoon black pepper

Creole Sauce

Creole sauce is a famous Louisiana sauce that can dress up any dish while giving it a distinctive Creole flavor. It can be made either with or without a roux as well as with butter or olive oil, depending upon which flavor you wish to lend to the sauce. Creole sauce is especially tasty on meats, fish, vegetables, or egg dishes.

2 tablespoons Seasoning Mix (see below)	½ cup chopped bell peppers	¼ cup red wine
1 tablespoon unsalted butter	¼ cup chopped celery	1 cup Chicken Stock (see page 132)
1 tablespoon all-purpose flour	1 tablespoon fresh chopped garlic	¼ teaspoon Worcestershire sauce
1 cup chopped onions	2 cups diced tomatoes	¼ teaspoon fresh lemon juice
	2 cups tomato purée	

In a mixing bowl combine all the the Seasoning Mix ingredients and mix well. If you want your blend to be a bit spicier, you can increase the amount of pepper. You may prepare the mixture in advance and store in an airtight jar in a cool, dry place.

In a heavy skillet over medium heat, melt the butter and add the flour, stirring with a wire whisk to make a medium brown roux. Add the onions, bell peppers, celery, and fresh chopped garlic, stirring well. Add the diced tomatoes while stirring. Add the tomato purée, red wine, chicken stock, Worcestershire sauce, lemon juice, and 2 tablespoons of Seasoning Mix. Stir well and simmer for 1 hour. **Makes about 8 cups of sauce.**

Seasoning Mix

Use 2 tablespoons of your favorite Cajun/ Creole Seasoning blend or 2 tablespoons of the following blend:

2 bay leaves

1 teaspoon sweet paprika

½ teaspoon dried thyme leaves

½ teaspoon dried sweet basil leaves

½ teaspoon dried oregano leaves

½ teaspoon garlic powder

½ teaspoon onion powder

¼ teaspoon black pepper

¼ teaspoon white pepper

¼ teaspoon cayenne pepper

¼ teaspoon salt

Béarnaise Sauce

Sauce Béarnaise is a classically French sauce which is an enriched version of Hollandaise with a stronger flavor. It is wonderfully rich and great on meats and seafood.

5 tablespoons coarsely chopped green onion	1 cup white wine	2 tablespoons chervil (optional)
1 tablespoon pepper	¾ cup cider vinegar	¾ cup Hollandaise Sauce
	1½ tablespoons thyme	
	1 tablespoon fresh parsley	

In a blender or food processor place all of the ingredients except for the Hollandaise Sauce. Blend at high speed for 30 seconds. Pour into a heavy saucepan and boil until the liquid is gone, about 30 minutes. Cool. Beat 1 teaspoon of this essence into the Hollandaise Sauce. Remaining essence may be frozen or refrigerated for several weeks. **Makes ¾ cup.**

Béchamel Sauce

This is basically a very rich, medium-thick cream sauce that is used in many meat and egg dishes. This sauce can also be used as a base for cheese sauce, mushroom sauce, or parsley sauce.

1¼ cups milk	1 slice onion	Pinch of pepper
1 tablespoon butter	8 peppercorns	Pinch of nutmeg
1½ tablespoons all–purpose flour	1 bay leaf	
	Pinch of salt	

In a small saucepan heat the milk. Add the onion, peppercorns, and bay leaf and bring to near boil. Remove from the heat and set aside, letting the flavors infuse for 20 minutes. Strain.

In another saucepan melt the butter and add the flour while stirring for 1 minute, making a blonde roux. Remove from the heat and gradually add the warm milk mixture, whisking constantly. Add the salt, pepper, and nutmeg. Place back on the heat and bring to a boil, whisking constantly, until the sauce thickens to a nice smooth consistency. **Makes about 1¼ cups.**

Creole Hollandaise Sauce

In Louisiana we make a Creole version of this classic French sauce, which we feel has a much more interesting flavor. It complements meats, seafood, vegetables, eggs, or whatever!

1	cup clarified butter	4	drops Tabasco sauce	1 tablespoon water
4	egg yolks	2	tablespoons fresh lemon	
1	fluid ounce white wine		juice	

To clarify butter, in a small saucepan melt 4 sticks of butter. Skim off the yellow top and measure enough remaining clear liquid to equal 1 cup. Set aside to cool slightly.

In a mixing bowl combine the eggs, wine, and Tabasco and beat well. Add the clarified butter slowly, beating constantly until the mixture thickens to a smooth pouring consistency. Add the lemon juice and water and mix well. **Makes 1½ cups.**

Creole Meuniere Sauce

This is a wonderfully delicious sauce for any fish or seafood, particularly trout.

4	ounces (1 stick) butter	1	tablespoon finely chopped	Juice of 2 lemons
½	teaspoon minced fresh		fresh parsley	1 tablespoon Worcestershire
	garlic	1	tablespoon finely chopped	sauce
			fresh thyme leaves	

This sauce should never be prepared in advance.

In a small skillet melt the butter over meat heat and then add the garlic, parsley, thyme, lemon juice, and Worcestershire sauce. Sauté until butter has turned slightly brown, about 30 to 45 seconds. Serve at once over any fish. **Makes ½ cup.**

Marchand de Vin Sauce

This sauce is great on beef, pork, lamb, and any type of red meat.

2 tablespoons unsalted butter	4 green onions, finely chopped	1 tablespoon chopped thyme leaves
2 tablespoons all–purpose flour	1 dozen fresh mushrooms, sliced	1 cup red wine
1 teaspoon chopped fresh garlic	1 tablespoon chopped parsley	1 cup Beef Stock (see page 135)

In a saucepan melt the butter and add the flour, stirring constantly over medium heat to make a dark brown roux. Add the garlic, onions, and mushrooms and sauté approximately 6 to 7 minutes. Add the parsley, thyme, and red wine, and beef stock. Cook at least 20 minutes.

Serve with beef, veal, or chicken. **Serves 8.**

Sassy Lemon Sauce

½ cup water	2 teaspoons cornstarch dis–solved in ¼ cup water
¼ cup sugar	½ teaspoon vanilla extract
2 tablespoons fresh lemon juice	½ teaspoon lemon extract

In a saucepan over medium heat combine the water, sugar, and lemon juice and bring to boil. Stir in the cornstarch mixture, and add the vanilla and lemon extracts. Boil for 1 minute, whisking constantly.

Serve warm over your favorite dessert. **Makes approximately ¾ cup.**

Cajun Sauce Piquant

This is a very spicy tomato-based sauce similar to a Sauce Creole but much spicier. It should be very flavorful and very hot!

---

2 to 3 tablespoons Seasoning Mix (see below)

1 tablespoon butter

1 tablespoon all-purpose flour

½ cup chopped onions

⅓ cup chopped bell pepper

¼ cup chopped celery

2 cups diced tomatoes

¼ cup dry red wine

½ teaspoon Worcestershire sauce

1 cup tomato purée

1 cup Chicken Stock (see page 132)

1 tablespoon tomato paste

1 tablespoon chopped garlic

¼ to ½ teaspoon Tabasco sauce

In a mixing bowl combine all of the Seasoning Mix ingredients and mix very well. If you want your blend to be a bit milder you can decrease the amount of pepper. You may prepare the Seasoning Mix in advance and store in an airtight jar in the refrigerator or in another cool, dry place.

In a heavy skillet over medium heat melt the butter and add the flour, and whisk constantly until it reaches a dark brown color. Add the onions, bell pepper, and celery to the pan, reduce the heat to a simmer, and mix all very thoroughly with a spoon. Add the tomatoes, red wine, and Worcestershire sauce, and continue to cook for 1 minute. Add the tomato purée, chicken stock, and tomato paste and continue to cook, stirring occasionally. Lastly, add the garlic, Tabasco sauce, and Seasoning Mix and stir well. Reduce heat to simmer and cook for 20 to 30 minutes, stirring occasionally. **Makes 4 cups.**

Seasoning Mix

Use 2 to 3 tablespoons of your favorite Cajun/Creole seasoning or:

1 teaspoon dried thyme

1 teaspoon dried sweet basil leaves

1 teaspoon dried parsley

1 teaspoon sweet paprika

½ teaspoon salt

½ teaspoon cayenne pepper

½ teaspoon black pepper

½ teaspoon white pepper

½ teaspoon garlic powder

½ teaspoon onion powder

Creole Mayonnaise

Creole Mayonnaise is similar to regular mayonnaise, but it features the addition of wonderful Creole flavors. Delicious on sandwiches or as a topping for a salad.

1 to 2 tablespoons Seasoning Mix (see below)	2 tablespoons chopped fresh garlic	2 teaspoons white wine vinegar
2 tablespoons unsalted butter	½ teaspoon dry mustard	2 organic, free–range eggs
	2 teaspoons lemon juice	2 cups olive oil

To make the Seasoning Mix, combine all of the Seasoning Mix ingredients and mix well. You may prepare it in advance and store in an airtight jar in a cool, dry place.

In a medium-sized saucepan melt the butter over medium heat and sauté the garlic, dry mustard, and Seasoning Mix for about 2 to 3 minutes, stirring occasionally. Then add the lemon juice and white wine vinegar stir until mixed well. Remove from the heat and let cool.

Place the eggs in a blender and blend on a low for approximately 30 seconds. Pour in the sautéed mixture and blend for another 15 seconds. Increase the blender speed to medium and slowly pour in the oil in a thin steady stream. Continue to process until all of the oil has been incorporated and the mayonnaise is thick and creamy. Store the mayonnaise in an airtight container in the refrigerator. **Makes 2½ cups.**

Seasoning Mix

Use 1 to 2 tablespoons of your favorite Cajun/ Creole seasoning or:

- ½ teaspoon salt
- ¼ teaspoon dried thyme leaves
- ¼ teaspoon dried sweet basil leaves
- ¼ teaspoon garlic powder
- ¼ teaspoon onion powder
- ¼ teaspoon white pepper
- ¼ teaspoon cayenne pepper
- 1 bay leaf

Whiskey or Rum Sauce

This is a sweet sauce made with whiskey or rum and is famous as the sauce served with bread puddings. It is has a bit of a kick and can be used on all sorts of desserts.

1 cup brown sugar	1 tablespoon unsalted butter	1 tablespoon bourbon
2 cups heavy cream	½ teaspoon cornstarch	whiskey or dark rum
Pinch of ground cinnamon	mixed with ¼ cup water	

In a saucepan combine the sugar, cream, cinnamon, and butter. Bring to a boil. Add the cornstarch mixture and cook, stirring, until sauce is thick. Remove from heat and stir in the bourbon or rum. **Makes 2 cups.**

Sauce Espagnole

This sauce is one of the three "Mother" sauces of Cajun/Creole cuisine from which so many other sauces descend. It goes back at least to the eighteenth century, if not further. It is a brown sauce and is usually made with red wine and beef stock and used on meat dishes.

2 tablespoons Seasoning Mix (see below)	2 tablespoons all-purpose flour	1 tablespoon lemon juice
2 tablespoons butter	1 cup beef stock, heated	2 tablespoons red wine
	3 tablespoons tomato paste	¼ tablespoon Tabasco sauce

To make the Seasoning Mix, in a mixing bowl combine all of the Seasoning Mix ingredients and mix well. You may prepare it in advance and store in an airtight jar in a cool, dry place.

In a heavy saucepan over medium heat melt the butter; add the flour and whisk the roux constantly until mahogany brown, about 10 minutes. Add the beef stock, tomato paste, lemon juice, wine, Tabasco, and the 2 tablespoons of Seasoning Mix. Stir until thick and smooth. **Makes 2 cups.**

Seasoning Mix

Use 1 to 2 tablespoons of your favorite Cajun/ Creole seasoning or:

2 teaspoons sweet paprika
1 teaspoon dried thyme leaves
1 teaspoon dried sweet basil leaves
½ teaspoon garlic powder
½ teaspoon onion powder
¼ teaspoon salt
¼ teaspoon black pepper
¼ teaspoon white pepper
¼ teaspoon cayenne pepper

Lemon Butter Sauce

This tart, lemony sauce is delectable on seafood or chicken but can also be used on meat or vegetables.

3 tablespoons lemon juice	¼ teaspoon salt	¾ cup (1½ sticks) butter,
1 tablespoon Dijon mustard	⅛ teaspoon white pepper	melted, but not separated
1 egg yolk	¼ teaspoon garlic powder	

In a bowl combine the lemon juice, mustard, egg yolk, salt, pepper, and garlic powder. Slowly add the melted butter in a stream, whisking until the sauce is thick. **Makes about 1 cup.**

Creole Cocktail Sauce

Here is the Creole version of traditional cocktail sauce for seafood.

2 tablespoons Seasoning Mix (see below)	¼ cup horseradish	1 tablespoon Tabasco sauce
2 cups tomato catsup	¼ cup Worcestershire sauce	1 tablespoon lemon juice
	¼ cup red wine vinegar	

To make the Seasoning Mix, in a mixing bowl combine all of the Seasoning Mix ingredients and mix well. You may prepare it in advance and store in an airtight jar in a cool, dry place.

To make the cocktail sauce, in a medium bowl combine all of the ingredients and stir to mix well. **Makes about 2¾ cups.**

Seasoning Mix

Use 2 tablespoons of your favorite Cajun/Creole seasoning or the following blend:

2 teaspoons sweet paprika
1 teaspoon dried thyme leaves
1 teaspoon dried sweet basil leaves
½ teaspoon garlic powder
½ teaspoon onion powder
¼ teaspoon salt
¼ teaspoon black pepper
¼ teaspoon white pepper
¼ teaspoon cayenne pepper

Praline Sauce

This sweet sauce, reminiscent of Praline candy, is tasty on cakes and desserts.

¾ cup white corn syrup	5 tablespoons unsalted	1 5.3–ounce can evaporated
1½ cups lightly packed light	butter	milk
brown sugar	1 teaspoon vanilla extract	1 cup chopped pecans

In a small skillet over medium heat combine the corn syrup, brown sugar, butter, and vanilla; heat, stirring constantly, until it just begins to boil. Once it is boiling, remove from the heat and add the evaporated milk and pecans; blend every well. Cool in the refrigerator. **Makes 2½ cups.**

White Wine Sauce

Fancy up a chicken, fish, or pasta dish at your next dinner party with this rich, elegant sauce.

¾ cup (1½ sticks) butter, cut into pieces	½ cup white wine	½ teaspoon lemon juice
¼ cup minced green onions	2 tablespoons heavy cream	1 teaspoon ground thyme
1 teaspoon fresh chopped garlic	⅓ teaspoon salt	
	¼ teaspoon pepper	

In a small, heavy saucepan over medium heat, melt 1 piece of the butter and sauté the green onions and garlic until soft. Add the wine and simmer until it is almost a glaze. Remove from the heat. Add the cream. Return to low heat and whisk in the remaining butter, 1 piece at a time, adding each additional piece of butter before previous one has completely melted, stirring constantly. Do not let the sauce get too hot or it will break. Add the salt, pepper, lemon juice, and ground thyme.

Serve immediately on any chicken, fish, or pasta dish. **Makes 1 cup.**

Breakfast Dishes

1. Calas

2. Beignets

3. Grillades and Grits

4. Eggs Sardou

5. Eggs Hussarde

6. Eggs Creole

7. Creole Crabmeat

Omelet Filling

8. Cajun Coush–Coush

9. Pain Perdu

Pain Perdu, page 116

Photo by Keith Dunn

107

Calas

Calas, a traditional New Orleans breakfast dish that originated in West Africa, are deep fried or panéed rice balls served with powdered sugar and/or syrup. This recipe requires some preparation the night before, but the results are well worth the effort.

½ cup warm water	3 eggs, beaten	¼ teaspoon cinnamon
2 tablespoons granulated sugar	1½ cups sifted all–purpose flour	¼ teaspoon allspice
1 package active dry yeast (about 1 tablespoon)	½ teaspoon salt	Vegetable oil
	½ teaspoon vanilla extract	Powdered sugar
1½ cups cooked white rice	¼ teaspoon nutmeg	

The night before you cook your calas, in a bowl combine the warm water with the granulated sugar and stir in the yeast. Let mixture stand until it becomes foamy (about 5 to 10 minutes).

Next, in a medium-sized bowl combine the yeast mixture and the cooked rice. Cover the bowl with plastic wrap and let it sit in a warm place overnight. (This process will make sour rice starter for your calas.)

The next morning, stir the sour rice starter thoroughly (it won't smell good, but it will make wonderful calas!). Add the beaten eggs, flour, salt, vanilla, nutmeg, cinnamon, and allspice and blend very well with a spoon. Cover the bowl with plastic wrap and let the mixture rise in a warm place for 1 hour.

Take some flour and place in a small bowl; sprinkle a little on your hands too. Spoon out about 1 tablespoon of the rice mixture and roll into a ball, and then roll the ball in the flour in the bowl.

In a large, heavy cast-iron skillet heat about 3 inches of vegetable oil over medium heat to about 365°F. Drop several of the balls at a time into the hot oil and fry until they are golden brown and crispy, about 4 to 5 minutes, moving them several times to ensure even cooking. When done, remove the calas from the skillet and drain on paper towels. Repeat with the remaining balls.

Serve dusted with powdered sugar or your favorite syrup. **Makes 2 dozen.**

Beignets

Beignets are French-Creole doughnuts that are square, lightly fried, and served dusted with powdered sugar. They are absolutely out of this world. It's no wonder everybody loves them.

1 cup half and half	2 eggs, beaten	Peanut oil for frying
1 cup sugar	1 cup (2 sticks butter), melted	Powdered sugar
1 cake yeast (three ¼ ounce packages of yeast equals activity of one 2–ounce yeast cake)	5 cups all–purpose flour	
	1 teaspoon allspice	

In a saucepan over medium heat combine the half and half and sugar and heat, stirring occasionally, but do not bring to a boil. Remove the pan from the heat. Combine the yeast with the beaten eggs and fold into the sugar and half and half mixture. Add the melted butter and stir. Next add the flour and allspice and mix well. Let this stand in a warm place for at least 2 hours until it has risen.

Once the dough has risen, roll it out on a floured board to 1-inch thickness and cut into squares. Let this dough continue to stand until it doubles in size.

Deep-fry your beignets squares in hot peanut oil (about 300°F) for about 5 minutes. Remove from oil, drain on paper towels, and sprinkle with powdered sugar. **Makes 2 dozen.**

Grillades and Grits

Grillades (Gree-yahds) are thin breakfast steaks (either beef round or veal) that are cooked in a Creole sauce and served alongside grits. This is a very hardy Louisiana-style breakfast, for true!

Grillades:

1 to 2 tablespoons Seasoning Mix (see below)

4 thin breakfast steaks (beef round or veal)

About 2 cups all-purpose flour

4 tablespoons olive oil or butter

2 medium onions, chopped

1 large green bell pepper, chopped

1 large celery stalk, chopped

4 large cloves garlic, chopped

3 tomatoes, chopped

¼ cup dry red wine

½ teaspoon Worcestershire sauce

2 cups pork or beef stock

¼ cup green onions, chopped

1 tablespoon tomato paste

To make the Seasoning Mix, in a mixing bowl combine all Seasoning Mix ingredients and mix well. If you want your blend to be a bit spicier, increase the amount of pepper. You may prepare this in advance and store in an airtight jar in a cool, dry place.

Using a meat tenderizer, pound the meat until flattened. Sprinkle about 1 teaspoon of Seasoning Mix onto both sides of the meat and rub into the meat very well. In a medium-sized bowl combine the flour with 1 teaspoon of Seasoning Mix and blend well. Dredge the meat in the flour and set aside.

In a large, heavy skillet heat the oil or butter over medium heat and fry the steaks very quickly on both sides. Remove the steaks from skillet and set aside. Add 2 tablespoons of flour to the skillet and begin stirring continuously with a wire whisk to make a medium brown roux. When the roux has reached the desired color add the onions, bell pepper, celery, and garlic and stir well, cooking the vegetables until they are slightly wilted and transparent, about 5 minutes. Stir in the tomatoes and add the wine and Worcestershire sauce; continue to cook for about 1 minute. Add the stock, tomato paste, and remainder of Seasoning Mix and stir until well combined.

Reduce heat to low, add cooked steaks and simmer for about 1 hour stirring occasionally. Meanwhile, cook the grits.

Continued on next page

Seasoning Mix

Use 1 to 2 tablespoons of your favorite Cajun/ Creole seasoning or:

1 teaspoon sweet paprika

1 teaspoon dried thyme

1 teaspoon dried sweet basil leaves

½ teaspoon salt

½ teaspoon garlic powder

½ teaspoon onion powder

¼ teaspoon cayenne pepper

¼ teaspoon black pepper

¼ teaspoon white pepper

Cheese Grits:

5 cups chicken stock	½ teaspoon black pepper	1 egg, beaten
1 cup slow–cooking grits	4 tablespoons unsalted but–ter softened	2 cups grated white Cheddar cheese
1 teaspoon salt		

In a large saucepan over medium heat bring the chicken stock to a boil. Once the stock has come to a good rolling boil, stir in the grits, salt, and pepper. Bring the stock back to a boil, then reduce the heat to low, cover, and cook until the grits have thickened, about 30 to 35 minutes, stirring occasionally. Once the grits have cooked, remove the pan from the heat and blend in the butter, egg, and cheese.

To serve, place each grillade on a plate with some sauce spooned over it and sprinkle with chopped green onion alongside a big helping of grits. **Serves 4.**

Eggs Sardou

Originally created at Antoine's Restaurant back in 1908, this classic New Orleans breakfast dish is made with creamed spinach, artichoke bottoms, and poached eggs smothered with a Hollandaise Sauce. Perfect to serve at an elegant Creole jazz brunch.

3 10-ounce bags fresh organic spinach	½ teaspoon fresh chopped garlic	¼ cup grated Parmigiano Reggiano cheese
2 cups Chicken Stock (see page 132)	½ teaspoon salt	8 cooked artichoke bottoms, fresh or canned
1½ tablespoons unsalted butter	¼ teaspoon freshly ground black pepper	8 poached eggs
¼ cup finely chopped green onions	½ teaspoon thyme	2 cups Creole Hollandaise Sauce (see page 98)
	1 cup Béchamel Sauce (see page 97)	

Wash the spinach thoroughly and discard the stems. Place the leaves into a large saucepan with 2 cups of Chicken Stock and simmer over moderate heat until the spinach is just wilted. Once the spinach is wilted, remove it from the heat, drain, and chop roughly. Set aside to cool.

In a large skillet over medium heat melt the butter and sauté the green onions and garlic, stirring occasionally, for about 2 minutes. Add the spinach, salt, black pepper, and thyme and continue to cook, stirring occasionally for about 2 more minutes. Stir in the Béchamel sauce and the Parmigiano Reggiano cheese and reduce the heat to low to keep warm.

Warm the artichoke bottoms by placing them on a baking sheet and putting them in a warm oven for about 5 minutes.

To serve, place a dollop of the creamed spinach onto a warmed plate and top with 2 warm artichoke bottoms. Place 2 poached eggs on each of the artichoke bottoms and spoon ½ cup of Hollandaise Sauce over the eggs. Serve immediately. **Serves 4.**

Eggs Hussarde

This recipe originated at Commander's Palace Restaurant in New Orleans and is a variation on the classical Eggs Bene-dict, but with the addition of grilled tomato and Marchand de Vin Sauce. While the original version has the tomatoes on the side, our adaptation incorporates the tomato into the dish.

12 thin slices fresh tomatoes	12 slices Canadian bacon	1½ cups Marchand de Vins
Salt and pepper or Cajun/	12 Holland rusks or 6	Sauce (see page 99)
Creole seasoning to taste	toasted English muffins,	12 soft poached eggs
1 tablespoon unsalted butter	split	1½ cups Creole Hollandaise
		Sauce (see page 98)

Place the tomato slices on a baking sheet. Sprinkle tomato slices with salt and pepper or Cajun/Cre-ole seasoning and then broil or bake the tomato slices until warmed through, about 5 minutes.

In a heavy skillet over medium heat melt the butter and quickly sauté the Canadian bacon, lightly browning it on both sides. Remove from the skillet and drain on paper towels. Set the toma-toes and bacon aside and keep warm.

For each serving, place 2 buttered Holland rusks or English muffin halves on a warmed plate. Next, put 1 slice of bacon on each and cover with Marchand de Vins sauce. Then lay a tomato slice on top of the sauce-covered bacon, top with a poached egg, and cover the egg with Hollandaise sauce. Serve immediately. **Serves 6.**

Eggs Creole

This is a simple, easy way to scramble eggs Creole style.

8 eggs	½ tablespoon fresh chopped garlic	Salt and pepper or Cajun/Creole seasoning to taste
1 tablespoon water	½ cup fresh peeled and chopped tomatoes	2 cups Creole Sauce (see page 95)
2 tablespoons unsalted butter		
¼ cup chopped onions		
¼ cup chopped bell pepper	1 cup shredded Cheddar cheese	

Crack the eggs into a mixing bowl, add the water, and beat with a wire whisk for about 1 minute. In a heavy skillet over medium heat melt the butter and sauté the onions, bell pepper, and garlic until soft. Add the tomatoes and pour in the beaten eggs and stir to scramble. When the eggs are almost done, sprinkle with shredded Cheddar cheese and salt and pepper or Cajun/Creole seasoning blend. Stir to incorporate. When eggs are done, remove from the heat and set aside.

To serve, place a serving of eggs onto a plate and cover with Creole Sauce. **Serves 4.**

Creole Crab Meat Omelet Filling

This recipe originally comes from Commander's Palace Restaurant in New Orleans; we have modified it just a bit. This filling is enough for four 4-egg omelets.

4 teaspoons Seasoning Mix (see below)	8 green onions, finely sliced	1 cup lump crab meat, shells carefully removed
4 tablespoons (½ stick) unsalted butter	½ teaspoon fresh chopped garlic	1 cup Creole Hollandaise Sauce (see page 98)
	1 tablespoon dry white wine	

To make the Seasoning Mix, in a mixing bowl combine all of the Seasoning Mix ingredients and mix well. If you want your blend to be a bit spicier, increase the amount of pepper. You may prepare this in advance and store in an airtight jar in a cool, dry place.

In a heavy skillet over medium heat melt the butter and sauté the green onions, garlic, and Seasoning Mix for about 2 minutes, stirring constantly. Deglaze the pan with the white wine and continue to stir for about 1 minute. Reduce the heat to low, add the crab meat, and mix gently; do not stir. When you are ready to make the omelets, add 4 tablespoons of Hollandaise Sauce to the mixture and fold in gently. Make 4 omelets, placing a fourth of the filling in each omelet, and top each with remaining Hollandaise Sauce. **Serves 4.**

Seasoning Mix

Use 4 teaspoons of your favorite Cajun/Creole seasoning or:

- 1 teaspoon dried thyme
- 1 teaspoon dried sweet basil leaves
- ½ teaspoon sweet paprika
- ¼ teaspoon salt
- ¼ teaspoon cayenne pepper
- ¼ teaspoon black pepper
- ¼ teaspoon white pepper
- ¼ teaspoon garlic powder
- ¼ teaspoon onion powder

Cajun Coush-Coush

Coush-Coush is a traditional Cajun breakfast dish of fried cornmeal served hot with a little syrup on top. It is very filling, not to mention delicious!

2	cups yellow cornmeal	¼	teaspoon salt	1½	cups milk
2	tablespoons of all-purpose flour	1	teaspoon baking powder	½	cup butter
		2	teaspoons sugar		

In a large bowl mix the cornmeal, flour, salt, baking powder, and sugar. Gradually add in the milk stirring until smooth. In a heavy skillet over medium heat melt the butter and add the cornmeal mixture, stirring it around in the pan. Let this cook, stirring occasionally, for about 5 minutes. Reduce the heat to simmer, cover the pan lightly, and cook for about 10 to 15 minutes stirring occasionally.

Serve hot in a bowl with sugar cane syrup drizzled on top. **Serves 6.**

Pain Perdu

Pain Perdu means "lost bread" and is a Creole version of French toast, which is made with stale French bread to use the bread before it spoiled or was "lost."

1	5-ounce can evaporated milk	½	cup of sugar	¼	teaspoon cinnamon
2	eggs, well beaten	½	teaspoon vanilla	6	slices of stale French bread
		¼	teaspoon allspice	1	cup (2 sticks) butter

In a large mixing bowl combine the evaporated milk, eggs, sugar, vanilla, allspice, and cinnamon and mix very well. Dip each slice of bread into this mixture and soak until it is well coated and saturated. In a large, heavy skillet over medium heat melt the butter and fry the bread slices until nice and brown on each side.

Drain on paper towels and serve with sugar cane syrup or powdered sugar. **Serves 6.**

Appetizers and Dips

Seafood Dip, page 125

Photo by Keith Dunn

1. Shrimp Rémoulade

2. Stuffed Mushrooms

3. Louisiana Crab Cakes

4. Creole–Stuffed Shrimp

5. Shrimp or Crawfish Boulettes

6. Cajun/Creole Seafood Dip

7. Oysters Bienville

8. Oysters Mosca

9. Spinach & Crab Meat Dip

10. Natchitoches Meat Pies

11. Crawfish Beignets

Shrimp Rémoulade

This classic Creole appetizer is an ideal first course to a sophisticated Creole meal. It is a bit spicy, but the intricate flavors that are blended in the sauce make it sumptuous and elegant. This recipe can be made with precooked shrimp, however, we have provided you with the option of cooking your own if you'd like to punch up the flavor. It is a true connoisseur's delight, yet very simple to prepare.

Sauce:

- ½ cup chopped celery
- 2 green onions, finely chopped
- 1 cup Creole mustard (or spicy, coarse-ground German mustard)
- 1 cup olive oil
- ½ cup horseradish
- 2 tablespoons Worcestershire sauce
- Dash Tabasco sauce
- ½ cup tomato ketchup
- ¼ cup white wine vinegar
- 2 tablespoons Seasoning Mix for sauce (optional)
- ¼ cup chopped fresh parsley
- ¼ cup chopped fresh thyme leaves
- 4 cloves fresh garlic, minced
- Juice of 1 lemon, freshly squeezed

If making the Seasoning Mix for the sauce, in a mixing bowl combine all Seasoning Mix ingredients and blend well. If you want your blend to be a bit spicier, increase the amount of pepper. You may prepare this in advance and store in an airtight jar in a cool, dry place.

To make the sauce, in a medium bowl combine the sauce ingredients and mix thoroughly with a whisk. Refrigerate mixture for at least 4 hours or up to overnight to let the flavors meld. The longer it sits in the refrigerator, the more flavorful (and hotter) it will become.

Shrimp:

- 1 pound large raw shrimp, peeled and deveined
- Juice of 1 lemon, freshly squeezed
- 4 tablespoons olive oil
- 2 tablespoons Seasoning Mix for Shrimp
- 2 tablespoons dry white wine
- Lettuce for serving

To make the shrimp, place the shrimp in a bowl and pour the lemon juice over them and mix well. Remove from the bowl and place on a paper towel to dry.

In a heavy skillet heat the olive oil over medium heat and sauté the shrimp, stirring them constantly, just until they turn pink. Sprinkle with Seasoning Mix for Shrimp and deglaze the pan with the white wine (pour in the white wine to loosen up any crusty bits that may have stuck to the bottom of the pan). Let this cook for just about 1 minute, then remove the shrimp from the skillet and let cool to room temperature. Place the shrimp in the refrigerator for a couple of hours to chill. If you like, you can marinate the shrimp in the Rémoulade sauce as well to give it even more flavor.

When you are ready to serve, remove the shrimp from the refrigerator and place them on a bed of lettuce. Spoon some of the sauce over them and enjoy! **Serves 4**.

Seasoning Mix for Sauce

A seasoning mix is actually optional in this recipe since there are so many different flavorful ingredients already in it. However, if you want to have even more flavor, you can add 2 tablespoons of your favorite Cajun/Creole seasoning the following:

- 2 teaspoons sweet paprika
- 1 teaspoon dried thyme leaves
- 1 teaspoon dried sweet basil leaves
- 1 teaspoon dried oregano leaves
- 1/2 teaspoon garlic powder
- 1/2 teaspoon onion powder
- 1/4 teaspoon salt
- 1/4 teaspoon cayenne pepper
- 1/4 teaspoon white pepper
- 1/4 teaspoon black pepper

Seasoning Mix for Shrimp

Use 2 tablespoons of your favorite Cajun/Creole Seasoning Blend or:

- 1 tablespoon dried thyme leaves
- 1 teaspoon dried sweet basil leaves
- 1/2 teaspoon sweet paprika
- 1/2 teaspoon garlic powder
- 1/2 teaspoon onion powder
- 1/4 teaspoon salt
- 1/4 teaspoon cayenne pepper
- 1/4 teaspoon white pepper
- 1/4 teaspoon black pepper

Stuffed Mushrooms

12 large, fresh mushrooms, stems removed	½ cup lump crab meat	½ teaspoon salt
8 tablespoons (1 stick) butter	2 tablespoons white wine	¼ teaspoon pepper
1 cup finely chopped onion	1 tablespoon chopped fresh parsley	1 cup Seasoned Bread–crumbs (see below)
1 tablespoon all–purpose flour	1 tablespoon chopped fresh thyme	

Preheat the oven to 325°.

Brush the mushrooms with a moist paper towel. Place the mushrooms caps, top side down, on a well-greased baking sheet. In a skillet melt 6 tablespoons of butter and sauté the onion until golden, about 5 minutes. Fold in the flour, crab meat, wine, parsley, thyme, salt, and pepper. Sauté for 2 to 3 minutes, stirring gently. Remove the pan from the heat and stuff the mushroom caps with crab meat mixture. Sprinkle with breadcrumbs and dot each cap with a pat of remaining butter. Bake for 20 minutes. Serve immediately. **Makes 12 stuffed mushrooms.**

Seasoned Breadcrumbs

We feel that the best breadcrumbs are home-made. To make your own, start with a crusty loaf of French bread (make sure that it is hard and crusty on the outside). Break off a few hunks of bread and grind them in a food processor or blender until they are nice and fine. Add a couple of tablespoons of your favorite Cajun/Creole seasoning, and you have seasoned breadcrumbs!

Louisiana Crab Cakes

½ cup (1 stick) unsalted butter

1 cup chopped white onions

1 cup chopped red bell pepper

1 cup chopped green bell pepper

½ cup chopped parsley

1 to 2 tablespoons fresh chopped garlic

1 tablespoon Dijon mustard

1 to 2 tablespoons Worcestershire sauce

1 pound fresh lump crab meat (picked through for any remaining pieces of shell)

Juice of ½ lemon, freshly squeezed

2 teaspoons ground thyme

2 teaspoons ground sweet basil

2 teaspoons salt

1 teaspoon garlic powder

1 teaspoon onion powder

1 teaspoon sweet paprika

¼ teaspoon black pepper

¼ teaspoon white pepper

¼ teaspoon cayenne pepper

3 cups Toasted Bread-crumbs (see below)

½ cup grated Romano cheese

1 egg, lightly beaten

½ cup heavy cream

Vegetable or olive oil

In a large skillet melt the butter on medium heat. Add the onions, bell peppers, and parsley and cook, stirring occasionally, until the onions are translucent, about 5 minutes. Add the garlic, mustard, and the Worcestershire sauce and continue to cook for another 1 to 2 minutes. Add the crabmeat, lemon juice, and seasonings, gently stirring to keep the crab meat in large chunks. Remove from the heat and set aside.

Place 2 cups of breadcrumbs in a large mixing bowl and add the crab mixture, Romano cheese, egg, and heavy cream. Mix well and place in the refrigerator for 1 to 2 hours to set.

Toasted Breadcrumbs

Make your own breadcrumbs by slicing 2 loaves of day-old French bread into small chunks and then grinding them up in a food processor or a blender. Spread the crumbs evenly in a pan and broil them until they turn a toasty brown. (Watch them carefully because they can burn very easily.) Another way to toast the crumbs is to put them in a skillet over medium to high heat and shake them, being sure to watch them carefully. Two loaves of bread will make about 3 cups of breadcrumbs.

Remove the crab mixture from the refrigerator and shape into 12 cakes. Roll them in the remaining cup of breadcrumbs.

Cover the bottom of a large, heavy skillet with oil and place over medium heat. Add the cakes about 4 at a time and lightly fry them, turning once, until they are golden brown and crispy on the outside. Serve this as an appetizer dish by itself or with a sauce such as tartar or Creole seafood. *Bon appetit!* **Makes about 12 medium-sized cakes.**

Creole Stuffed Shrimp

Stuffed shrimp is one of the most delicious appetizers you will ever have, a bit involved but well worth the effort. They can be prepared ahead of time and then deep-fried right before serving. Everyone will rave about these.

2 to 3 tablespoons Seasoning Mix (see next page)	2 tablespoons fresh chopped parsley	1 dozen extra-large shrimp peeled, deveined, and butterflied (see below)
1½ sticks unsalted butter	1 pound fresh lump crab meat (picked through for shells)	1 cup all-purpose flour
3 to 4 green onions, finely chopped		2 large eggs beaten with 1 tablespoon of milk
4 cloves fresh garlic, chopped	2 cups Seasoned Bread-crumbs (see below)	Vegetable oil for deep frying

To make the Seasoning Mix, in a mixing bowl combine all of the Seasoning Mix ingredients and mix well. If you want your blend to be a bit spicier, increase the amount of pepper. You may prepare this in advance and store in an airtight jar in a cool, dry, place.

In a large, heavy skillet melt the butter over medium heat and sauté the onions, garlic, and parsley until soft, about 2 to 3 minutes. Add the crab meat and about 1 tablespoon of the Seasoning Mix and stir in, cooking for about 1 minute. Add ½ to 1 cup of the seasoned breadcrumbs (depending on how you like the consistency of your stuffing) and mix thoroughly, When your stuffing has reached the desired consistency, remove the pan from the heat and prepare to stuff the shrimp.

After the stuffing has cooled off enough for you to handle, scoop out a small amount and and fill the split in a shrimp with the stuffing, pressing it firmly between your

Butterflied Shrimp

To butterfly shrimp, first peel the shrimp from the shell, leaving the tip of the tail. Next, using a small sharp knife, make a small incision down the groove along the back starting at the tip of the head and going all the way down to the tail. Remove the black vein and spread open the back. You have a small area that you can now stuff with your stuffing.

Seasoned Breadcrumbs

We feel that the best breadcrumbs are home-made. To make your own, start with a crusty loaf of French bread (make sure that it is hard and crusty on the outside). Break off a few hunks of bread and grind them in a food processor or blender until they are nice and fine. Add a couple of tablespoons of your favorite Cajun/Creole seasoning, and you have seasoned breadcrumbs!

hands to make it stick. Continue to do this until all of the shrimp are stuffed in this manner. Roll the shrimp in the flour, then in the egg wash, and then in the rest of the seasoned breadcrumbs. Make sure that all of the stuffed shrimp are thoroughly coated. Place them in the refrigerator for a couple of hours to let the mixture set.

continued on next page

Now you are ready to fry. In a medium-sized pot heat enough oil for deep frying to about 350 degrees and drop in the stuffed shrimp a few at a time. Fry them until they are a light, crispy, golden brown. Drain on paper towels. You can serve these by themselves or with a nice dipping sauce. Enjoy! **Serves 4**.

Seasoning Mix

Use 2 to 3 tablespoons of your favorite Cajun/ Creole seasoning or:

- 1 tablespoon dried thyme leaves
- 1 tablespoon dried sweet basil leaves
- 1 teaspoon garlic powder
- 1 teaspoon onion powder
- 1/2 teaspoon salt
- 1/4 teaspoon cayenne pepper
- 1/4 teaspoon white pepper
- 1/4 teaspoon black pepper

Shrimp or Crawfish Boulettes

In Louisiana a boulette is a small appetizer, usually made with seafood, rolled into a little ball and deep-fried. These mouth-watering delights are sure to be the hit of any party. You won't be able to make enough of these for everybody!

1 pound raw medium shrimp, peeled, deveined, and chopped into small pieces (or boiled crawfish tails cut up the same way)

1½ cups Seasoned Bread-crumbs (see below)

1 large egg, beaten

2 to 3 green onions, finely chopped

4 to 5 cloves garlic, finely chopped

3 tablespoons finely chopped fresh parsley

½ cup grated Parmigiano Reggiano cheese

¼ teaspoon salt

¼ teaspoon cayenne pepper

¼ teaspoon black pepper

½ teaspoon dried thyme leaves

¼ teaspoon dried sweet basil leaves

¼ teaspoon garlic powder

½ teaspoon Worcestershire sauce

Vegetable oil for frying (enough to cover the balls in the pan)

In a large mixing bowl combine the shrimp, ½ cup seasoned breadcrumbs, and remaining ingredients. Place the remaining breadcrumbs in a shallow dish. Scoop out about 1 tablespoon of shrimp mixture and roll in your hand to form a small ball. Roll it in the reserved seasoned breadcrumbs. Repeat this process until all of the mixture has been rolled into small balls. Refrigerate for at least 2 hours to set the balls and make frying easier.

When you are ready to cook the boulettes, heat the vegetable oil in a heavy skillet to 350°F. Drop the boulettes into the hot oil a few at a time and fry them until they are a light golden brown, about 4 to 5 minutes per batch, depending upon how hot you have your oil. Serve either alone or with cocktail or tarter sauce. Enjoy! **Serves 4.**

Seasoned Breadcrumbs

We feel that the best breadcrumbs are home-made. To make your own, start with a crusty loaf of French bread (make sure that it is hard and crusty on the outside). Break off a few hunks of bread and grind them in a food processor or blender until they are nice and fine. Add a couple of tablespoons of your favorite Cajun/Creole seasoning, and you have seasoned breadcrumbs!

Cajun/Creole Seafood Dip

This terrific party dip is very easy to make and gets more flavorful the longer it sits out.

---

2 tablespoons Seasoning Mix (see below)

1 cup sour cream

1 cup mayonnaise

8 ounces fresh lump crab meat (picked through for any remaining pieces of shell)

¼ pound fresh cooked shrimp, chopped

¼ cup chopped green onions

1 tablespoon fresh lemon juice

¼ cup chopped fresh parsley

¼ cup chopped fresh thyme

1 teaspoon chopped fresh garlic

To make the Seasoning Mix, in a mixing bowl combine all of the Seasoning Mix ingredients and mix well. You may prepare this in advance and store in an airtight jar in a cool, dry place.

Combine all ingredients in a mixing bowl and blend very well. This dip can be made the day before your party—as it sits in the refrigerator it will become even more flavorful. Serve with crackers or sliced vegetables.

Seasoning Mix

Use 2 tablespoons of your favorite Cajun/Creole seasoning blend or:

2 teaspoons sweet paprika

1 teaspoon ground thyme

1 teaspoon ground sweet basil

1 teaspoon garlic powder

1 teaspoon onion powder

½ teaspoon salt

½ teaspoon black pepper

½ teaspoon white pepper

½ teaspoon cayenne pepper

Oysters Bienville

6 tablespoons unsalted butter	2 tablespoons Cajun/Creole seasoning	⅓ cup grated Parmigiano Reggiano cheese
¼ cup all–purpose flour	½ cup chopped mushrooms	½ cup Seasoned Bread-crumbs (see below)
4 green onions, finely chopped	½ pound boiled shrimp, peeled, deveined, and chopped	Rock salt
2 tablespoons fresh chopped parsley	1 cup whipping cream	24 shucked oysters, well drained
4 cloves garlic, finely chopped	2 egg yolks, beaten	24 well–scrubbed oyster shells
	¼ cup dry white wine	

In a heavy skillet melt the butter over medium heat; add the flour, stirring constantly with a wire wisk to make a blond roux (about 4 minutes). When the roux has reached the desired color, add the green onions, parsley, garlic, mushrooms, and 1 tablespoon of Cajun/Creole seasoning and cook until the vegetables are soft, about 2 to 3 minutes. Add the shrimp and cook until the vegetables are pink, about 3 to 4 minutes. Slowly add the cream, stirring it very gently until everything is blended together. Next, fold in the egg yolks, white wine, and remaining 1 tablespoon of Cajun/Creole seasoning and cook, stirring occasionally, until the mixture begins to thicken, about 4 to 5 minutes. Remove from the heat and set aside.

In a small mixing bowl mix the Parmigiano Reggiano cheese and breadcrumbs; set aside.

Preheat the oven to 400°. Sprinkle a large baking pan with the rock salt. Nestle the cleaned oyster shells in the rock salt on the baking pan. Pat dry the oysters with a paper towel; place a dried oyster onto each of the oyster shells. Spoon out some of the shrimp and cream mixture onto each oyster and then sprinkle with the cheese and breadcrumb mixture. Bake for about 10 to 15 minutes or until each oyster is crispy brown. **Serves 6.**

Seasoned Breadcrumbs

We feel that the best breadcrumbs are home-made. To make your own, start with a crusty loaf of French bread (make sure that it is hard and crusty on the outside). Break off a few bunks of bread and grind them in a food processor or blender until they are nice and fine. Add a couple of tablespoons of your favorite Cajun/Creole seasoning and you have seasoned breadcrumbs!

Oysters Mosca

Oysters Mosca originally comes from Mosca's restaurant in New Orleans and is a delicious way to prepare oysters. Basically it is baked, breaded oysters with a most wonderful Creole flavor!

1⅓ cups Seasoned Bread-crumbs (see facing page)	1 teaspoon dried thyme	½ cup chopped green onions
½ cup grated Parmigiano Reggiano cheese	1 teaspoon dried oregano	¼ cup chopped fresh parsley
	1 tablespoon Worcestershire sauce	2 tablespoons minced fresh garlic
1 teaspoon salt	1 teaspoon Tabasco sauce	2 pints oysters, drained
1 teaspoon black pepper	1 cup clarified butter	
1 teaspoon dried sweet basil	½ cup olive oil	

Preheat the oven to 425°.

In a medium bowl combine the breadcrumbs, Parmigiano Reggiano cheese, seasonings, Worcestershire sauce, and Tabasco. Be sure to mix thoroughly.

In a large skillet heat the clarified butter and olive oil over medium heat and sauté the green onions, parsley, and garlic until they are nice and soft, about 3 to 5 minutes. Add the seasoned breadcrumb mixture and stir to mix. Remove the pan from the heat and fold the oysters in very gently until they are nicely mixed in and covered. Once this is done, transfer the mixture to a 2-quart casserole dish. Bake for about 15 minutes or until the mixture is browned and crusty.

Serve as an appetizer or as a main dish with some crusty French bread and a nice salad. *Bien mangé.* **Serves 6.**

Spinach & Crab Meat Dip

1   10–ounce package frozen chopped spinach, thawed
1   pound lump crab meat (picked through for any remaining pieces of shell)
1   teaspoon salt
¼   teaspoon pepper
⅛   teaspoon dried thyme
⅛   teaspoon dried sweet basil
¼   teaspoon garlic powder
⅛   teaspoon Tabasco sauce
1   cup sour cream
½   cup mayonnaise
½   cup finely chopped fresh parsley
½   cup minced green onion
1   teaspoon lemon juice

Drain and squeeze the spinach to remove excess liquid. In a large bowl mix the spinach with the remaining ingredients. Cover and refrigerate overnight.

Serve with crusty French bread. **Makes 4 cups.**

Natchitoches Meat Pies

Pastry:

- 2½ cups all-purpose flour
- 1 teaspoon sugar
- 1 teaspoon salt
- ½ cup unsalted butter, cold
- ½ cup milk

Filling:

- 4 tablespoons olive oil
- ½ pound lean ground beef

- 2 tablespoons fresh rubbed sage
- 2 tablespoons Cajun/Creole seasoning
- ¼ cup all-purpose flour
- 1 onion, finely chopped

- 4 green onions, finely chopped
- 1 bell pepper, finely chopped
- 2 cups fresh chopped mushrooms
- 1 egg, slightly beaten
- 2 tablespoons milk

To prepare the pastry, in a large bowl add the flour, sugar, and salt and stir until blended. Cut the butter into 1-inch chunks; add to the flour mixture. Blend until the butter has broken into bits. Next, pour the milk into the bowl, mixing until the dough begins to come together. Place the dough on a lightly floured surface; shape it into 2 flat pieces. Wrap in plastic wrap and refrigerate until it is chilled (up to 24 hours).

To prepare the filling, in a large, heavy skillet heat the olive oil over medium heat. Add the ground beef, fresh rubbed sage, and 1 tablespoon Cajun/Creole seasoning and sauté until the beef is thoroughly cooked, about 8 minutes. Remove the meat from the skillet with a slotted spoon and place it in a bowl, leaving the oil in the pan; set aside. Add the flour to the skillet and stir with a wire whisk constantly to make a medium-brown roux. When the roux has reached the color that you want, add the onions, bell pepper, mushrooms, and remaining 1 tablespoon of Cajun/Creole seasoning and cook until the vegetables are soft, about 5 to 6 minutes. Add the ground beef back to the skillet and continue to cook, stirring occasionally, until the mixture is blended well. Remove from the heat, spoon the mixture into a bowl, and refrigerate until it is chilled.

To complete the pies, preheat the oven to 375°. Lightly grease 2 baking pans. Roll out the pastry dough on a floured surface into 2 flat circles about ⅟₁₆ of an inch thick. Using a 4-inch cookie cutter, cut 12 circles out of each of the 2 large circles of dough. Place a spoonful of the meat mixture into the center of each circle.

In a small bowl, beat the egg and 2 tablespoons of milk until it is blended. Using a pastry brush, paint a ½-inch border of egg wash around the edge of each of the 24 circles; fold the dough in half to encase the filling. Seal the edges of each pie by pressing the tines of a fork along the edges of each circle. (Be sure to turn each pie over to seal the edges on both sides.) When finished, place the pies onto the prepared baking pans and bake for 15 minutes. Turn the pies over and continue to bake for another 10 minutes. Serve hot. **Makes 24 meat pies.**

Crawfish Beignets

A savory twist on the traditional beignet.

2 tablespoons butter	2 tablespoons chopped garlic	½ cup shredded white
⅓ cup chopped green onions	½ pound crawfish tails	Cheddar cheese
⅓ cup chopped bell peppers	2 tablespoons Cajun/	2½ cups Bisquick
1 tablespoon fresh chopped	Creole seasoning	½ cup warm beer
parsley		Peanut Oil for frying

In a heavy skillet over medium heat melt the butter and sauté the green onions, bell peppers, parsley, and garlic until tender (about 3 to 4 minutes). Next, add in the crawfish tails and Cajun/Creole seasoning and reduce the heat to low and simmer, stirring occasionally, for about 2 minutes. Add the cheese and continue to simmer, stirring the mixture very well until the cheese has melted (about another 2 to 3 minutes). When the cheese has all melted out, remove the skillet from the heat and set aside.

In a large bowl mix the Bisquick and the warm beer and stir very well with a large fork to make a dough. Roll the dough out onto a well-floured cutting board and cut into 4-inch squares. Place a small dollop of the crawfish mixture onto one corner of a dough square. Fold this over into a diamond shape and seal the edges with a floured fork. Continue to do this until all of the dough squares are filled.

In a medium-sized saucepan heat the peanut oil to about 350° (over medium heat on most stoves). Be sure that you have enough oil to cover the surface of your beignets for deep frying. Deep fry the beignets a couple at a time until they are golden brown and crispy. **Makes 1 dozen.**

Stocks

1. Chicken Stock

2. Seafood Stock

3. Pork Stock

4. Beef Stock

5. Vegetable Stock

Photo by Keith Dunn

Chicken Stock

All stocks are made by simmering bones with various vegetables and aromatic herbs, creating a liquid that will give dishes a richer flavor than just using water.

1 large onion quartered (with the skin still on)

2 ribs celery, cut up (with the leaves still on)

2 large carrots, cut up (scrubbed and preferably unpeeled)

1 large bud garlic, broken up with all of the cloves crushed

1 whole chicken carcass (or as many chicken bones as you can acquire to equal a chicken carcass in size)

2 bay leaves

1 bunch fresh parsley

1 bunch fresh herbs (In this case a "bunch" is the amount that can fit into the palm of your hand. We recommend using two fresh herbs, such as sweet basil and thyme, but you may use any combination you prefer.)

Place the vegetables and the bones in a large 8- to 10-quart stockpot and cover entirely with *cold* water (about 3 to 4 quarts). Bring the water to a good rolling boil. Once it is boiling, a film of fat will rise to the top. Skim this off if you wish to make the stock less oily. After you have skimmed off as much of the fat as you wish, add bay leaves and fresh herbs and continue to boil for 2 to 3 minutes. Reduce the heat, cover the pot, and simmer for at least 4 hours. The ideal cooking time is 8 hours. Remember, the longer you simmer the pot, the more flavorful the stock will become. Every hour or so, stir the stock.

Remove the pot from heat and let the stock cool to room temperature. Strain the liquid into a smaller container. This can then be placed in the refrigerator to cool down further. After several hours in the refrigerator you will notice a film appear on the top of the stock. This is more fat that has risen to the top. You can skim this off to make the stock less fatty as well. This stock will give a wonderful flavor to a soup, stew, or gumbo. **Makes approximately 2 quarts of stock.**

For Richer Stock

To make your stock even richer, you can roast the bones and vegetables on a pan in the oven at 350° for about 2 hours, turning them over about every 30 minutes until they have formed a nice brown crust. For more details about making stock, see "Basic Stock" on page 28.

Seafood Stock

All stocks are made by simmering bones with various vegetables and aromatic herbs, creating a liquid that will give dishes a richer flavor than just using water.

Several large fish heads, fish bones, shrimp shells, crab claws, or other types of seafood bones and shells. (If you can, get shrimp heads as well, as they will have a lot of flavor.)

1 large onion, quartered (with the skin still on)

2 ribs of celery cut up (with the leaves still on)

2 large carrots cut up (scrubbed and preferably unpeeled)

1 large bud garlic broken up with all of the cloves crushed

1 large lemon, quartered

2 bay leaves

1 bunch fresh parsley

1 bunch fresh herbs (In this case a "bunch" is the amount that can fit into the palm of your hand. We recommend using two fresh herbs, such as sweet basil and thyme, but you may use any combination you prefer.)

Place the bones and/or shells, vegetables, and lemon in a large 8- to 10-quart stockpot and cover entirely with *cold* water (about 3 to 4 quarts). Bring the water to a good rolling boil. Once it is boiling, a film of fat will rise to the top. Skim this off if you wish to make the stock less oily. After you have skimmed off as much of the fat as you wish, add the bay leaves and fresh herbs and continue to boil for 2 to 3 minutes. Reduce the heat, cover the pot, and simmer for at least 4 hours. The ideal cooking time is 8 hours. Remember, the longer you simmer the pot, the more flavorful the stock will become. Every hour or so stir the stock.

Remove the pot from heat and let the stock cool to room temperature. Strain the liquid into a smaller container. This can then be placed in the refrigerator to cool down further. After several hours in the refrigerator, you will notice a film appear on the top of the stock. This is more fat that has risen to the top. You can skim this off to make the stock less fatty as well. Now you have a good batch of stock for a soup, stew, or gumbo that will make your dishes taste wonderful! **Makes approximately 2 quarts of stock.**

All stocks are made by simmering bones with various vegetables and aromatic herbs, creating a liquid that will give dishes a richer flavor than just using water.

1 large onion, quartered (with the skin still on)

2 ribs celery, cut up (with the leaves still on)

2 large carrots, cut up (scrubbed and preferably unpeeled)

1 large garlic bud broken up with all of the cloves crushed

1 large, meaty ham bone or several pork bones, such as necks or feet

2 bay leaves

1 bunch fresh herbs (In this case a "bunch" is the amount that can fit into the palm of your hand. We recommend using two fresh herbs, such as sweet basil and thyme, but you may use any combination you prefer.)

Place the bones and the vegetables in a large 8- to 10-quart stockpot and cover entirely with *cold* water (about 3 to 4 quarts). Bring the water to a good rolling boil. Once it is boiling. a film of fat will rise to the top. Skim this off if you wish to make the stock less oily. After you have skimmed off as much of the fat as you wish, add the bay leaves and fresh herbs and continue to boil for 2 to 3 minutes. Reduce the heat, cover the pot, and simmer for at least 4 hours. The ideal cooking time is 8 hours. Remember, the longer you simmer the pot, the more flavorful the stock will become. Every hour or so, stir the stock.

Remove the pot from heat and let the stock cool to room temperature. Strain the liquid into a smaller container. This can then be placed in the refrigerator to cool down further. After several hours in the refrigerator, you will notice a film appear on the top of the stock. This is more fat that has risen to the top. You can skim this off to make the stock less fatty as well. Now you have a good batch of stock for a soup, stew, or gumbo! **Makes approximately 2 quarts of stock.**

For Richer Stock

To make your stock even richer, you can roast the bones and vegetables on a pan in the oven at 350° for about 2 hours, turning them over about every 30 minutes until they have formed a nice brown crust. For more details about making stock, see "Basic Stock" on page 28.

4. Beef Stock

All stocks are made by simmering bones with various vegetables and aromatic herbs, creating a liquid that will give dishes a richer flavor than just using water.

- 1 large onion, quartered (with the skin still on)
- 2 ribs of celery, cut up (with the leaves still on)
- 2 large carrots, cut up (scrubbed and preferably unpeeled)
- 1 large bud garlic, broken up with all of the cloves crushed
- 1 large, meaty beef bone or several steak bones
- 2 bay leaves
- 1 bunch fresh parsley
- 1 bunch fresh herbs (In this case a "bunch" is the amount that can fit into the palm of your hand. We recommend using two fresh herbs, such as sweet basil and thyme, but you may use any combination you prefer.)

Place the bones and the vegetables in a large 8- to 10-quart stockpot and cover entirely with *cold* water (about 3 to 4 quarts). Bring the water to a good rolling boil. Once it is boiling a film of fat will rise to the top. Skim this off if you wish to make the stock less oily. After you have skimmed off as much of the fat as you wish, add the bay leaves and fresh herbs and continue to boil for 2 to 3 minutes. Reduce the heat to a simmer, cover the pot, and simmer for at least 4 hours. The ideal cooking time is 8 hours. Remember, the longer you simmer the pot, the more flavorful the stock will become. Every hour or so, stir the stock.

Remove the pot from heat and let the stock cool to room temperature. Strain the liquid into a smaller container. This can then be placed in the refrigerator to cool down further. After several hours in the refrigerator, you will notice a film appear on the top of the stock. This is more fat that has risen to the top. You can skim this off to make the stock less fatty as well. Now you have a good batch of stock for a soup, stew, or gumbo! **Makes approximately 2 quarts of stock.**

Vegetable Stock

For those of you non-carnivores, we have included a recipe for a vegetarian stock. This stock is made the same way as a meat stock but with more vegetables in place of the meat bones. You can put any sort of vegetables you would like in this, which allows a lot of creativity.

1	large onion, quartered (with the skin still on)	1	large bud garlic, broken up with all of the cloves crushed	1	bunch fresh herbs (In this case a "bunch" is the amount that can fit into the palm of your hand. We recommend using two fresh herbs, such as sweet basil and thyme, but you may use any combination you prefer.)
2	ribs celery, cut up (with the leaves still on)	1	large zucchini squash, sliced into chunks		
2	large carrots, cut up (scrubbed and preferably unpeeled)	1	large tomato, quartered		
		1	large potato, quartered		
		2	bay leaves		
		1	bunch fresh parsley		

Place all the vegetables in a large 8- to 10-quart stockpot and cover entirely with *cold* water (about 3 to 4 quarts). Bring the water to a good rolling boil. After the water has boiled for a minute or two, add the bay leaves and fresh herbs and continue to boil for 2 to 3 minutes. Reduce the heat to a simmer, cover the pot, and simmer for at least 4 hours. The ideal cooking time is 8 hours. Remember, the longer you simmer the pot, the more flavorful the stock will become. Every hour or so stir the stock.

Remove the pot from heat and let the stock cool to room temperature. Strain the liquid into a smaller container. This can then be placed in the refrigerator to cool down further. Now you have a good batch of vegetarian stock for a soup, stew, or gumbo! **Makes approximately 2 quarts of stock.**

For Richer Stock

To make your stock even richer, you can roast the vegetables on a pan in the oven at 350° for about 2 hours, turning them over about every 30 minutes, until they have formed a nice brown crust. For more details about making stock, see "Basic Stock" on page 28.

Soups and Gumbos

1. Louisiana Turtle Soup

2. Oyster and Artichoke Bisque

3. Shrimp and Crab Meat Bisque

4. Creole Vegetable Soup

5. Crawfish Bisque

6. Bouillabaisse Louisiane

7. Chicken Sausage Gumbo

8. Seafood Okra Gumbo

9. Gumbo Z'Herbes

10. Seafood Filé Gumbo

11. Pot–au–Feu à la Creole

12. Creole Potato Soup

13. Cream of Asparagus Soup

14. Cajun–Style Pumpkin Soup

15. Corn and Crab Meat Soup

16. Creole French Onion Soup

17. Duck and Sausage Gumbo

Photo by Keith Dunn

Cajun-Style Pumpkin Soup, page 151

Louisiana Turtle Soup

¼ cup (½ stick) unsalted butter	2 pounds turtle meat, trimmed, cut into ½ inch cubes	¼ teaspoon mace
¼ cup all–purpose flour		½ teaspoon dried sweet basil
1 large onion, finely chopped	2 large tomatoes, peeled and chopped	1 bay leaf
1 bell pepper, finely chopped	1 teaspoon salt	1½ quarts Pork Stock (see page 134)
2 tablespoons fresh chopped parsley	½ teaspoon black pepper	½ teaspoon Worcestershire sauce
4 cloves fresh garlic, chopped	½ teaspoon ground allspice	1 tablespoon fresh lemon juice
1 pound smoked ham, cut into ½–inch cubes	¼ teaspoon freshly grated nutmeg	¼ cup sherry
	1 teaspoon dried thyme	
	½ teaspoon ground cloves	

In a heavy 4- to 5-quart soup pot melt the butter over medium heat. Add the flour and stir constantly with a wire whisk to make a light brown roux, about 15 minutes. When the roux has reached the desired color, add the onion, bell pepper, parsley, garlic, ham, and turtle meat and cook until the vegetables are soft, about 5 to 6 minutes. Add the tomatoes and all of the seasonings and continue to cook for about 3 to 4 minutes. Slowly add the Pork Stock along with the Worcestershire sauce and lemon juice and bring to a boil, stirring occasionally, until the soup begins to thicken. Then, reduce the heat to a simmer and cover partially and cook for about 2 hours, stirring occasionally.

When you are ready to serve, add the sherry. **Serves 6**.

Oyster and Artichoke Bisque

4 fresh artichokes	4 cloves fresh garlic, chopped	½ teaspoon dried sweet basil
3 tablespoons butter	½ teaspoon dried thyme	½ teaspoon Worcestershire sauce
3 tablespoons all–purpose flour	1 bay leaf	1 quart oysters and their liquid
1 cup chopped onions	1½ quarts Seafood Stock, warmed (see page 133)	1 teaspoon lemon juice
1 cup chopped bell pepper	¼ teaspoon cayenne pepper	¼ cup dry white wine
1 tablespoon finely chopped fresh parsley	1 teaspoon salt	¼ cup heavy cream

Steam the artichokes. Scrape the leaves, chop the hearts, and reserve. In a heavy 4- to 5-quart pot melt the butter. Add the flour and stir constantly with a wire whisk to make a blonde roux, about 4 to 5 minutes. When the roux has reached the desired color, add the onions, bell pepper, parsley, and garlic and cook until the vegetables are tender, about 3 to 4 minutes. Add the artichoke mixture and blend in well. Slowly add the Seafood Stock along with the seasonings and the Worcestershire sauce; reduce the heat to low and simmer, stirring occasionally, for about 15 minutes.

Add the oysters (including the oyster liquid) and continue to simmer for about 5 minutes. Add the lemon juice, white wine, and heavy cream and blend together until smooth. **Serves 6.**

Shrimp and Crab Meat Bisque

6 tablespoons (¾ stick) butter

3 tablespoons grated onion

6 tablespoons all-purpose flour

½ teaspoon dry mustard

2 cups whole milk, warmed

4 cups half and half, warmed

2 teaspoons chopped fresh parsley

1 pound lump crab meat (picked through for any remaining pieces of shell)

2 tablespoons dry sherry

2 teaspoons Worcestershire sauce

¼ teaspoon Tabasco

2 teaspoons salt

White pepper to taste

2 pounds shrimp, peeled and deveined

In a heavy pot melt the butter. Add the onion and sauté for 5 minutes. Stir in the flour and cook for 2 minutes. Add the dry mustard and stir well. Lower the heat and whisk in the milk and half and half. Add this mixture to pot and stir in the parsley, crab meat, sherry, Worcestershire sauce, Tabasco, salt, and pepper. Simmer for ½ hour over low heat.

Before serving, add the shrimp and heat until the shrimp turn pink. Serve with a crusty loaf of French bread. **Serves 6.**

Creole Vegetable Soup

This vegetarian recipe will make enough soup to last for a week!

2 tablespoons Seasoning Mix (see below)

2 quarts Vegetable Stock (see page 136)

2 bay leaves

¼ cup fresh chopped parsley

¼ cup fresh chopped thyme leaves

¼ cup fresh chopped sweet basil

2 cups fresh lima beans or 10-ounce package of frozen lima beans

2 large potatoes, peeled and cubed

3 tablespoons olive oil

1 tablespoon chopped fresh garlic

3 cups sliced zucchini squash

3 cups sliced mushrooms

2 cups chopped onions

2 cups chopped green bell pepper

1 cup chopped celery

2 cups diced tomatoes

2 28-ounce cans tomato purée

1 tablespoon Worcestershire sauce

½ cup dry white wine

1 tablespoon lemon juice

To make the Seasoning Mix, in a mixing bowl combine all of the Seasoning Mix ingredients and mix well. You may prepare this in advance and store in an airtight jar in a cool, dry place.

In a large stockpot bring the vegetable stock to a boil with the bay leaves, fresh herbs, lima beans, and potatoes. Cover, reduce the heat, and simmer. Meanwhile, in a large skillet heat the oil over medium heat and sauté the remaining vegetables, except tomatoes, for about 2 to 3 minutes. Add tomatoes and 2 tablespoons of Seasoning Mix, stirring for 1 to 2 minutes. Add the tomato purée, Worcestershire sauce, white wine, and lemon juice and bring to a simmer, stirring occasionally. Add the skillet mixture to the stockpot and bring back to a boil. Cover the pot, reduce the heat, and simmer for a minimum of 4 hours. The longer it simmers on a low heat, the more flavorful it will become.

This recipe can be made the day before and re-heated the next day. Cool the soup slightly before re-frigerating. The soup will be even *more* flavorful the second day! *Bon appetit!* **Makes about 4 quarts of soup.**

Seasoning Mix

Use 2 tablespoons of your favorite Cajun/ Creole seasoning blend or:

1 teaspoon dried thyme leaves

1 teaspoon dried sweet basil leaves

1 teaspoon dried oregano leaves

1 teaspoon sweet paprika

½ teaspoon salt

½ teaspoon garlic powder

½ teaspoon onion powder

½ teaspoon black pepper

½ teaspoon white pepper

½ teaspoon cayenne pepper

Crawfish Bisque

¼ cup olive oil	½ cup chopped green onions	3 pounds crawfish tails
¼ cup all–purpose flour	3 cloves garlic, minced	1 cup heavy cream
1½ cups chopped yellow onions	¼ cup chopped fresh parsley	Salt to taste
1½ cups chopped celery	1 bay leaf	Pepper to taste
½ cup chopped green pepper	½ teaspoon dried thyme	Cayenne pepper to taste
	4 cups Seafood Stock (see page 133)	Worcestershire sauce to taste
		3 cups steamed rice

In a large cast-iron pot heat the oil and gradually add the flour, stirring constantly, until the roux is blonde. Add the onions, celery, green pepper, green onions, garlic, parsley, bay leaf, and thyme. Cook until tender, stirring often. Slowly add the stock, stirring constantly. Cover and simmer for 1 hour, stirring occasionally.

Two minutes before serving, add the crawfish tails and stir in the cream; add salt, pepper, cayenne, and Worcestershire sauce to taste. Stir and serve over rice. **Serves 6.**

Bouillabaisse Louisiane

This dish is similar to its French cousin except that it has different seafood and is a bit spicier with haughty Creole flavor.

2 quarts Seafood Stock (see page 133)	1 pint oysters	1 teaspoon fresh chopped garlic
1 cup dry white wine	1 10–ounce can whole crushed tomatoes	Salt and pepper to taste
1 pound red snapper fillets	Pinch of saffron	
1 lobster tail (cubed)	½ teaspoon cayenne pepper	
1 pound shrimp, shelled and deveined	1 tablespoon thyme	

In a 4-quart stockpot bring the Seafood Stock and wine to a boil. Add the fish, tomatoes, and seasonings and bring back to a boil. Reduce the heat and simmer gently for 10 minutes.

Serve with crusty baguettes of French bread. **Serves 4.**

Chicken Sausage Gumbo

2 to 3 tablespoons Seasoning Mix (see below)

4 cups Chicken Stock

2 tablespoons olive oil

1 pound smoked sausage, sliced

1 whole chicken, cut up

2 cups fresh sliced okra

¼ cup olive oil

¼ cup all-purpose flour

2 cups chopped onions

1 cup chopped green bell pepper

½ cup chopped celery

4 cloves fresh garlic, chopped

2 cups diced tomatoes

½ teaspoon Worcestershire sauce

1 bay leaf

1 teaspoon dried thyme

1 teaspoon dried sweet basil

3 cups Louisiana Tasty Rice (see page 156)

1 jar filé powder (optional)

½ cup fresh chopped parsley for garnish

½ cup chopped green onions for garnish

To make the Seasoning Mix, combine all Seasoning Mix ingredients in a mixing bowl and mix well. If you want your blend to be a bit milder, decrease the amount of pepper. You may prepare this in advance and store in an airtight jar in a cool, dry place.

Place the chicken stock into a large stockpot and bring to a good boil then reduce the heat to a low simmer.

In a large cast-iron skillet heat 1 tablespoon of olive oil over medium heat and sauté the sausage and the chicken pieces until they are cooked, about 5 to 7 minutes. When the meat is done, remove from skillet and drain on paper towels. Next, heat another skillet over medium heat with 1 table-spoon of olive oil and cook the okra until it is a bit crispy and all of the slime is cooked out of it, about 5 minutes. Drain on paper towels.

Seasoning Mix

Use 2 to 3 tablespoons of your favorite Cajun/ Creole seasoning or:

1 teaspoon sweet paprika

1 teaspoon dried thyme

1 teaspoon dried sweet basil leaves

1 teaspoon dried parsley

½ teaspoon salt

½ teaspoon cayenne pepper

½ teaspoon black pepper

½ teaspoon white pepper

½ teaspoon garlic powder

½ teaspoon onion powder

In a heavy cast-iron skillet over medium heat, heat up the ¼ cup olive oil and gradually add in the flour, stirring constantly with a wire whisk to make a dark-brown roux. When the roux has reached the color that you want, reduce the heat to low and add the onions, bell pepper, celery, and garlic and cook until the vegetables are soft, about 5 minutes, stirring occasionally, and then remove from the heat.

Meanwhile, bring the Chicken Stock back to a good rolling boil and add the roux, chicken and sausage pieces, okra, tomatoes, Worcestershire sauce, and the rest of your seasonings. Bring all of this back to a good boil and then reduce the heat to low and let simmer for about 2 hours, stirring occasionally.

To serve, place a small amount of Tasty Rice in a bowl and spoon out some of the gumbo on top of it. If you wish to make it a bit thicker, sprinkle a small amount of filé powder into each bowl and stir. Garnish each bowl with fresh chopped parsley and green onions. **Serves 6.**

Seafood Okra Gumbo

2 quarts Seafood Stock (see page 133)

4 tablespoons olive oil

2 cups fresh sliced okra

3 tablespoons all-purpose flour

2 cups chopped onions

1 cup chopped green bell pepper

1 cup chopped red bell pepper

½ cup chopped celery

2 cups fresh sliced mushrooms

2 tablespoons fresh minced garlic

6 tablespoons of your favorite Cajun/Creole seasoning

2 tablespoons Worcestershire sauce

2 whole bay leaves

½ sliced lemon

2 pounds raw shrimp, peeled and deveined

1 pound fresh lump crab meat (picked through for any remaining pieces of shell)

3 catfish fillets

Filé powder (optional)

1 cup Louisiana Tasty Rice (see page 156)

Fresh chopped green onions and parsley for garnish

In a large stockpot begin to simmer the Seafood Stock. In a large skillet heat 1 tablespoon of olive oil and sauté the okra over medium heat for about 5 to 10 minutes, until it has browned and is less slimy. Once it has browned, set it aside.

In another larger, heavy cast iron skillet heat 3 tablespoons of olive oil over medium heat and add the flour, stirring with a wire whisk to make a roux. The roux is ready when it has turned a dark chocolate brown color. Remember to keep stirring the roux constantly while you are cooking it. As long as you keep it moving, it will not burn. Once your roux has reached the color you want, turn the heat off and add the onions, bell peppers, celery, and mushrooms, stirring constantly. As it begins to cook add the garlic, 3 tablespoons of Cajun/Creole seasoning, and 1 tablespoon of Worcestershire sauce. When the mushrooms are soft, transfer the roux mixture into the stock and bring it all to a good rolling boil. Stir in the okra, bay leaves, lemon, remaining Cajun/Creole seasoning, and 1 tablespoon of Worcestershire sauce. Stir well and bring back to a boil. Cover, reduce the heat, and simmer for about 2 hours.

When ready to serve the gumbo, add in the seafood. (Remember, the seafood needs only to poach. Once the shrimp has turned pink and the catfish is opaque and flakes easily, the gumbo is ready to serve.) Remove the bay leaves. You may want to add a tablespoon of filé powder to thicken the gumbo. To serve, spoon out some of the cooked rice into a bowl and top with gumbo. Garnish the bowl with a few fresh chopped green onions and some fresh chopped parsley. **Serves 8.**

Gumbo Z'Herbes

This vegetarian gumbo is traditionally served during Lent since this is a time when many people give up meat—which means they can have their gumbo and eat it too!

10 ounces fresh spinach or 1 10-ounce pkg. frozen leaf spinach, thawed	4 quarts Vegetable Stock (see page 136)	½ teaspoon freshly ground black pepper
10 ounces fresh mustard greens or 1 10-ounce pkg. frozen mustard greens, thawed	2 tablespoons vegetable oil	½ teaspoon cayenne pepper
	2 large onions, chopped	2 tablespoons sugar
	2 ribs celery, chopped	1 teaspoon salt
	1 large green bell pepper, chopped	½ teaspoon Worcestershire sauce
10 ounces fresh turnip greens or 1 10-ounce pkg. frozen turnip greens, thawed	4 large cloves garlic, chopped	3 cups Louisiana Tasty Rice (see page 156)
	2 bay leaves	1 jar filé powder (optional)
	1 teaspoon dried thyme leaves	½ cup chopped green onions for garnish
10 ounces fresh collard greens or 1 10-ounce pkg. frozen collard greens, thawed	1 teaspoon dried sweet basil leaves	½ cup fresh chopped parsley for garnish
½ medium cabbage, shredded	1 teaspoon dried oregano leaves	

Wash the fresh greens and cabbage and tear into small pieces, removing the stems. Place into a large stockpot and add the Vegetable Stock and bay leaves and bring to a boil. Reduce the heat to a simmer and cover.

Meanwhile, in a large skillet heat the vegetable oil over medium heat and sauté the onions, celery, and bell peppers along with the garlic and all of the herbs and spices and cook until the vegetables are soft, about 5 minutes. Transfer the cooked vegetables to the simmering pot along with the sugar, salt, and Worcestershire sauce. Cover and continue to simmer for 2 hours, stirring occasionally.

To serve, place a small amount of the Tasty Rice into each serving bowl and spoon out some of the gumbo over the rice. If you like your gumbo a little thicker, sprinkle some of the filé powder into each bowl and stir. Garnish each bowl with the fresh chopped green onions and parsley. **Serves 8.**

Seafood Filé Gumbo

¼ cup olive oil

¼ cup all-purpose flour

1 large onion, chopped

1 medium green bell pepper, chopped

¼ cup chopped celery

4 medium cloves garlic, finely minced

3 quarts Seafood Stock (see page 133)

2 bay leaves

1 teaspoon Worcestershire sauce

Juice of ½ lemon

1 teaspoon dried thyme leaves

1 teaspoon dried sweet basil leaves

1 teaspoon dried oregano leaves

1 teaspoon freshly ground black pepper

½ teaspoon cayenne pepper

Salt to taste

1 pound lump crab meat, (picked through for any remaining pieces of shell)

2 pounds raw shrimp,

peeled and deveined

1 pint oysters

1 pound redfish or red snapper fillets, cut into bite-sized nuggets

1 pound bay scallops

3 cups hot cooked rice

1 jar filé powder (optional)

½ cup fresh chopped green onions for garnish

½ cup fresh chopped parsley for garnish

In a large, heavy cast-iron skillet heat the olive oil over medium heat and add the flour, stirring constantly to make a dark brown roux. Add the onion, bell pepper, celery, and garlic, cooking until the vegetables are nice and soft, about 5 minutes.

Meanwhile, in a large saucepan bring the stock to a boil. Slowly whisk the roux into boiling stock until all has been added. Add the bay leaves, Worcestershire sauce, and lemon juice along with the herbs and spices. Reduce the heat and simmer 2 hours.

Add the crab meat, shrimp, oysters, fish, and scallops. Cook over medium heat for 5 minutes. Taste for seasoning; adjust if necessary.

To serve, place a small amount of Tasty Rice in each bowl and spoon out some of the gumbo on top of it. Sprinkle with a little bit of the filé powder and stir to make the gumbo thick. Garnish with the fresh chopped green onions and parsley. **Serves 8**.

Pot-au-Feu à la Creole

This historic recipe is a classic French beef soup from a bygone era. This version is taken from the 1987 reprint of The Picayune's Creole Cookbook, *first published in 1901 by The Times-Picayune. Reviewing this recipe gives us a snapshot of Creole life at the turn of the twentieth century.*

4 pounds of lean beef	A cupful of tomatoes, cup–up	A small piece of lemon peel	
6 quarts of cold water (or beef stock)	2 whole cloves	A bunch each of celery leaves and parsley, chopped	
2 small turnips	A bay leaf		
2 onions	A clove of garlic	A pinch each of salt and black pepper	
2 carrots	5 allspice		
A parsnip	2 Irish potatoes	A sprig of cabbage	

This Pot-au-feu, properly made, is truly delicious, savory and delicately odorous. The best cut from this is from the round lower end of the beef. It is important to have good beef, and that it be as freshly killed as can be had. Many of the Creoles add the beef spleen or brisket to the soup. This is rich and juicy, and gives nutritive value to the dish.

Put the meat into beef stock, heating by slow degrees, in order that it may gradually penetrate the meat, softening it and dissolving the non-nutritive portion, which rises to the top of the liquid as a scum. As the scum becomes thicker, remove it. After having skimmed well, set the soup back where it can be kept on a gentle but steady boil; when the soup is well skimmed, add the vegetables, which have been cut to proper fineness, and a little salt to suit the taste, and let the soup continue to boil from five to six hours, remembering strictly the two essential rules given. By following this recipe you will have an excellent soup for family use.

The Creoles often serve the Pot-au-Feu with croutons, small squares of dry or toasted bread, put into the tureen, and the hot soup is poured over the moment of serving.

Should the flavor of the garlic, allspice, cloves or bay leaf be disagreeable, they may be omitted. But they are essential ingredients of the Creole Pot-au-Feu.

A particularly delicate flavor is often obtained by adding to the beef some pieces of raw fowl, or the remains of a cooked fowl, more especially the carcass. But never add remains of mutton, pork or veal as these may impart an acrid color, detracting from the perfection of the Pot-au-Feu.

*Cook's Note:
To jazz up your pot-au-feu, we recommend using beef stock instead of water.

Creole Potato Soup

(Potage au Pom de Terre)

2 onions, finely chopped
2 tablespoons butter
8 potatoes, washed, peeled, and quartered

2 quarts Chicken Stock, homemade or organic (see page 132)
Pinch grated nutmeg
2 tablespoons of your favorite Cajun/Creole seasoning

Salt and pepper to taste
1 cup cream
Croutons
Chopped fresh chives

In a small saucepan sauté the onions in 1 tablespoon butter until they are very soft. Place the potatoes in a large pot and add about 2 quarts of Chicken Stock. Bring to a boil, cooking until the potatoes are very tender. Transfer to a blender, and the onions, and blend until smooth. Return the soup to the pot. Add the seasonings and remaining 1 tablespoon butter. Bring to a boil, remove from the heat, and add the cream. Serve immediately with croutons and chives. **Serves 6.**

Cream of Asparagus Soup

Crème d'Asparges

1½ pounds fresh asparagus	6 cups Chicken Stock,	Salt and pepper to taste
2 tablespoons butter	homemade or organic	⅔ cup heavy cream
2 onions, peeled and	(see page 132)	
chopped		

Cut the tips off the asparagus spears and cook gently in salted water for 3 to 5 minutes. Drain and set aside for use as garnish. Trim and discard the woody ends of remaining the asparagus. Slice the spears into ½-inch pieces.

In a large saucepan melt the butter, add the asparagus and onions, cover, and cook over medium heat until the vegetables begin to soften. Add the stock and salt and pepper to taste. Bring to a boil and simmer until the asparagus and onions are tender, 30 to 40 minutes. Remove the saucepan from heat and let cool slightly. Transfer to a blender and purée until smooth. Return the soup to the pot. Stir in the cream and serve immediately. Garnish with reserved tips. **Serves 6.**

Cajun-Style Pumpkin Soup

4 cups Vegetable Stock, homemade or organic (see page 136)	4 cloves fresh garlic, chopped	1 teaspoon salt
1 bay leaf	2 cups boiled potatoes, peeled and mashed	1 teaspoon ground thyme
1 tablespoon butter	6 cups puréed pumpkin, fresh or canned	¼ teaspoon black pepper
1 cup finely chopped onions	1 teaspoon ground sweet basil	2 cups heavy cream
1 cup chopped bell peppers		Grated nutmeg for garnish
		Fresh chopped chives for garnish

Place the Vegetable Stock into a 4-quart pot along with the bay leaf and bring to a boil. Reduce heat to low and simmer.

In a large saucepan melt the butter and sauté the onions and bell peppers along with the garlic until they are nice and soft, about 5 minutes. Add the potatoes, puréed pumpkin, and the seasonings and simmer for about 15 minutes, stirring occasionally. Remove the pan from the heat and allow to cool for a short while (about 10 minutes). When cooled, pour the mixture into a blender and purée. Pour the puréed mixture into the simmering vegetable stock and add the cream. Allow to simmer for about 10 minutes more, stirring occasionally.

This soup may be served hot or cold. Garnish each bowl with a little freshly grated nutmeg and some fresh chopped chives. **Serves 6.**

Corn and Crabmeat Soup

3 tablespoons unsalted butter	2 cups fresh or frozen whole-kernel corn	1 pint heavy cream (2 cups)
3 tablespoons all-purpose flour	1 teaspoon dried thyme leaves	1 pound lump crab meat (picked through for any remaining pieces of shell)
1 large onion, chopped	1 bay leaf	
1 bell pepper, chopped	½ teaspoon salt	½ cup fresh chopped parsley for garnish
4 cloves garlic, chopped	½ teaspoon freshly ground black pepper	½ cup fresh chopped green onions for garnish
4 cups Seafood Stock (see page 133)	¼ teaspoon cayenne pepper	

In a large, heavy stockpot melt the butter over medium heat. Add the flour and stir constantly with a wire whisk to make a blonde roux, about 4 to 5 minutes. When the roux has reached the desired color, add the onion, bell pepper, and garlic and sauté until the vegetables are nice and soft, about 4 to 5 minutes. Slowly pour in the Seafood Stock and bring to a boil, stirring occasionally. Add the corn and the seasonings and reduce the heat to a simmer. Allow the pot to simmer for 30 minutes.

Stir in the cream and continue to simmer for about 10 more minutes, stirring occasionally. Gently fold in the crab meat and simmer another 5 minutes. Serve hot and garnish each bowl with fresh chopped parsley and green onions. **Serves 8.**

Creole French Onion Soup

4 tablespoons butter

3 yellow onions, peeled and thinly sliced

1 tablespoon all-purpose flour

3½ cups Beef Stock (see page 135)

Salt to taste

Pepper to taste

1 bay leaf

1 tablespoon minced garlic

1 teaspoon chopped fresh thyme leaves

¼ teaspoon cayenne pepper

½ loaf French bread

¾ cup shredded Gruyère cheese

4 ovenproof soup bowls

In a large saucepan melt the butter. Add the onions and cook slowly until golden brown, 15 to 20 minutes. Stir in the flour and cook, stirring for 1 minute. Add the stock and seasonings. Bring to boil, reduce the heat, and simmer for 30 to 40 minutes.

Cut the bread diagonally into ½-inch slices. Toast lightly on both sides. Place 2 slices of bread in each ovenproof bowl and ladle hot soup over the bread. Sprinkle liberally with cheese to form a thick layer. Under a preheated broiler, heat the cheese until melted and bubbly. Serve immediately. **Makes 4 servings.**

Duck and Sausage Gumbo

For the Ducks and Stock:

2	ducks, cleaned (gutted), plucked, and washed	2 onions, quartered	2 bay leaves
	Water to cover	2 ribs celery	Several sprigs fresh parsley,
		2 whole carrots, peeled and sliced	sweet basil, and thyme
		1 whole garlic bulb, crushed	

To prepare the ducks and stock, place the ducks in a large pot and cover with water. Add the onions, celery, carrots, celery, garlic, bay leaves, and fresh herbs and bring to a boil. Once the pot is boiling, reduce the heat to a simmer and cook for 1 hour. Remove ducks, then skin, debone, and cut up the meat and lay aside. Strain the stock and reserve the liquid.

For the Gumbo:

3 quarts duck stock	½ cup chopped celery	1 tablespoon ground sweet basil
1 bay leaf	4 tablespoons fresh chopped garlic	3 cups Louisiana Tasty Rice (see page 156)
2 pounds smoked sausage, sliced	2 cups sliced mushrooms	1 jar filé powder (optional)
¼ cup olive oil	½ teaspoon salt	½ cup chopped fresh parsley for garnish
¼ cup all-purpose flour	¼ teaspoon black pepper	
2 cups chopped onions	¼ teaspoon cayenne pepper	½ cup chopped green onions for garnish
1 cup chopped green bell peppers	1 tablespoon ground thyme	

Place the duck stock in a large stockpot along with the bay leaf and bring to a simmering boil over medium heat. While the pot is simmering, in a large, heavy skillet over medium heat, sauté the smoked sausage until it is cooked, about 5 to 6 minutes, stirring occasionally. Remove from the skillet and drain on paper towels.

In another skillet heat the olive oil and add the flour, stirring constantly with a wire whisk to make a dark-brown roux. When the roux has reached the color that you want, add the onions, bell peppers, celery, garlic, mushrooms, and seasonings and sauté until the vegetables are nice and soft, about 5 to 6 minutes. Add the roux, sausage, and duck meat to the simmering pot and bring to a boil. Once the pot is boiling, reduce the heat to a simmer and cook for 1 hour, stirring occasionally.

To serve, spoon out a small amount of the Tasty Rice into a bowl and pour some gumbo over it. Sprinkle a small amount of filé powder into the bowl and stir to make it thick. Garnish with fresh chopped parsley and green onions. **Serves 8.**

Vegetable Dishes

1. Basic Louisiana Tasty Rice
2. Brown Rice
3. Cajun Maque Choux
4. Creole Stewed Okra and Tomatoes
5. Beef–Stuffed Bell Peppers
6. Cajun "Dirty" Rice
7. Cajun Corn Pudding
8. Cajun Collard Greens
9. Creole Zucchini and Tomatoes
10. Fried Okra
11. Creole Red Beans and Rice
12. Congri
13. Pecan Rice
14. Cajun Potato Fries
15. Fried Sweet Potato and Onion
16. Creole String Beans
17. Roasted Pecan and Sausage Stuffing
18. New Year's Day Hoppin' John
19. Hush Puppies
20. Seafood–Stuffed Bell Pepper
21. Stuffed Eggplant
22. Brabant Potatoes
23. Smothered Cabbage

Photo by Keith Dunn

Basic Louisiana Tasty Rice

Rice is an integral part of any Louisiana meal and is used in virtually all Cajun/Creole dishes. If a dish does not have rice in it, such as Jambalaya, then it is usually served over rice. Therefore, how you cook your rice is very important. It is easy to cook white rice and does not take long at all. The recipe for brown rice is almost the same but takes just a bit longer. We have included some ways for you to make what we call "Tasty Rice," the most flavorful rice you will ever eat, for true!

1 tablespoon Seasoning Mix (see below)	2 cups Chicken Stock (see page 132)	1 cup raw white rice
	1 tablespoon butter	

To make the Seasoning Mix, in a mixing bowl combine all of the Seasoning Mix ingredients and mix well. You may prepare this in advance and store in an airtight jar in a cool, dry place.

In a saucepan bring the stock to a boil with the butter and Seasoning Mix. Add the rice and bring back to a boil. (Stir this a few times so the rice does not stick to the bottom of the pan.) Reduce the heat to simmer, cover the pan, and cook for approximately 20 minutes, without peeking. **Makes 3 cups of cooked rice.**

Seasoning Mix

Use 1 tablespoon of your favorite Cajun/Creole seasoning blend or 1 tablespoon of the following:

1 teaspoon sweet paprika
½ teaspoon ground thyme leaves
½ teaspoon ground sweet basil leaves
½ teaspoon ground oregano leaves
½ teaspoon garlic powder
½ teaspoon onion powder
¼ teaspoon salt
¼ teaspoon black pepper
¼ teaspoon white pepper
¼ teaspoon cayenne pepper

Brown Rice

1 tablespoon Seasoning Mix (see below)	2½ cups Chicken Stock (see page 132)	¼ teaspoon Worcestershire sauce
	1 tablespoon butter	1 cup raw brown rice

To make the Seasoning Mix, in a mixing bowl combine all of the Seasoning Mix ingredients and mix well. You may prepare this in advance and store in an airtight jar in a cool, dry place.

In a saucepan bring the chicken stock to a boil with the butter, Worcestershire sauce, and Seasoning Mix. Add the rice and bring back to a boil. (Stir this a few times so the rice does not stick to the bottom of the pan.) Reduce the heat to simmer, cover the pan, and cook for approximately 40 minutes, without peeking. After 40 minutes you can lift the lid off the pot and *voila!* You now have tasty brown rice! **Makes 2 cups of cooked rice.**

Seasoning Mix

Use 1 tablespoon of your favorite Cajun/Creole seasoning blend or:

1 teaspoon sweet paprika
½ teaspoon ground thyme leaves
½ teaspoon ground sweet basil leaves
½ teaspoon garlic powder
½ teaspoon onion powder
¼ teaspoon salt
¼ teaspoon black pepper
¼ teaspoon white pepper
¼ teaspoon cayenne pepper

Cajun Maque Choux

12 ears fresh yellow corn on the cob, shucked

¼ pound (1 stick) butter

2 cups chopped onions

1 cup chopped bell pepper

½ cup chopped celery

2 tablespoons fresh chopped garlic

2 large fresh tomatoes, peeled and chopped

1 cup Vegetable Stock (see page 136)

Salt and cayenne pepper to taste

1 tablespoon ground thyme

1 tablespoon ground sweet basil

¼ cup heavy cream

Using a sharp knife, slice the corn off of the cob and then scrape the cob to remove the "milk" from the corn; place the corn mixture in a bowl. In a heavy pot over medium heat melt the butter and sauté the onions, bell peppers, and celery along with the garlic until the vegetables are nice and soft, about 4 to 5 minutes. Add the corn, tomatoes, Vegetable stock, and seasonings and cook until the corn is tender, about 5 to 10 minutes, stirring occasionally. Lastly, add the heavy cream and stir well to blend all the ingredients. **Serves 8.**

Creole Stewed Okra and Tomatoes

3 tablespoons olive oil	½ teaspoon salt	1 tablespoon fresh chopped parsley
1 cup chopped onion	½ teaspoon freshly ground black pepper	1 cup Chicken Stock, homemade or organic (see page 132)
1 cup chopped bell pepper	¼ teaspoon cayenne pepper	
4 cloves chopped garlic	½ teaspoon sugar	
40 medium–sized okra pods, sliced	1 tablespoon ground thyme	
4 medium–sized tomatoes, peeled and diced	1 tablespoon ground sweet basil	

In a heavy skillet heat the olive oil over medium heat and sauté the onion, bell pepper, garlic, and okra until the vegetables have softened and reduced in size. Then add in the tomatoes, all of the seasonings, and the Chicken Stock, and simmer for about ½ hour, stirring occasionally. **Serves 6.**

Beef-Stuffed Bell Peppers

This is classic Cajun cookin' at its best. . . . bell peppers stuffed with ground beef and Cajun spices. Very delicious indeed.

6 large bell peppers	1 28–ounce can diced tomatoes	1 cup Seasoned Bread–crumbs (see below)
1 recipe Cajun "Dirty" Rice (see page 161)		

Preheat the oven to 350°.

Cut the tops off the bell peppers and remove the stems and seeds. Stuff with Cajun "Dirty" Rice. Pour the canned tomatoes on the bottom of a 2-quart casserole dish. Place the stuffed peppers on top of the tomatoes and top each with 2 tablespoons of breadcrumbs. Cover the dish and bake for 30 minutes or until the tops become crusty and brown and the peppers are soft.

To serve, place one bell pepper on each plate and spoon tomatoes with juice on top. **Serves 6.**

Seasoned Breadcrumbs

We feel that the best breadcrumbs are home-made. To make your own, start with a crusty loaf of French bread (make sure that it is hard and crusty on the outside). Break off a few hunks of bread and grind them in a food proces-sor or blender until they are nice and fine. Add a couple of tablespoons of your favorite Cajun/Creole seasoning and you have sea-soned breadcrumbs!

Cajun "Dirty" Rice

In the old days, dirty rice was cooked with the gizzard, liver, and other parts of the chicken that are normally thrown away. The finished dish looked a bit "dirty" at a glance, which is where the name comes from. Today we use not only chicken but also ground beef to make the dish even more satisfying.

½ pound chicken livers and gizzards

3 tablespoons olive oil

2 cups finely chopped onion

1 cup finely chopped green bell pepper

½ cup finely chopped celery

2 tablespoons Cajun/Creole seasoning

4 cloves fresh garlic, chopped

1 pound ground beef

¼ cup Chicken Stock, homemade or organic (see page 132)

1 teaspoon Worcestershire sauce

3 cups cooked Basic Louisiana Tasty Rice (see page 156)

¼ cup fresh chopped parsley for garnish

¼ cup fresh choped green onions for garnish

Remove the tough outer skin from the gizzards by scraping it with a sharp knife. Chop the chicken gizzards and liver and set aside.

In a deep, heavy skillet or pot heat the olive oil over medium heat and sauté the vegetables along with 1 tablespoon of the Cajun/Creole seasoning and the garlic until soft, about 4 to 5 minutes. Add the chicken livers and gizzards and ground beef and continue to sauté along with 1 more tablespoon of the Cajun/Creole seasoning until the meat is cooked, about 5 to 6 minutes. Add the Chicken Stock and Worcestershire sauce and scrape the bottom of the pan to release any browned bits of meat. Fold in the cooked rice and mix thoroughly until everything is blended and warm. Serve garnished with parsley and green onions. **Serves 8.**

Cajun Corn Pudding

2 tablespoons butter	1 cup canned creamed corn	½ cup grated white Cheddar cheese
½ cup chopped onion	2 tablespoons sugar	
½ cup chopped bell pepper	½ teaspoon salt	3 organic, free–range eggs, beaten
1 cup fresh whole–kernel corn	¼ teaspoon black pepper	

In a large skillet over medium heat melt the butter and sauté the onion and bell pepper until soft, about 4 to 5 minutes. Add the corn, creamed corn, sugar, salt, and pepper and continue to cook, stirring occasionally, for about 15 to 20 minutes.

Add the Cheddar cheese and beaten eggs and blend well to incorporate. Pour into a greased casserole dish and bake in the oven at 350 degrees for 35 minutes. **Serves 6.**

Cajun Collard Greens

2 slices bacon	1 bunch of collard greens, cleaned and chopped	1 tablespoon ground thyme
1 medium onion, chopped		Pinch of sugar
1 medium bell pepper, chopped	1 quart Vegetable Stock (see page 136)	Salt and pepper to taste

In a large skillet fry the bacon pieces with a slotted spoon and reserve. Add the onion and bell pepper and sauté until onion is translucent. In a large stockpot combine bacon pieces and drippings with all other ingredients. Cook until the greens are tender, about 10 to 20 minutes. **Serves 4.**

Creole Zucchini and Tomatoes

When these two vegetables are cooked together, it is truly a marriage made in heaven and will make a wonderful side dish for any entrée that you want to serve!

1 tablespoon Seasoning Mix (see below)	1 small onion, chopped	1 tablespoon Worcestershire sauce
2 tablespoons olive oil	2 zucchini squash, sliced	
	2 fresh tomatoes, peeled and chopped	

To make the Seasoning Mix, in a mixing bowl combine all of the Seasoning Mix ingredients and mix well. You may prepare this in advance and store in an airtight jar in a cool, dry place.

In a pan melt the butter over low heat. Sauté the onions until clear, about 4 to 5 minutes. Add the zucchini, tomatoes, Worcestershire sauce, and Seasoning Mix. Cover and simmer until the zucchini is tender, about 10 to 20 minutes. **Serves 6.**

Seasoning Mix

Use 1 tablespoon of your favorite Cajun/Creole seasoning blend or:

1 teaspoon dried thyme

1 teaspoon dried sweet basil leaves

1 teaspoon sweet paprika

½ teaspoon salt

½ teaspoon garlic powder

½ teaspoon onion powder

¼ teaspoon cayenne pepper

¼ teaspoon black pepper

¼ teaspoon white pepper

Fried Okra

1 to 2 tablespoons Seasoning Mix (see below)	1 cup all–purpose flour	2 eggs, beaten
2 pounds okra, with tops removed and cut into ¾–inch pieces	1 cup white corn meal	Vegetable oil for frying

To make the Seasoning Mix, in a mixing bowl combine all of the Seasoning Mix ingredients and mix well. You may prepare this in advance and store in an airtight jar in a cool, dry place.

In a shallow dish combine the flour, cornmeal, and Seasoning Mix. Dip the okra into the eggs and then into the flour-cornmeal mixture. Deep fry in oil at 375° until golden brown, about 5 minutes or less; drain on paper towels. **Serves 6**.

Seasoning Mix

Use 1 to 2 tablespoons of your favorite Cajun/ Creole seasoning blend or:

1 teaspoon sweet paprika
1 teaspoon dried thyme
1 teaspoon dried sweet basil leaves
½ teaspoon salt
½ teaspoon garlic powder
½ teaspoon onion powder
¼ teaspoon cayenne pepper
¼ teaspoon black pepper
¼ teaspoon white pepper

Creole Red Beans and Rice

This dish is traditionally served on Mondays in Louisiana, because in bygone days Monday was wash day and the ease of preparation of red beans and rice gave the wives time to wash the clothes and still have a meal on the table at the end of the day.

1 tablespoon Seasoning Mix (see below)	4 large cloves garlic, minced	1 12-ounce can beer
2 pounds dried red kidney beans	1 ham bone (about 1½ pounds)	About 2 quarts Pork Stock (see page 134)
¼ cup bacon drippings or olive oil	Salt to taste	3 tablespoons olive oil
2 large onions, chopped	Freshly ground black pepper to taste	2 pounds smoked sausage, sliced
1 large green bell pepper, chopped	2 bay leaves	Hot cooked Louisiana Tasty Rice (see page 156)
½ cup chopped celery	1½ tablespoons fresh chopped thyme leaves	12 green onions, thinly sliced
		½ cup minced parsley

To make the Seasoning Mix, in a mixing bowl combine all of the Seasoning Mix ingredients and mix well. You may prepare this in advance and store in an airtight jar in a cool, dry place.

Pick through the beans; discard any bad ones. Rinse the beans; set aside. In a large stockpot or Dutch oven heat the drippings and saute the onions, bell pepper, celery, and garlic until the vegetables are wilted. Add the rinsed beans, ham bone, bay leaves, Seasoning Mix, beer, and enough pork stock to cover. Bring to a boil. Reduce the heat, cover, and simmer until the beans are soft and the juice has thickened, about 3 hours, stirring occasionally. Add more stock, if necessary. Discard the bay leaves.

In a heavy 12-inch skillet heat the oil over medium heat. Add the sliced sausage and cook, turning often, until browned, about 10 to 15 minutes. Add to the beans.

To serve, spoon rice on each plate; ladle the beans and sausage mixture over the rice. Sprinkle with green onions and parsley. **Serves 8.**

Seasoning Mix

Use 1 tablespoon of your favorite Cajun/Creole seasoning blend or:

1 teaspoon dried thyme leaves
1 teaspoon dried sweet basil leaves
½ teaspoon garlic powder
½ teaspoon onion powder
¼ teaspoon black pepper
¼ teaspoon white pepper
¼ teaspoon cayenne pepper
¼ teaspoon salt

Cook's Note:

Here is a trick that New Orleans' restaurants use to give this dish incredible flavor: Instead of using olive oil, sauté your vegetables in bacon drippings. Also, after your beans have finished cooking, melt one stick of butter in the pot and let it cream out before serving. Of course, you won't want to do this if you are heart conscious or are trying to watch your cholesterol.

Congri

Congri is black beans and rice and is very similar to its brother, red beans and rice, the only difference being the type of bean that is used. The dish dates back to at least the mid-eighteenth century, with the name (and possibly the recipe) being mostly of African origin.

1 to 2 tablespoons Seasoning Mix (see below)

2 pounds dried black beans

¼ cup bacon drippings or olive oil

2 large onions, chopped

1 large green bell pepper, chopped

½ cup chopped celery

4 large garlic cloves, minced

1 ham bone (about 1½ pounds)

2 bay leaves

1½ tablespoons fresh chopped thyme leaves

1 12–ounce can beer

About 2 quarts Pork Stock (see page 134)

3 tablespoons olive oil

2 pounds smoked sausage, sliced

Hot cooked Louisiana Tasty Rice (see page 156)

12 green onions, thinly sliced

½ cup minced parsley, preferably flat–leaf

To make the Seasoning Mix, in a mixing bowl combine all of the Seasoning Mix ingredients and mix well. You may prepare this in advance and store in an airtight jar in a cool, dry place.

Pick through the beans; discard any bad ones. Rinse the beans; set aside. In a large stockpot or Dutch oven heat the drippings and sauté the onions, bell pepper, celery, and garlic until the vegetables are wilted. Add the rinsed beans, ham bone, bay leaves, Seasoning Mix, thyme, beer, and enough pork stock to cover. Bring to a boil. Reduce the heat, cover, and simmer until the beans are soft and the juice has thickened, about 3 hours, stirring occasionally. Add more stock, if necessary. Discard the bay leaves.

In a heavy 12-inch skillet heat the oil over medium heat. Add the sliced sausage and cook, turning often, until browned, about 10 to 15 minutes. Add to the beans.

To serve, spoon rice on each plate; ladle the beans and sausage mixture over the rice. Sprinkle with green onions and parsley. **Serves 8.**

Seasoning Mix

Use 1 to 2 tablespoons of your favorite Cajun/ Creole seasoning blend or:

2 teaspoons sweet paprika

1 teaspoon dried thyme leaves

1 teaspoon dried sweet basil leaves

½ teaspoon garlic powder

½ teaspoon onion powder

¼ teaspoon salt

¼ teaspoon black pepper

¼ teaspoon white pepper

¼ teaspoon cayenne pepper

Pecan Rice

¼	cup unsalted butter	½	teaspoon salt	½	teaspoon freshly ground
1	cup chopped onions	1	cup chopped pecans		pepper
½	cup chopped bell pepper	¼	teaspoon Worcestershire	½	teaspoon ground thyme
¼	cup chopped celery		sauce	2	cups cooked Konrico wild
1	teaspoon chopped fresh	2	tablespoons minced parsley		pecan rice
	garlic				

Melt the butter in a large, heavy skillet over medium heat and sauté the onions, bell pepper, and celery along with the garlic until the vegetables are soft, about 3 to 4 minutes. Add in pecans, Worcestershire sauce, and seasonings and stir, cooking until the pecans have browned, about 2 minutes. Reduce the heat to simmer and fold in the cooked rice, stirring well to blend all ingredients. Serve hot. **Serves 6.**

Cajun Potato Fries

These are the Colonel's famous French fries!

1 tablespoon Seasoning Mix (see below)	Enough oil to cover bottom of a heavy skillet	5 large potatoes, sliced

To make the Seasoning Mix, in a mixing bowl combine all of the Seasoning Mix ingredients and mix well. You may prepare this in advance and store in an airtight jar in a cool, dry place.

In a heavy skillet heat oil over medium heat. Add the potato slices and fry, turning frequently, until the potatoes are nice and crispy and brown. Once the fries are golden and crispy, remove them from the skillet and drain on a paper towel. Sprinkle generously with the Seasoning Mix on both sides. Serve immediately. **Serves 6.**

Seasoning Mix

Use 1 tablespoon of your favorite Cajun/Creole seasoning blend or:

1	teaspoon sweet paprika
½	teaspoon dried thyme leaves
½	teaspoon dried sweet basil leaves
½	teaspoon dried oregano leaves
½	teaspoon garlic powder
½	teaspoon onion powder
¼	teaspoon salt
¼	teaspoon black pepper
¼	teaspoon white pepper
¼	teaspoon cayenne pepper

Fried Sweet Potato and Onion

Enough olive oil to cover bottom of a heavy skillet	1 large red onion, julienne cut
4 medium–sized sweet potatoes, peeled and cut into bite–sized cubes	2 tablespoons Cajun/ Creole seasoning

In a heavy skillet heat the olive oil over medium-low heat and sauté the sweet potatoes, stirring them often to keep them from burning. When the sweet potatoes are just brown and crispy on all sides, sprinkle on the Cajun seasoning and cover the potatoes with the red onions slices to let them sweat. When the onions have turned opaque, stir all the ingredients in the pan and serve immediately. **Serves 4.**

Cook's Note

This dish may also be cooked with bacon. Fry 6 slices of bacon until crisp and then add potatoes, onion, and seasonings. Continue cooking as directed.

Creole String Beans

8   ounces (2 sticks) butter
1   pound tasso, cut into pieces (may substitute smoked sausage)

2   medium onions, finely chopped
2   pounds fresh green beans or 2 pounds frozen green beans

2   tablespoons fresh chopped garlic
½   teaspoon Worcestershire sauce
2   tablespoons Cajun/Creole seasoning

In a large cast-iron pot over medium heat melt the butter. Add the tasso, stir, and cook for 3 to 4 minutes, stirring occasionally. Add the onions, beans, garlic, Worcestershire sauce, and Cajun/Creole seasoning and cook for about 30 minutes, stirring occasionally, until the beans are nice and tender. **Serves 6**.

Roasted Pecan and Sausage Stuffing

This Louisiana-style stuffing goes wonderfully with Thanksgiving or Christmas Turkey.

2 tablespoons Seasoning Mix (see below)

1 pound smoked sausage, cut in small pieces

1 large onion, chopped

1 medium bell pepper, chopped

2 ribs celery, chopped

1 cup sliced mushrooms

4 cloves garlic, chopped

1 tablespoon fresh rubbed sage

1 tablespoons Worcestershire sauce

1 cup roasted chopped pecans

2 cups Toasted Bread-crumbs (see below)

1 cup Chicken Stock (see page 132)

To make the Seasoning Mix, in a mixing bowl combine all of the Seasoning Mix ingredients and mix well. You may prepare this in advance and store in an airtight jar in a cool, dry place.

In a large, heavy skillet over medium heat sauté the sausage until it is nearly done, about 5 to 10 minutes. Add the onions, bell pepper, and celery and continue cooking until they are soft. Add the mushrooms, garlic, sage, Worcestershire sauce, and Seasoning Mix. Continue to cook for about another minute or 2, stirring occasionally. Add the roasted pecans and continue to cook for another minute, stirring occasionally. Reduce the heat to low and add the breadcrumbs, stirring until everything is well combined. Finally, add the chicken stock and stir the pan well. Taste the stuffing and adjust the seasoning; see if the texture suits you. You may want to add more breadcrumbs or more stock, depending on your own taste. Serve with turkey at Thanksgiving or anytime of the year. **Serves 6.**

Toasted Breadcrumbs

Make your own breadcrumbs by slicing 2 loaves of day-old French bread into small chunks and then grinding them up in a food processor or a blender. Spread the crumbs evenly in a pan and broil them until they turn a toasty brown. (Be very careful to watch them carefully because they can burn very easily.) Another way to toast the crumbs is to put them in a skillet over medium to high heat and shake them, being sure to watch them carefully. Two loaves of bread will make about 3 cups of breadcrumbs.

Seasoning Mix

Use 2 tablespoons of your favorite Cajun/Creole seasoning blend or:

2 teaspoons sweet paprika

1 teaspoon dried thyme leaves

1 teaspoon dried sweet basil leaves

½ teaspoon garlic powder

½ teaspoon onion powder

¼ teaspoon salt

¼ teaspoon black pepper

¼ teaspoon white pepper

¼ teaspoon cayenne pepper

New Year's Day
Hoppin' John

Hoppin' John is traditionally served on New Year's Day, as it is generally believed that if you eat this dish it will bring you good luck for the coming year. In most of the South, Hoppin' John is simply black-eyed peas and rice cooked together. However, in Louisiana, it is made more like a black-eyed pea jambalaya. It is very filling and very delicious!

- 2 tablespoons Seasoning Mix (see below)
- 2 tablespoons olive oil
- 1 pound sliced smoked sausage or ham
- 3 boneless chicken breasts or thighs, cut up
- 1 cup chopped onions

- 1 cup chopped bell peppers
- ½ cup chopped celery
- 5 cloves garlic, chopped
- 3 tablespoons Worcestershire sauce
- 2 cups Basic Louisiana Tasty Rice (see page 156)

- 2 cans black-eyed peas precooked, drained, and set aside
- Chopped green onions and parsley for garnish

To make the Seasoning Mix, in a mixing bowl combine all of the Seasoning Mix ingredients and mix well. You may prepare this in advance and store in an airtight jar in a cool, dry place.

In a very large heavy skillet heat the olive oil over medium heat and sauté the sausage and the chicken until they are just about done, about 5 minutes. Add the vegetables, garlic, Worcestershire sauce, and Seasoning Mix. The mixture will be done when the vegetables are soft and the chicken is nice and firm, about 5 more minutes. Add the cooked rice and black-eyed peas, and mix thoroughly. Heat through before serving.

Serve on pretty plates with some fresh chopped green onions and parsley for garnish. If you clean your plate, you will have good luck all year round! **Serves 6.**

Seasoning Mix

Use 2 tablespoons of your favorite Cajun/Creole seasoning blend or:

- 2 teaspoons sweet paprika
- ½ teaspoon dried thyme leaves
- ½ teaspoon dried sweet basil leaves
- ½ teaspoon garlic powder
- ½ teaspoon onion powder
- ¼ teaspoon salt
- ¼ teaspoon black pepper
- ¼ teaspoon white pepper
- ¼ teaspoon cayenne pepper

Hush Puppies

1 tablespoon Seasoning Mix (see below)	³⁄₄ cup (1½ sticks) unsalted butter	1½ teaspoons baking powder
1½ cups Chicken Stock (see page 132)	2 cups plus 2 tablespoons yellow cornmeal, preferably stone–ground	⅓ cup finely chopped green onions
		⅓ cup fresh chopped parsley Vegetable oil

To make the Seasoning Mix, in a mixing bowl combine all of the Seasoning Mix ingredients and mix well. You may prepare this in advance and store in an airtight jar in a cool, dry place.

Place the Chicken Stock and the butter into a large saucepan over a medium heat and bring to a boil. Meanwhile, in a large bowl combine the cornmeal, Seasoning Mix, baking powder, green onions, and parsley. Once the Chicken Stock has come to a boil, pour the stock into the cornmeal mixture and stir until it is nice and moist. Once the moist mixture has cooled down just a bit, form the dough into small balls by rolling them in your hands.

Fry the balls of dough in a large skillet filled with the vegetable oil at 350° until the balls are golden brown and crispy. This will work best if you will deep fry them or at least have enough oil to almost cover them. Fry only a few balls at a time —do not crowd the skillet. Turn them once in the pan while they are frying. The balls will take about 2 minutes per side to cook. Drain on paper towels. Serve hot. **Makes 32 hush puppies.**

Seasoning Mix

Use 1 tablespoon of your favorite Cajun/Creole seasoning blend or:

  1 teaspoon dried sweet basil leaves
  1 teaspoon sweet paprika
  1 teaspoon dried thyme
  ½ teaspoon salt
  ½ teaspoon garlic powder
  ½ teaspoon onion powder
  ¼ teaspoon cayenne pepper
  ¼ teaspoon black pepper
  ¼ teaspoon white pepper

Seafood-Stuffed Bell Peppers

½ cup olive oil	1 tablespoon ground thyme	2 organic, free-range eggs
1 pound shrimp, peeled, deveined, and chopped	1 tablespoon ground sweet basil	1 cup Toasted Bread-crumbs (see below)
1 large bell pepper, finely chopped	Salt and black pepper to taste	6 bell peppers, halved
½ cup chopped onion	1 pound lump crab meat (picked through for any remaining pieces of shell)	
¼ cup chopped celery		
1 teaspoon cayenne pepper		

In a large skillet heat the oil and cook the shrimp until they just turn pink. Add the bell pepper, onion, and celery and sauté until the vegetables are soft, about 5 minutes. Add the seasonings. Remove the skillet from the heat to cool. Add the crab meat, shrimp, eggs, and breadcrumbs and mix well. Stuff into the uncooked pepper shells. Place in a baking dish with enough water to cover the bottom. Bake at 350° for 20 minutes or until the peppers are tender. **Serves 6.**

Toasted Breadcrumbs

Make your own breadcrumbs by slicing 2 loaves of day-old French bread into small chunks and then grinding them up in a food processor or a blender. Spread the crumbs evenly in a pan and broil them until they turn a toasty brown. (Watch carefully because they can burn very easily.) Another way to toast the crumbs is to put them in a skillet over medium to high heat and shake them, being sure to watch them carefully. Two loaves of bread will make about 3 cups of breadcrumbs.

Stuffed Eggplant

3 eggplants	¼ cup chopped fresh parsley	½ teaspoon sweet basil
6 tablespoons butter		½ teaspoon oregano
2 cups chopped onions	1 pound raw shrimp, chopped	½ teaspoon salt
1 cup chopped green bell pepper		½ teaspoon black pepper
½ cup chopped celery	½ teaspoon Worcestershire sauce	¼ cup homemade seasoned breadcrumbs
4 cloves fresh garlic, chopped	½ teaspoon dried thyme	

Preheat the oven to 350°.

Wash and slice the eggplants in half lengthwise. Place into a large pot and cover with cold water. Bring the pot to a simmering boil and cook for about 30 minutes, being careful to not let the eggplant break; drain and cool. Scoop out the meat from the eggplant and set aside, leaving about ½ inch of shell. Place the shells onto a baking sheet.

In a large, heavy skillet over medium heat melt the butter and sauté the onions, bell pepper, celery, garlic, and parsley until the vegetables are soft, about 5 minutes. Add the chopped shrimp, eggplant meat, Worcestershire sauce, and seasonings and continue to cook, stirring until everything has cooked and is blended well, about 6 to 7 minutes. Fold in the seasoned breadcrumbs and blend together. Remove the pan from the heat and fill the eggplant shells with the cooked mixture. Place the stuffed shells in the oven and bake for 30 minutes. **Serves 6.**

Seasoned Breadcrumbs

We feel that the best breadcrumbs are homemade. To make your own, start with a crusty loaf of French bread (make sure that it is hard and crusty on the outside). Break off a few hunks of bread and grind them in a food processor or blender until they are nice and fine. Add a couple of tablespoons of your favorite Cajun/Creole seasoning, and you have seasoned breadcrumbs!

Brabant Potatoes

2 cups Vegetable Stock (see page 136)	3 large potatoes, peeled and washed	1 teaspoon finely chopped fresh parsley
½ stick butter		Salt to taste

In a large saucepan heat the Vegetable Stock over medium heat. Add the potatoes and cook until you can stick a toothpick in them. Remove and drain the potatoes and let cool to touch. Using a melon baller, form small potato balls.

In a skillet melt the butter, add potato balls, and sauté until browned and crispy. Add parsley and salt to taste. **Serves 4.**

Smothered Cabbage

1 large head cabbage, cut into large pieces with core removed	Pinch baking soda	1 quart Vegetable Stock (see page 136)
1 large onion, chopped	2 tablespoons Cajun/Creole seasoning	1 tablespoon butter
	Salt, black pepper, and cayenne pepper, to taste	

In a large, heavy saucepan place the cabbage, onion, baking soda, and seasoning. Add enough Vegetable Stock to cover the vegetables halfway. Boil until all of the liquid evaporates and continue cooking until the cabbage starts to brown. Add the butter and stir. **Serves 4.**

Meat Entrées

1. Steak Louisiane

2. Marinated Steak
   with Mushrooms

3. *Cotelettes Creole de Cochon*

4. Pecan–and–Herb–Encrusted
   Prime Rib Roast

5. Cajun–Style Barbeque Ribs

6. Creole Panéed Veal

7. Cajun Jambalaya

8. New Orleans Creole Jambalaya

9. Beef Bordelaise

10. Daubé Glacé

11. Cajun Pork Roast

12. *Cochon de Lait*

Photo by Keith Dunn

Steak Louisiane

These fancy steaks make for an elegant presentation. They will be particularly succulent if you marinate them.

Seasoning Mix to taste (see below)

2 tablespoons olive oil

2 tablespoons unsalted but–ter

4 1–inch–thick ribeye steaks

2 tablespoons all–purpose flour

¼ cup chopped onions

¼ cup chopped bell peppers

1 cup sliced mushrooms

2 tablespoons chopped garlic

2 tablespoons chopped fresh parsley

2 tablespoons chopped fresh thyme

2 tablespoons chopped fresh sweet basil

½ teaspoon Worcestershire sauce

½ cup dry red wine

1 cup Beef Stock (see Stocks section)

2 tablespoons heavy cream (optional)

4 green onions, freshly chopped for garnish

¼ cup freshly chopped parsley for garnish

Now, many people have very decided opinions on just how they like their steaks to be seasoned. Some people like nothing more than just salt and pepper. In Louisiana we tend to like to use either a good Cajun/Creole seasoning blend or make our own herb and spice blend. If you want to season your steaks with more than just salt and pepper but do not have a Cajun/Creole seasoning blend on hand, you can make you own blend from the recipe for the Seasoning Mix for the sauce below. If you choose to make the Seasoning Mix below for both the steaks and the sauce, you may need to make several batches.

Sprinkle some Cajun Seasoning on each of the steaks (or season them as you like) and let sit for a couple of hours in the refrigerator to allow the flavors to blend. When you are ready to cook, in a heavy skillet heat the olive oil and butter over medium heat. Sauté the steaks until they are cooked to your de-sire doneness. (About 4 to 6 minutes for rare and 6 to 8 minutes for medium, depending upon the thickness of the steaks. Be sure to turn the steaks over about every minute while you are cooking them.) When the steaks are done, remove from the pan and drain on a plate with paper towels.

Add the flour to the skillet and begin to stir with a wire whisk to make a nice medium-brown roux. Con-tinue to stir with the whisk constantly to make sure you do not burn the roux. The longer you cook it the darker in color it will become. As long as you keep stir-ring the roux, it will not burn. When the roux has reached the desired color, add the onions, bell pep-

Seasoning Mix

Use 2 tablespoons of your favorite Cajun/Creole seasoning blend or:

½ teaspoon dried thyme leaves

½ teaspoon dried sweet basil leaves

½ teaspoon sweet paprika

¼ teaspoon salt

¼ teaspoon garlic powder

¼ teaspoon onion powder

¼ teaspoon black pepper

¼ teaspoon white pepper

¼ teaspoon cayenne pepper

pers, and mushrooms and sauté them in the roux until the vegetables are soft. Add the Seasoning Mix, garlic, fresh herbs, and Worcestershire sauce and continue to stir. Add the red wine to deglaze the pan (breaking up any crusty bits that have stuck to the bottom of the skillet). Add the Beef Stock and let this come to a simmering boil for about 3 to 4 minutes. As the sauce simmers for a few minutes it will reduce in volume. At this point you will want to taste it to adjust your seasonings.

Lastly, if you like, add in the splash of heavy cream and stir it into the sauce, turning it down to low and let it simmer. This will give your sauce a velvety texture and make it very rich. Stir well with a spoon and let simmer for 2 to 3 minutes to let all of the flavors meld.

To serve, spoon some of the sauce over the steaks and garnish each with fresh chopped green onions and parsley. Now enjoy! **Serves 4.**

Marinated Steak with Mushrooms

This is an easy and delicious way to serve up a great steak that will satisfy even the most serious carnivore.

For the Steaks:

- 2 tablespoons Seasoning Mix (see below)
- 2 cups dry red wine (or as needed)
- 2 cups olive oil (or as needed)

- 1 teaspoon fresh chopped parsley
- 1 teaspoon fresh chopped thyme
- 1 teaspoon fresh chopped sweet basil

- 2 tablespoons honey
- 2 tablespoons chopped garlic
- 1 tablespoon Worcestershire sauce
- 2 large steaks (sirloin, porterhouse, or rib eye)

To make the Seasoning Mix, in a mixing bowl combine all of the Seasoning Mix ingredients and mix well. You may prepare this in advance and store in an airtight jar in a cool, dry place.

For this steak first we make a marinade. In a medium-sized casserole dish or large bowl combine the red wine and olive oil. (The amount you need depends upon the size of your steaks, but you want equal amounts of both the wine and the olive oil to try and just cover the top of the steak with the marinade once the steaks are put in.) To the red wine and olive oil mixture add the parsley, thyme, sweet basil, honey, garlic, and Worcestershire sauce. This will make a lovely marinade that will both tenderize and flavor your steaks.

Wash the steaks and pat dry with a paper towel. Rub 1 teaspoon of Seasoning Mix onto each side of the steaks. Place the steaks in the red wine and olive oil mixture and refrigerator for at least 4 hours or overnight if possible. Just remember that the longer you leave the steaks in the marinade, the more flavorful they will become. Turn the steaks over about once an hour or so if you can.

Grill the steaks on your barbeque until they are almost done to taste. Right before they are done, season with salt and pepper or sprinkle 1 teaspoon of Seasoning Mix on each side of the steaks. They will be extremely juicy and tender and full of rich flavor.

Seasoning Mix

The following blend yields 4 tablespoons. Use 2 tablespoons for the steaks and 2 tablespoons for the mushrooms:

- 2 teaspoons dried thyme leaves
- 2 teaspoons dried sweet basil leaves
- 1 teaspoon salt
- 1 teaspoon onion powder
- 1 teaspoon black pepper
- 1 teaspoon white pepper
- 1 teaspoon cayenne pepper
- 1 teaspoon sweet paprika
- 1 teaspoon garlic powder

For the Mushrooms:

6 tablespoons unsalted butter

2 tablespoons fresh chopped green onions

1 tablespoon chopped garlic

2 cups sliced fresh mush-rooms

3 tablespoons dry white wine

½ teaspoon Worcestershire sauce (for the mush-rooms)

2 tablespoons Seasoning Mix

1 sprig fresh parsley

1 sprig fresh thyme

1 sprig fresh sweet basil

2 green onions, freshly chopped for garnish

2 tablespoons, freshly chopped parsley for garnish

To make the mushrooms, in a skillet melt the butter over a medium heat. Add the green onions along with 1 tablespoon of garlic and sauté for about 1 minute. Add in the sliced mushrooms and continue to sauté them, stirring (or flipping them if you have the talent for that) in the pan until they begin to get soft, about 5 minutes. Deglaze the pan with the white wine and add ½ teaspoon of Worces-tershire sauce, the remaining Seasoning Mix, parsley, thyme, and sweet basil. Continue to sauté until everything done.

Spoon the mushrooms with some of the white wine butter sauce onto the steaks, garnish each with fresh chopped green onions and parsley, and enjoy a real Louisiana-style treat. *Bon appetit, cher!* **Serves 2.**

Cotelettes Creole de Cochon

(Creole Pork Chops)

This is one of the Colonel's original recipes and is a wonderful way to dress up an ordinary pork chop while giving it a real Creole touch! This recipe is especially good with the Colonel's Cajun/Creole seasonings.

2 cups all-purpose flour
4 tablespoons Seasoning Mix (see below)
4 loin pork chops
½ cup peanut oil (to fry the pork chops in)
2 tablespoons olive oil (to make the sauce)
1 cup chopped onions
½ cup chopped bell pepper

¼ cup chopped celery
1 tablespoon chopped fresh garlic
1 cup sliced mushrooms
2 cups diced tomatoes
½ cup dry red wine
2 tablespoons tomato paste
1 cup Beef Stock (see page 135)

1 teaspoon Worcestershire sauce
2 tablespoons heavy cream
¼ cup fresh chopped green onions for garnish
¼ cup fresh chopped parsley for garnish

To make the Seasoning Mix, in a mixing bowl combine all of the Seasoning Mix ingredients and mix well. You may prepare this in advance and store in an airtight jar in a cool, dry place.

In a shallow dish mix the flour and 1 tablespoon of Seasoning Mix. Then sprinkle 1 tablespoon of Seasoning Mix over the pork chops, seasoning both sides, and then dredge them in the flour. In a heavy skillet heat the peanut oil and cook the pork chops over medium heat until they are golden brown, about 4 to 5 minutes. Remove from the skillet and drain on a paper towel.

In another skillet heat 2 tablespoons of olive oil and sauté the onions, bell peppers, celery, garlic, mushrooms, and tomato until soft, about 5 to 6 minutes. Add in the red wine to deglaze the pan and scrape the bottom for any browned bits. Add the tomato paste, Beef Stock, Worcestershire sauce, and 1–2 table-spoons Seasoning Mix and let the sauce come to a soft boil. Add the heavy cream and stir until well mixed. Reduce the heat to low and let the sauce gently simmer for about 30 minutes. Serve the pork chops with the sauce spooned over them. Sprinkle the chops with some chopped green onions and parsley as a garnish. **Serves 4.**

Seasoning Mix

Use 4 tablespoons of your favorite Cajun/Creole seasoning blend or:

2 teaspoons dried thyme leaves
2 teaspoons dried sweet basil leaves
1 teaspoon salt
1 teaspoon garlic powder
1 teaspoon onion powder
1 teaspoon black pepper
1 teaspoon white pepper
1 teaspoon cayenne pepper
1 teaspoon sweet paprika

Pecan-and-Herb-Encrusted Prime Rib Roast

Everyone will be impressed with your culinary skills when they taste this delectable roast. The pecan and herb crust is so delicious that it makes this the King of Prime Rib Roasts, for true!

¾ cup Seasoning Mix (see below)	¼ cup fresh chopped sweet basil	1 large prime rib beef roast (about 5 to 6 pounds)
¼ cup fresh chopped parsley	2 tablespoons fresh chopped garlic	2 thick carrots, cut into chunks
¼ cup fresh chopped sage	1 cup finely chopped pecans	2 large potatoes, peeled and quartered
¼ cup fresh chopped rose-mary		
¼ cup fresh chopped thyme	1 bottle olive oil (about 17 ounces)	1 large onion, peeled and quartered

To make the Seasoning Mix, in a mixing bowl combine all of the Seasoning Mix ingredients and mix well. You may prepare this in advance and store in an airtight jar in a cool, dry place.

In a small mixing bowl combine the fresh herbs, garlic, pecans, and Seasoning Mix. Make sure that everything is very finely chopped and then mixed together thoroughly. Add 2 tablespoons of olive oil and mix well to make a sort of paste. Stand the roast in a roasting pan and with your hands spread olive oil all over the meat. Rub the herb and nut paste mixture evenly all over the roast, being sure to cover as much of the meat as you can. (Once this is done you can let it stand in the refrigerator for about an hour or two to marinate the meat, if you wish).

Preheat the oven to 350°.

Arrange the carrots, potatoes, and onion around the roast and bake for about 20 minutes per pound. The total cooking time can be any where from 1½ to 3 hours, depending on the roast. Test for doneness with a meat thermometer. The internal temperature should be around 120 to 125° for medium-rare. Carve it up and enjoy! **Serves 6.**

Seasoning Mix

Use ¾ cup of your favorite Cajun/Creole Seasoning or ¾ cup of the following blend:

3	tablespoons ground thyme
3	tablespoons ground sweet basil
3	teaspoons garlic powder
3	teaspoons onion powder
1½	teaspoons salt
¾	teaspoon black pepper
¾	teaspoon white pepper
¾	teaspoon cayenne pepper
½	teaspoon sweet paprika

Cajun-Style Barbequed Ribs

Pork ribs have always been a mainstay at Cajun barbeques, and these ribs are so easy to make and deliciously spiced that they will most definitely be the hit of your next barbeque.

Seasoning Mix (see below)
1   bottle olive oil (about 17 ounces)

2   sides meaty pork spareribs

To make the Seasoning Mix, in a mixing bowl combine all of the Seasoning Mix ingredients and mix well. You may prepare this in advance and store in an airtight jar in a cool, dry place.

Spread olive oil all over both sides of each rack of ribs. Generously rub Seasoning Mix all over both sides of each rack of ribs, being sure to spread it evenly. Place the ribs in a large pan with the bone side of the ribs facing up and cover loosely with wax paper or plastic wrap. Refrigerate anywhere from 4 to 8 hours to let all of the flavors blend into the meat.

Prepare a slow-burning grill and cook the ribs. Remember, the longer the ribs take to cook on a lower heat, the more juicy and tender they will become. If you can, use indirect heat with the coals pushed to the sides of your grill.

If you had rather roast the ribs in the oven, preheat the oven to about 350°. Place the ribs in a roasting pan on the center rack of the oven. Cook on one side for 45 minutes, and then turn the ribs over and cook for another 45 to 60 minutes.

Once they have been grilled or baked to your satisfaction, serve with your favorite side dish and enjoy! **Serves 4.**

Seasoning Mix

Use 1 jar of your favorite Cajun/Creole Seasoning or desired amount of following blend:

4   tablespoons dried thyme leaves
4   tablespoons dried sweet basil leaves
4   tablespoons dried parsley leaves
2   teaspoons garlic powder
2   teaspoons onion powder
1   teaspoon salt
1   teaspoon sweet paprika
½   teaspoon black pepper
½   teaspoon white pepper
½   teaspoon cayenne pepper

Creole Panéed Veal

This is a classic New Orleans Creole veal dish that is truly delectable!

1 pound veal cutlets	1 teaspoon garlic powder	8 tablespoons (1 stick) un-salted butter
2 cups Toasted Bread-crumbs (see below)	1 tablespoon ground sweet basil	½ cup fresh chopped parsley for garnish
2 teaspoons salt	½ cup olive oil	½ cup fresh chopped green onions for garnish
2 teaspoons freshly ground pepper	2 cups all-purpose flour	
1 tablespoon ground thyme	2 eggs beaten with 1 table-spoon milk	
¼ teaspoon cayenne pepper	½ cup dry white wine	

Trim the veal cutlets and pound flat with a meat mallet until they are very thin. Set aside.

In a medium-sized bowl combine the breadcrumbs with the salt, pepper, and herbs and set aside. Dredge the veal cutlets in the flour and shake off any excess flour. Then, dip them in the egg wash mixture and then dredge again in the seasoned breadcrumbs to coat very well. Place the cutlets on a plate and put in the refrigerator to let the breading mixture set (about 1 hour). After the cutlets have set in the refrigerator, heat the olive oil in a large, heavy skillet over medium heat and sauté the cutlets very quickly, about 2 minutes on each side, until they are all done. Drain on paper towels.

Drain the oil from the skillet, leaving the browned bits at the bottom. Return the skillet to medium heat and add the white wine. Scrape the bottom of the pan to remove any charred bits. Add the stick of butter and stir constantly until it has all melted out. Remove from the heat.

Serve the veal cutlets on a plate with the butter sauce drizzled over it. Garnish with the fresh chopped parsley and green onions. **Serves 4.**

Toasted Breadcrumbs

Make your own breadcrumbs by slicing 2 loaves of day-old French bread into small chunks and then grinding them up in a food processor or a blender. Spread the crumbs evenly in a pan and broil them until they turn a toasty brown. (Watch them carefully because they can burn very easily.) Another way to toast the crumbs is to put them in a skillet over medium to high heat and shake them, being sure to watch them carefully. Two loaves of bread will make about 3 cups of breadcrumbs.

Cajun Jambalaya

Jambalaya dates from the Spanish colonial period in Louisiana and is similar to a Spanish dish called paella. This recipe is a Cajun version of this traditional Louisiana dish.

3 tablespoons vegetable or olive oil	2 cups chopped onions	2 cups uncooked rice
4 boneless, skinless chicken thighs, cut in pieces	1 cup chopped bell pepper	2 tablespoons Worcester-shire sauce
1 pound smoked sausage, sliced	½ cup chopped celery	Chopped green onions
2 tablespoons Cajun/Creole seasoning	1 tablespoon minced garlic	Chopped fresh parsley
	3 cups chicken stock	
	2 whole bay leaves	
	2 tablespoons Kitchen Bouquet	

In heavy skillet heat the oil and sauté the chicken and sausage together with ½ tablespoon of Cajun/Creole seasoning until browned. Remove the meat from the pan with a slotted spoon. Add the onions, bell pepper, celery, garlic, and ½ tablespoon Cajun/Creole seasoning to the skillet and sauté until soft.

In a large pot combine the meat, cooked vegetables, and stock. Add the bay leaves and Kitchen Bouquet and bring to boil. Add the rice, Worcestershire sauce, and 1 tablespoon of Cajun/Creole seasoning. Bring back to a boil, being careful to stir so the rice will not stick to the bottom of the pot. Cover the pot, reduce the heat, and simmer for 20 minutes. Remove the lid and stir. Recover and cook for 10 more minutes or until all liquid has been absorbed and the rice is done. Discard the bay leaves. Serve with chopped green onions and chopped parsley. **Serves 5.**

New Orleans Creole Jambalaya

The people of New Orleans make a red (a.k.a. Creole) Jambalaya. The rich tomato flavor stems from an Italian influence.

3   boneless, skinless chicken breasts, diced
1   pound smoked sausage, sliced
1   tablespoon olive oil
2   cups chopped onions
1   cup chopped bell pepper
½   cup chopped celery
2   cups sliced mushrooms

2   cups chopped fresh tomatoes
3   tablespoons Cajun/Creole seasoning
1   cup chicken stock
1   15-ounce can tomato purée
1   teaspoon Worcestershire sauce
1   teaspoon lemon juice

1   bay leaf
1   pound raw shrimp, peeled and deveined
2   cups cooked Louisiana Tasty Rice (see page 156)
¼   cup fresh chopped parsley for garnish
¼   cup fresh chopped green onions for garnish

In a large skillet sauté the chicken and sausage in the olive oil over medium heat until cooked through, about 5 to 6 minutes. Add all the vegetables and 1 tablespoon of the Cajun/Creole seasoning, and continue to cook until the vegetables are soft. Add the chicken stock, tomato purée, Worcestershire sauce, lemon juice, bay leaf, and remaining Cajun/Creole seasoning. Bring to a boil. Reduce heat and simmer for 30 minutes.

Add the shrimp and cook until just pink, about 2 minutes. Stir in the rice and blend very well. Garnish with the fresh chopped parsley and green onions. **Serves 5.**

Beef Bordelaise

2 tablespoons Seasoning Mix (see below)	2 green onions, finely chopped	1 tablespoon fresh chopped garlic
1 3–pound boneless sirloin strip	1 teaspoon fresh chopped parsley	¼ teaspoon Worcestershire sauce (optional)
1 tablespoon olive oil	1 teaspoon fresh chopped thyme	2 tablespoons dry red wine
1 stick unsalted butter		

To make the Seasoning Mix, in a mixing bowl combine all of the Seasoning Mix ingredients and mix well. You may prepare this in advance and store in an airtight jar in a cool, dry place.

Preheat the oven to 400°.

Season the beef with your Seasoning Mix. In a large skillet over medium heat sauté the steak in the olive oil very quickly on both sides to seal in the juices. Place in a roasting pan fitted with a rack and bake for 15 to 20 minutes until medium rare. While the steak is cooking, pour out the excess olive oil from the skillet and then return the pan to the heat. Melt the stick of butter and sauté the green onions, parsley, thyme, and garlic for about 1 to 2 minutes. Then, deglaze the pan with the red wine and remove from the heat. When the steak is done, serve on a plate with the Bordelaise sauce drizzled over it. **Serves 6.**

Seasoning Mix

Use 1 to 2 tablespoons of your favorite Cajun/ Creole seasoning blend or:

1 teaspoon sweet paprika
1 teaspoon dried thyme
1 teaspoon dried sweet basil leaves
½ teaspoon salt
½ teaspoon garlic powder
½ teaspoon onion powder
¼ teaspoon cayenne pepper
¼ teaspoon black pepper
¼ teaspoon white pepper

Daubé Glacé

1 teaspoon salt	2 tablespoons dried oregano leaves	1 10–pound boneless beef round roast
½ teaspoon black pepper		
2 tablespoons dried thyme leaves	4 cloves fresh garlic, chopped	2 quarts Beef Stock (see page 135)
2 tablespoons dried sweet basil leaves	½ cup fresh chopped green onions	1 cup dry white wine
½ cup fresh chopped parsley	¼ cup olive oil	

Preheat oven to 300°.

In a shallow dish combine your seasonings along with the fresh herbs, garlic, and green onions and mix well. Rub the olive oil on the roast and then sprinkle all of the seasoning mixture over the roast, being sure to coat all sides as much as possible. Place the roast in a dry roasting pan and bake uncovered for 30 minutes. Remove from the oven and pour the beef stock and white wine over the roast; cover the pan and put back in the oven, increasing the temperature to 350°. Cook for 3 hours, basting the meat every 30 minutes. Slice the roast when ready to serve. **Serves 16.**

Cajun Pork Roast

1 cup chopped onion	¼ teaspoon black pepper	4 cloves fresh garlic,
1 cup chopped bell pepper	¼ teaspoon white pepper	chopped
¼ cup chopped celery	¼ teaspoon Cayenne pepper	1 4-pound pork roast
1 tablespoon ground thyme	1 teaspoon salt	¼ cup olive oil
1 tablespoon ground sweet basil	¼ cup fresh chopped parsley	2 cups Pork Stock (see page 134)

Preheat the oven to 350 degrees.

In a small bowl combine the vegetables, spices, herbs, and garlic and blend very well. Make several slits in the roast and stuff the vegetable/herb mixture into them. Once you have filled several slits in the roast, rub the remaining vegetable mixture on the outside of the meat. In a large, heavy pot big enough to hold the roast (a cast-iron pot works best for this) heat the olive oil and brown the roast on all side very quickly. Next, add the Pork Stock, cover the pot, and bake in the oven for about 3 hours, basting the meat every 30 minutes. Cook until the roast is tender and done inside. **Serves 8.**

Cochon de Lait

(Roast Suckling Pig)

1 10–pound suckling pig, cleaned of hair and eyes removed	1 teaspoon Worcestershire sauce	1 tablespoon salt
	2 tablespoons rubbed sage	1 teaspoon black pepper
1 stick unsalted butter	2 tablespoons dried thyme leaves	½ teaspoon white pepper
2 cups chopped onions		½ teaspoon Cayenne pepper
2 cups chopped bell pepper	2 tablespoons dried sweet basil leaves	4 cups Pork Stock (see page 134)
2 cups sliced mushrooms		1 cup dry white wine
6 cloves fresh garlic, chopped	8 skewers	1 small apple
	1 cup olive oil	2 cherries

Thoroughly wash the pig both inside and out with cold running water and scrape off any remaining hair on the outside of the skin. Dry off with paper towels. In a heavy skillet over medium heat melt the butter and sauté the vegetables along with 2 cloves of garlic, the Worcestershire sauce, and 1 tablespoon each of the sage, thyme, and sweet basil until the vegetables are nice and soft, about 3 to 4 minutes. After the vegetables have cooled down a bit, stuff them inside the cavity of the pig.

Now, run four skewers through both sides of the cavity and skewer the front and back legs in place. The front legs are extended with the head in between them and the back legs are folded under the pig's rump. Cover the pigs ears and tail with aluminum foil and insert a ball of foil into both eyes and the mouth. If you are not ready to cook the pig it can be covered and refrigerated, but be sure to remove the pig 3 hours prior to cooking it.

To cook your pig, preheat the oven to 450°. Cross 2 large sheets of heavy aluminum foil on a rack in a shallow roasting pan. Place the pig on the rack and cover it over with the aluminum foil to catch the dripping juices. Rub the pig with the olive oil and cover with the remaining seasonings. Pour the Pork Stock and white wine in the bottom of the pan and put the pig in the oven to roast. Roast the pig for 15 minutes and then baste. Then, roast for another 15 minutes and baste again. Reduce the heat to 350° and continue to baste every 20 minutes. The total roasting time is 3 hours or until a meat thermometer reads 165° when stuck into the thickest part of the pig's thigh. After the pig is done, turn the oven off and let it cool down in the oven for about 30 minutes before carving. To serve, remove the pig from the roasting pan and place onto a platter. Remove all of the skewers and the foil and place a small apple into its mouth and the cherries in its eyes. *Bon apetit!* **Serves 8.**

Chicken Entrées

1. Creole Chicken Salad

2. Chicken Sauce Piquant

3. Chicken Espagnole

4. Chicken Étouffée

5. Pecan-Crusted Chicken with Cream Sauce

6. Chicken Jean Laffite

7. Chicken in White Wine Sauce

8. Cajun Fried Chicken

9. Chicken Florentine

Photo by Keith Dunn

Chicken Jean Laffite, page 201

195

Creole Chicken Salad

This is a wonderfully delicious Creole-style Chicken Salad that's dressed up with the addition of sweet red bell pepper and roasted pecans. It is considered improper in the South to make chicken salad with anything other than white meat, which is why we use chicken breasts. Be careful not to overcook them.

3 teaspoons Seasoning Mix (see below)	bell pepper	½ cup mayonnaise
4 tablespoons olive oil	1 teaspoon green onions finely chopped	¼ cup finely chopped roasted pecans (see below)
2 large boneless, skinless chicken breasts	1 teaspoon fresh chopped garlic	2 teaspoons fresh chopped parsley
¼ cup finely chopped red	¼ cup finely chopped celery	

To make the Seasoning Mix, in a mixing bowl combine all of the Seasoning Mix ingredients and mix well. You may prepare this in advance and store in an airtight jar in a cool, dry place.

In a large, heavy skillet heat the olive oil over medium heat and sauté the chicken breasts. Turn them over once or twice and then sprinkle them with 1 teaspoon each of Seasoning Mix, ½ teaspoon per side. Once the chicken has cooked, about 8 to 10 minutes, drain it on a paper towel. Refrigerate for 1 hour or so, until chilled.

Chop the chicken. Into a mixing bowl combine the chicken, bell pepper, green onions, garlic, celery, pecans, parsley, and 1 teaspoon of the remaining Seasoning Mix. Stir well then add the mayonnaise. Continue to stir nicely mixed and smooth and creamy. Taste to see if you want to adjust the seasoning. Refrigerate for another hour or so to let the spices and flavors mix together if desired. This recipe doubles easily. **Serves 4.**

To Toast Pecans

Place the pecans on cookie sheet and bake at 350° for a couple of minutes. Watch very carefully so the pecans do not burn. This process is very short, and there is a very fine line between roasting them and burning them, but the flavor of freshly roasted pecans makes it worth the effort. For this recipe we recommend that you chop the pecans before you roast them and that you stir them every minute or so while roasting.

Seasoning Mix

Use 3 teaspoons (½ teaspoon for each side of the chicken breasts, and 1 teaspoon for the chicken salad) of your favorite Cajun/Creole seasoning blend or:

1 teaspoon ground thyme
1 teaspoon ground sweet basil
½ teaspoon garlic powder
½ teaspoon onion powder
½ teaspoon sweet paprika
¼ teaspoon salt
¼ teaspoon black pepper
¼ teaspoon white pepper
¼ teaspoon cayenne pepper

Chicken Sauce Piquant

2 to 3 tablespoons Seasoning
Mix (see below)

⅓ cup olive oil

4 to 6 boneless, skinless,
chicken breasts and
thighs, cut into bite–size
nuggets

⅓ cup all–purpose flour (to
make sauce)

2 cups chopped onions

1 cup chopped bell pepper

½ cup chopped celery

2 cups sliced mushrooms

1 tablespoon chopped garlic

2 cups diced tomatoes

¼ cup dry white wine

½ teaspoon Worcestershire
sauce

¼ to ½ teaspoon Tabasco
sauce

1 cup tomato purée

2 cup Chicken Stock (see
page 132)

1 teaspoon lemon juice

1 tablespoon tomato paste

Hot Louisiana Tasty Rice
(see page 156)

½ cup chopped fresh parsley

6 green onions, chopped

To make the Seasoning Mix, in a mixing bowl combine all of the Seasoning Mix ingredients and mix well. You may prepare this in advance and store in an airtight jar in a cool, dry place.

In a heavy skillet heat the olive oil over medium heat and sauté the chicken nuggets with 1 tablespoon of Seasoning Mix until they are about done, about 5 to 6 minutes; then remove the chicken from the skillet. Add the flour and stir the roux constantly with a wire whisk until it reaches a dark brown color. Add the onions, bell pepper, celery, and sliced mushrooms to the pan and mix very thoroughly with a spoon. Add the garlic, tomatoes, wine, Worcestershire sauce, Tabasco, and Seasoning Mix and continue to cook for 1 minute. Add the tomato purée, Chicken Stock, lemon juice, and tomato paste and continue to cook, stirring occasionally. Add the chicken meat back into the skillet, reduce the heat to a simmer, and cook for 20 to 30 minutes, stirring occasionally.

When you are ready to serve, make a bed of cooked rice on a plate, spoon some of the chicken and sauce on the rice, and garnish with the fresh chopped parsley and green onions. **Serves 6.**

Seasoning Mix

*Use 2 tablespoons of your favorite Cajun/
Creole seasoning blend or:*

2 teaspoons sweet paprika

1 teaspoon dried thyme

1 teaspoon dried sweet basil leaves

1 teaspoon dried parsley

1 teaspoon garlic powder

1 teaspoon onion powder

½ teaspoon salt

½ teaspoon cayenne pepper

½ teaspoon black pepper

½ teaspoon white pepper

Chicken Espagnole

Chicken Espagnole is similar to an étouffée, but the sauce is made with red wine and a little beef stock. It is one of the three "Mother sauces" from which most other sauces in Louisiana cuisine descend. This recipe is usually made with whole boned chicken instead of boneless chicken, which can make it a bit messy to eat!

1 whole chicken, cut into pieces, including the bones	1 cup finely chopped green bell pepper	½ teaspoon white pepper
2 cups all–purpose flour	½ cup finely chopped celery	½ teaspoon cayenne pepper
Olive oil (enough to cover the bottom of a pan up to 1 inch deep to fry chicken in)	2 cups mushrooms, sliced	½ teaspoon salt
	½ teaspoon Worcestershire sauce	½ teaspoon garlic powder
	1 teaspoon chopped fresh garlic	½ teaspoon onion powder
¾ cup (1½ sticks) butter	¼ cup dry red wine	2 cups Beef Stock (see page 135)
¾ cup all–purpose flour	1 cup tomato purée	Hot Louisiana Tasty Rice (see page 156)
2 cups finely chopped onion	1 teaspoon thyme	½ cup chopped parsley
	½ teaspoon black pepper	½ cup thinly sliced green onions

Dredge the chicken pieces in the 2 cups of flour. In a large, heavy skillet heat 1 inch of olive oil over medium heat and fry the chicken pieces until they are nice and crispy and golden brown. Remove the chicken from the skillet and set aside.

In another large, heavy-bottomed skillet melt the butter over medium heat. Add the flour and stir continuously with a wire whisk to make a dark brown roux. Add the onion, bell pepper, celery, mushrooms, Worcestershire sauce, and fresh garlic, and stir them all in very well. Deglaze the pan with the red wine, add in the tomato purée, and continue to cook, stirring occasionally, for about 1 to 2 minutes. Add in the rest of the seasonings and the Beef Stock, reduce the heat to a simmer, and continue to cook for 1 to 2 minutes, stirring occasionally. Lastly, put the chicken pieces into the pan, cover, and simmer for about 20 to 30 minutes, stirring and scraping the bottom of the pan from time to time.

Serve the chicken over a bed of cooked rice, spooning lots of sauce over the rice and the chicken pieces, and garnish with the fresh chopped parsley and green onions. **Serves 6 to 8.**

Chicken Étouffée

2 tablespoons Seasoning Mix (see below)

⅓ cup olive oil

4 to 6 boneless, skinless chicken breasts and thighs cut into bite–sized nuggets

⅓ cup all–purpose flour

2 cups chopped onions

1 cup chopped bell pepper

½ cup chopped celery

2 cups sliced mushrooms

¼ cup dry white wine

½ teaspoon Worcestershire sauce

1 tablespoon chopped garlic

2 cups Chicken Stock (see page 132)

Hot Louisiana Tasty Rice (see page 156)

½ cup chopped fresh parsley

6 green onions, chopped

To make the Seasoning Mix, in a mixing bowl combine all of the Seasoning Mix ingredients and mix well. You may prepare this in advance and store in an airtight jar in a cool, dry place.

In a heavy skillet heat the olive oil over medium heat and sauté the chicken nuggets with 1 teaspoon of Seasoning Mix until they are just about done, about 5 to 6 minutes. Remove the chicken from the skillet. Add the flour to the skillet and make a dark brown roux, stirring the mixture constantly with a wire whisk until it reaches the color that you like. Add the onions, bell peppers, celery, and mushrooms to the pan and mix all very thoroughly with a spoon. Add the wine, Worcestershire sauce, garlic, and the rest of the Seasoning Mix and continue to cook for about 1 minute. Add the chicken stock and continue to cook, stirring occasionally. Return chicken meat to the skillet, reduce the heat to a simmer, and cook for 20 to 30 minutes, stirring occasionally.

When you are ready to serve, make a bed of cooked rice on a plate, spoon some of the chicken and sauce over the rice and garnish with the fresh chopped parsley and green onions. **Serves 4 to 6.**

Seasoning Mix

Use 2 tablespoons of your favorite Cajun/Creole seasoning blend or:

1 teaspoon sweet paprika

1 teaspoon dried thyme

1 teaspoon dried sweet basil leaves

1 teaspoon dried oregano leaves

1 teaspoon dried parsley

½ teaspoon garlic powder

½ teaspoon onion powder

¼ teaspoon salt

¼ teaspoon cayenne pepper

¼ teaspoon black pepper

¼ teaspoon white pepper

Pecan-Crusted Chicken with Cream Sauce

For the Cream Sauce:

2	tablespoons unsalted butter	2	cups milk or heavy cream	¼	teaspoon salt
2	tablespoons all–purpose flour	2	tablespoons dry white wine	¼	teaspoon garlic powder
		½	cup grated Parmigiano Reggiano cheese	¼	teaspoon white pepper
				¼	teaspoon onion powder

To make the sauce, in a small, heavy saucepan or skillet melt the butter over low to medium heat, add the flour, and begin to stir constantly with a wire whisk to make a blonde roux. Cook for about 5 minutes or so, stirring constantly, as you do not want this to change color at all. Add the milk or cream and continue to stir to incorporate the mixture in the pan. Reduce the heat to simmer and add the wine, Parmigiano Reggiano, salt, garlic powder, pepper, and onion powder. Stir until well blended. Cook for about another 5 minutes, continuing to stir to incorporate everything and avoid getting lumps. The longer you keep this on the heat, the more it will reduce and get thick, so keep stirring it and taste occasionally to see if the flavor and thickness is to your liking. After about 5 minutes of cooking and stirring, remove from the sauce from the heat and let it cool. **Makes about 2 cups of sauce.**

For the Chicken:

2	tablespoons Seasoning Mix (see below)	1	cup grated Parmigiano Reggiano cheese	4	boneless skinless chicken breasts or thighs
2	cups finely chopped pecans	4	eggs		Peanut oil for frying (enough to cover the bottom of the pan with about an inch of oil)
2	cups seasoned bread– crumbs (see pg. 223)	1	tablespoon of milk		

Seasoning Mix

Use 2 tablespoons of your favorite Cajun/ Creole seasoning blend or:

1	teaspoon sweet paprika
1	teaspoon dried thyme leaves
1	teaspoon dried sweet basil leaves
1	teaspoon dried parsley leaves
½	teaspoon garlic powder
½	teaspoon onion powder
¼	teaspoon cayenne pepper
¼	teaspoon white pepper
¼	teaspoon black pepper
¼	teaspoon salt

To make the Seasoning Mix, in a mixing bowl combine all of the Seasoning Mix ingredients and mix well. You may prepare this in advance and store in an airtight jar in a cool, dry place.

In a large mixing bowl combine the pecans, breadcrumbs, and Parmigiano Reggiano cheese and set aside. In another mixing bowl combine the eggs and milk, whip for about a minute, and set aside.

Lightly season the chicken pieces on both sides with the Seasoning Mix, then roll in the bowl with the pecan mixture, coating very well. Dredge in the egg mixture, and then roll them once again in the pecan mixture. Refrigerate for about 2 hours to let the coating mixture set on the meat.

In a heavy skillet heat the oil over medium heat and fry the chicken until crispy and brown, about 20 to 25 minutes. **Serves 4.**

Chicken Jean Laffite

This recipe originally comes from Chef John Folse, owner of Lafitte's Landing Restaurant in Donaldsonville, Louisiana. With respect to Chef Folse, we have modified it just a bit with the addition of our own Classic White Cream Sauce.

6 chicken breasts, skinned and deboned	½ pound lump crab meat
Salt and cayenne pepper	½ cup chopped parsley
2 tablespoons butter	1 ounce (2 tablespoons) white wine
½ cup chopped onions	½ cup seasoned Italian breadcrumbs
½ cup chopped green onions	¼ pound (1 stick) butter
½ cup chopped celery	2 tablespoons all-purpose flour
	1 recipe Classic White Cream Sauce (see page 93)

Preheat the oven to 350°. Pound the chicken breasts to flatten. Season to taste with salt and cayenne pepper. In a skillet melt 2 tablespoons of butter and sauté the onions and celery until tender. Add the crab meat and blend well. Add the parsley, white wine, and Italian breadcrumbs. Fill each breast with equal amounts of mixture. Roll and secure with a toothpick or string. In a heavy skillet melt ¼ pound of butter. Dust the chicken breast with flour and sauté until done, approximately 20 minutes, turning constantly. Place the chicken in a casserole dish, top with Cream Sauce, and bake in a 350° oven for approximately 30 minutes. **Serves 6.**

Chicken in White Wine Sauce

4	boneless, skinless chicken breasts, halved	1	tablespoon olive oil	1	teaspoon dried sweet basil leaves	
½	teaspoon salt	1	tablespoon flour (for sauce)	1	teaspoon lemon juice	
¼	teaspoon white pepper	1	cup dry white wine	¼	cup fresh chopped parsley	
2	cups flour (to dredge chicken in)	½	teaspoon garlic powder	¼	cup fresh chopped green onions	
5	tablespoons butter	1	teaspoon dried thyme leaves			

Sprinkle each chicken half with salt and pepper to taste and dredge in flour. In a large skillet heat 3 tablespoons of butter and the oil. Sauté the chicken until light brown. Remove the pieces and keep warm. Add the remaining butter and 1 tablespoon of flour and stir continuously to make a blonde roux, about 2 to 3 minutes. Add the wine, seasonings, and lemon juice and cook for about 2 minutes, stirring occasionally, until sauce thickens slightly. When the sauce is ready, place the chicken on a plate and spoon some of the sauce over it. Garnish with the fresh chopped parsley and green onions. **Serves 4.**

Cajun Fried Chicken

2 tablespoons Seasoning
   Mix (see below)

1 3-pound chicken washed
   and cut into pieces

1 quart buttermilk

3 cups all-purpose flour

3 organic free-range eggs,
   beaten

1 cup whole milk

Peanut oil for frying

To make the Seasoning Mix, in a mixing bowl combine all of the Seasoning Mix ingredients and mix well. You may prepare this in advance and store in an airtight jar in a cool, dry place.

In a dish just big enough to hold all of the chicken, pour the buttermilk over the chicken. The buttermilk should completely cover the chicken. Place in the refrigerator and let soak overnight.

Gather 3 medium bowls to create a production line.

In the first bowl combine 1½ cups of flour and half of the Seasoning Mix and mix well. In the second bowl combine the beaten eggs and milk, whisking them thoroughly to make an egg wash. Put the other 1½ cups of flour in the third bowl, which should be closest to stove.

Remove the chicken from the buttermilk and drain. Next, dredge the chicken 1 piece at a time in the bowl of seasoned flour, thoroughly coating it. Dip the chicken in the egg wash, then dredge in the bowl of plain flour.

In a large, heavy pot or cast iron skillet, heat 3 inches of peanut oil to 375°. Carefully place the chicken in the pan, arranging the bigger pieces in the center of the pan and the smaller pieces around the edge, being careful not to overcrowd the pan. It is helpful to have a splatter screen to place over the pan while frying. Cook the chicken until golden brown on both sides, turning once. Remove from the pan and drain on paper towels. **Serves 4.**

Seasoning Mix

Use 2 to 3 tablespoons of your favorite Cajun/ Creole seasoning blend or:

1 teaspoon sweet paprika

1 teaspoon dried thyme

1 teaspoon dried sweet basil leaves

1 teaspoon dried parsley

½ teaspoon salt

½ teaspoon cayenne pepper

½ teaspoon black pepper

½ teaspoon white pepper

½ teaspoon garlic powder

½ teaspoon onion powder

Chicken Florentine

For the Chicken:

- 1 cup all–purpose flour
- Salt and pepper to taste
- 1 tablespoon ground thyme
- 1 tablespoon ground sweet basil
- 1 teaspoon garlic powder
- 1 teaspoon onion powder
- 4 whole chicken breasts, skin intact

For the Cream Sauce:

- 4 tablespoons unsalted butter
- 4 tablespoons all–purpose white flour
- 4 cups milk or heavy cream
- 4 tablespoons dry white wine
- ¼ teaspoon salt
- ½ teaspoon garlic powder
- ½ teaspoon white pepper
- ½ teaspoon onion powder
- 1½ cups grated Parmigiano Reggiano cheese

For the Spinach:

- 10 tablespoons (1 stick plus 2 tablespoons) unsalted butter
- 4 cups cream sauce
- 2 10–ounce packages frozen spinach, thawed
- 2 tablespoons chopped fresh parsley
- 2 tablespoons chopped fresh thyme

Preheat the oven to 375°.

To make the chicken, in a shallow dish combine the flour, salt, pepper, thyme, basil, garlic powder, and onion powder. Dredge the chicken in the flour mixture. In a skillet melt the butter over medium heat and saute the chicken breasts until tender and brown, about 6 to 7 minutes on each side). When the chicken is cooked, set it aside.

To make the cream sauce, in a small, heavy saucepan or skillet melt the butter for the cream sauce over low to medium heat, add the flour, and begin to stir constantly with a wire whisk to make a blonde roux. Cook this for about 5 minutes or so, stirring constantly, so that it does not change color at all. Add the milk or cream and continue to stir to incorporate the mixture in the pan. Reduce the heat to a simmer. Add the white wine, seasonings, and 1 cup of the grated Parmigiano Reggiano cheese, blending well. Cook for another 5 minutes, continuing to stir to incorporate everything and avoid getting lumps. The longer you keep this on the heat, the more it will reduce and get thick, so keep stirring it and taste occasionally to see if the flavor and thickness are to your liking. Adjust the seasonings to taste. After about 5 minutes of cooking and stirring, remove the sauce from the heat and let cool.

To make the spinach, while your sauce is cooling cook the spinach according to the directions on the package. Drain and combine with 2 cups of the Cream Sauce in the bottom of a large casserole dish. Place the cooked chicken breasts on the spinach mixture and cover with the remaining sauce. Sprinkle with the remaining ½ cup of Parmigiano Reggiano cheese and bake for about 10 minutes or until the cheese has melted and everything is warm and creamy. Sprinkle the finished dish with the fresh parsley and thyme. **Serves 4.**

Game Entrées

1. Alligator Sauce Piquant

2. *Lapin Au Sauce Piquant*

3. Cajun Venison Roast

4. Cajun Roasted Duck

5. Quail Étouffée

Cajun Roasted Duck, page 209

Alligator Sauce Piquant

Alligator meat is a choice delicacy in Louisiana. Since an alligator is a reptile, the meat is very lean and low in fat and is similar in taste and texture to seafood. The most commonly eaten part is the tail, which is cut up into bite-size nuggets.

2 to 3 tablespoons Seasoning Mix (see below)

2½ pounds alligator meat, cut into cubes

Salt and black pepper to taste

2 cups all-purpose flour

½ cup olive oil

⅓ cup (5½ tablespoons) butter

⅓ cup all-purpose flour

2 cups chopped onions

1 cup chopped bell pepper

½ cup chopped celery

2 cups diced tomatoes

¼ cup dry white wine

½ teaspoon Worcestershire sauce

1 tablespoon chopped garlic

¼ to ½ teaspoon Tabasco sauce

1 cup tomato purée

2 cups Seafood Stock (see page 133)

1 teaspoon of lemon juice

1 tablespoon tomato paste

Hot Louisiana Tasty Rice (see page 156)

½ cup chopped fresh parsley

6 green onions, chopped

To make the Seasoning Mix, in a mixing bowl combine all of the Seasoning Mix ingredients and mix well. You may prepare this in advance and store in an airtight jar in a cool, dry place.

Season the alligator meat with salt and black pepper to taste. Dredge in the 2 cups of flour. In a large, heavy skillet heat the oil over medium heat and sauté the alligator meat in batches until all the meat has been cooked, about 5 to 6 minutes per batch. Set aside.

In another heavy skillet over a medium heat melt the butter, add the ⅓ cup of flour, and stir the roux constantly until it reaches a dark brown color. Add the onions, bell pepper, and celery to the pan and mix very thoroughly. Add the tomatoes, wine, Worcestershire sauce, garlic, Tabasco, and the Seasoning Mix and continue to cook for 1 minute. Add the tomato purée, Seafood Stock, lemon juice, and tomato paste and continue to cook, stirring occasionally. Add the alligator meat, reduce the heat to simmer, and cook for 20 to 30 minutes, stirring occasionally.

When you are ready to serve, make a bed of cooked rice on a plate, spoon some alligator meat and sauce over the rice, and garnish with the fresh chopped parsley and green onions. **Serves 4 to 6.**

Seasoning Mix

Use 2 to 3 tablespoons of your favorite Cajun/Creole seasoning blend or:

2 teaspoons sweet paprika

1 teaspoon dried thyme

1 teaspoon dried sweet basil leaves

1 teaspoon dried parsley

1 teaspoon garlic powder

1 teaspoon onion powder

½ teaspoon salt

½ teaspoon cayenne pepper

½ teaspoon black pepper

½ teaspoon white pepper

Lapin au Sauce Piquant

(Rabbit Sauce Piquant)

Rabbit was a staple of the Cajun diet during the Colonial Period. The sauce piquant gives it a delectable Cajun flavor.

2 to 3 tablespoons Seasoning Mix (see below)

1 large rabbit, cut into serving pieces

Salt and black pepper to taste

2 cups all–purpose flour

¼ cup olive oil

¼ cup all–purpose flour (to make sauce)

½ cup chopped onions

⅓ cup chopped bell pepper

¼ cup chopped celery

2 cups diced tomatoes

¼ cup dry red wine

½ teaspoon Worcestershire sauce

1 tablespoon chopped garlic

¼ to ½ teaspoon Tabasco sauce

1 cup tomato purée

2 cups Beef or Pork Stock (see pages 134–35, or you can go to the trouble of making a rabbit stock)

1 tablespoon tomato paste

Hot Louisiana Tasty Rice (see page 156)

½ cup chopped fresh parsley

6 green onions chopped

To make the Seasoning Mix, in a mixing bowl combine all of the Seasoning Mix ingredients and mix well. You may prepare this in advance and store in an airtight jar in a cool, dry place.

Season the rabbit meat with salt and black pepper to taste. Dredge in the 2 cups of flour. In a large, heavy skillet heat the oil over medium heat and sauté the rabbit meat until browned. Remove the rabbit from skillet.

Return the heavy skillet to medium heat and add ¼ cup of flour. Stir the mixture constantly until it reaches a dark brown color. Add the onions, bell pepper, and celery to the pan and mix very thoroughly. Add the tomatoes, wine, Worcestershire sauce, garlic, Tabasco, and the Seasoning Mix and continue to cook for 1 minute. Add the tomato purée, stock, and tomato paste and continue to cook, stirring occasionally. Add the rabbit meat, reduce the heat to a simmer, cover, and cook for 2 hours.

When you are ready to serve, make a bed of cooked rice on each plate, spoon some rabbit meat and sauce over the rice, and garnish with the fresh chopped parsley and green onions. **Serves 4 to 6.**

Seasoning Mix

Use 2 to 3 tablespoons of your favorite Cajun/Creole seasoning blend or:

1 teaspoon sweet paprika

1 teaspoon dried thyme

1 teaspoon dried sweet basil leaves

1 teaspoon dried parsley

½ teaspoon salt

½ teaspoon cayenne pepper

½ teaspoon black pepper

½ teaspoon white pepper

½ teaspoon garlic powder

½ teaspoon onion powder

Cajun Venison Roast

Roast venison is every hunter's delight. This recipe has a succulent flavor due to the Cajun spices and the addition of a little syrup, which adds a slight sweetness to the meat. In Louisiana we would use pure cane syrup, but any syrup will work.

- 1 to 2 tablespoons Seasoning Mix (see below)
- 2 cups olive oil
- 2 cups red wine
- 1 tablespoon Worcestershire sauce
- 1 cup syrup (see above)
- 5 to 6 pounds venison roast
- 2 large onions, peeled and quartered
- 2 large potatoes, peeled and quartered
- 2 large carrots, peeled and halved

To make the Seasoning Mix, in a mixing bowl combine all of the Seasoning Mix ingredients and mix well. You may prepare this in advance and store in an airtight jar in a cool, dry place.

In a large pan or casserole dish big enough to hold the roast combine the olive oil, red wine, Worcestershire sauce, and syrup. Place the roast in the pan and place in the refrigerator. Marinate overnight, turning the roast over every few hours.

Place the roast in a large roasting pan. Cover the roast with Seasoning Mix and place the onions, potatoes, and carrots around it. Bake the roast in the oven at 350° for about 20 minutes per pound. The total cooking time can be anywhere between 1½ to 3 hours, depending upon the size of the roast. The internal temperature should be around 120° to 125°F for medium rare.

When the roast is ready, slice and serve it with the potatoes, carrots, and onions alongside. **Serves 8.**

Seasoning Mix

Use 1 to 2 tablespoons of your favorite Cajun/Creole seasoning blend or:

- 1 tablespoon dried thyme
- 1 tablespoon dried sweet basil leaves
- 1 tablespoon dried parsley
- 1 teaspoon sweet paprika
- ½ teaspoon garlic powder
- ½ teaspoon onion powder
- ¼ teaspoon salt
- ¼ teaspoon cayenne pepper
- ¼ teaspoon black pepper
- ¼ teaspoon white pepper

Cajun Roasted Duck

This recipe is a great way to season a wild duck and give it some Louisiana flavor.

1 to 2 tablespoons Seasoning Mix (see below)

2 cups Chicken Stock (see page 132)

1 cup white wine

1 tablespoon Worcestershire sauce

1 wild duck

½ cup olive oil

To make the Seasoning Mix, in a mixing bowl combine all of the Seasoning Mix ingredients and mix well. You may prepare this in advance and store in an airtight jar in a cool, dry place.

Preheat the oven to 325°.

In a large roasting pan combine the Chicken Stock, white wine, and Worcestershire sauce. Rub the duck thoroughly with the olive oil, then sprinkle with Seasoning Mix. Place the duck in the roasting pan and cover the pan loosely with aluminum foil to make a tent. Place in the oven and cook for about 2 hours, basting often. Serve with your choice of side vegetables. **Serves up to 4**, depending on the size of the duck.

Seasoning Mix

Use 1 to 2 tablespoons of your favorite Cajun/ Creole seasoning blend or:

1 teaspoon dried thyme

1 teaspoon dried sweet basil leaves

1 teaspoon dried parsley

½ teaspoon sweet paprika

½ teaspoon garlic powder

½ teaspoon onion powder

¼ teaspoon salt

¼ teaspoon cayenne pepper

¼ teaspoon black pepper

¼ teaspoon white pepper

Quail Étouffée

Étouffée means "smothered" in Louisiana French. This is a delicious way to prepare quail: smothered in a thick, rich Cajun-style sauce.

1 to 2 tablespoons Seasoning
   Mix
8 quail, cleaned
Salt and pepper to taste
⅓ cup olive oil
⅓ cup all–purpose flour

2 cups chopped onions
1 cup chopped bell pepper
½ cup chopped celery
½ cup dry white wine
½ teaspoon Worcestershire
   sauce

1 tablespoon chopped garlic
2 cups Chicken Stock (see
   page 132)
Hot Louisiana Tasty Rice
   (see page 156)

To make the Seasoning Mix, in a mixing bowl combine all of the Seasoning Mix ingredients and mix well. You may prepare this in advance and store in an airtight jar in a cool, dry place.

Season the quail with salt and black pepper to taste. In a large, heavy skillet heat the oil over medium heat and brown the quail in the oil. Remove the quail from the skillet. Add the flour and stir the mixture constantly until it reaches a dark brown color. Add the onions, bell pepper, and celery to the pan and mix all thoroughly. Add the white wine, Worcestershire sauce, garlic, and Seasoning Mix and continue to cook for 1 minute. Add the chicken stock and continue to cook, stirring occasionally. Add the quail to the pan, reduce the heat to a simmer and cook for about 45 minutes, stirring occasionally.

When you are ready to serve, make a bed of cooked rice on each plate, place a quail on the rice, and cover with sauce. **Serves 4.**

Seasoning Mix

Use 1–2 tablespoons of your favorite Cajun/ Creole seasoning blend or:

1 teaspoon dried thyme
1 teaspoon dried sweet basil leaves
1 teaspoon dried parsley
½ teaspoon salt
½ teaspoon sweet paprika
½ teaspoon garlic powder
½ teaspoon onion powder
¼ teaspoon cayenne pepper
¼ teaspoon black pepper
¼ teaspoon white pepper

Seafood Entrées

1. *Pompano en Papillote*
2. Creole Shrimp and Crab Meat au Gratin
3. Shrimp Creole
4. Shrimp Clemenceau
5. Creole Barbecued Shrimp
6. Trout Marguery
7. Creole-Style Tuna Fish Salad
8. Redfish Courtbouillon
9. Pecan-Crusted Catfish with Mushroom Sauce
10. Fried Creole Mustard Catfish
11. Shrimp or Crawfish Étouffée
12. Blackened Redfish
13. New Orleans-Style Spinach and Crab Meat Casserole
14. Louisiana-Styled Boiled Shrimp
15. Boiled Crawfish
16. Creole Shrimp and Crab Meat Quiche
17. Louisiana-Style Shrimp Stir-fry
18. Trout Amandine
19. Crawfish Pie
20. Crawfish Fettuccine
21. Crab and Shrimp Étouffée
22. Shrimp-Stuffed Mirlitons
23. Cajun Fried Crawfish Tails
24. Trout Meuniere
25. Crab Meat Ravigote

Shrimp Clemenceau, page 216

Photo by Keith Dunn

Pompano en Papillote

This classic New Orleans Creole dish of fresh Gulf Pompano fish is made in several steps before everything is combined and cooked in a paper bag in the oven. If pompano is unavailable, use a firm-flesh fish such as salmon fillets.

For the Pompano:
Seasoning Mix (see below)
6 fresh Pompano fillets
Juice of 2 lemons
1 small bottle olive oil

For the Filling:
½ pound raw shrimp, peeled
2 pints raw oysters
1 cup sliced mushrooms
½ cup chopped onions
½ cup chopped bell pepper
2 tablespoons unsalted butter

2 tablespoons chopped fresh thyme
½ cup sherry
¼ cup chopped green onions and chopped fresh parsley for garnish
1 roll parchment paper

For the Poaching Liquid:
Seafood Stock (enough to cover the fish fillets)
Several sprigs each of fresh parsley, thyme, and sweet basil

2 bay leaves
Juice of ¼ lemon
1 teaspoon Worcestershire sauce
¼ cup dry white wine

For the Cream Sauce:
4 tablespoons unsalted butter
4 tablespoons all-purpose flour
3 cups half and half
1 cup grated Parmesan cheese
¼ cup dry white wine

To make the Seasoning Mix, in a mixing bowl combine all of the Seasoning Mix ingredients and mix well. You may prepare this in advance and store in an airtight jar in a cool, dry place.

In a large pot place enough Seafood Stock to cover the fish. Add the sprigs of parsley, thyme, basil, bay leaves, Worcestershire sauce, and wine. Bring the liquid to a boil. Reduce the heat to low and place the fish in the liquid. Let the fish poach in this liquid for no more than 5 minutes. Remove the fish from the liquid and set aside.

In a small skillet melt the butter over medium heat and add in the flour, stirring with a wire whisk for about 1 or 2 minutes to make a blonde roux. Add the half and half, white wine, and Parmesan cheese and continue to stir to make a cream sauce. When completed, set the sauce aside.

In a large, deep, heavy skillet heat 2 tablespoons of butter over medium heat and sauté the shrimp, oysters, mushrooms, onions, bell peppers, and the 2 tablespoons of Seasoning Mix. Sauté, stirring occasionally, for about 2 to 3 minutes, until the shrimp are just pink. Season with salt and pepper to taste. Add the sherry and cream sauce and continue to stir to mix all ingredients. Simmer for about 5 minutes, and set the filling aside.

Seasoning Mix

Use your favorite Cajun/Creole seasoning blend or:
2 teaspoons salt
3 tablespoons ground thyme
3 tablespoons ground sweet basil
3 tablespoons ground parsley
2 tablespoons paprika
1 tablespoon black pepper
½ teaspoon cayenne pepper

Preheat the oven to 350°.

Spread out the parchment paper and grease both sides of the paper with olive oil. Next, spoon some of the sauce on each sheet of paper and place a fish fillet on the sauce. Cover the fish with the remainder of the sauce and sprinkle with the green onions and a small amount of fresh chopped parsley. Fold up the paper to wrap up the fish and seal. Place each the wrapped fish on a baking sheet and bake for 5 minutes.

Serve with a vegetable side dish and some crusty French bread. To eat, simply cut into the parchment and enjoy this New Orleans classic. **Serves 6.**

To Make a Parchment Bag

For each fillet, cut a piece of parchment paper into a rectangle large enough to form a pouch to hold the fish. Lightly oil both sides of the paper with a pastry brush and fold the paper in half. Place the fish inside the folded paper along with some sauce. Fold each of the three open ends over an inch or so to create a pouch. Roll the edges up and twist the ends slightly to seal.

Creole Shrimp and Crab Meat au Gratin

4 tablespoons butter

4 tablespoons all–purpose flour

3 cups heavy cream

¼ teaspoon salt

¼ teaspoon cayenne pepper

1 cup grated Parmigiano

Reggiano cheese

2 cups chopped, cooked, peeled, and deveined shrimp

½ pound fresh lump crab meat, thoroughly checked for shell

1 tablespoon minced garlic

1 teaspoon ground sweet basil

1 teaspoon ground thyme

¼ cup white wine

In a medium saucepan melt the butter over medium heat and stir in the flour. Add the cream, salt, and cayenne pepper. Bring the mixture to a boil and add the grated cheese, shrimp, crab meat, garlic, basil, thyme, and wine. Pour the mixture into 8 ramekins. Bake in a 350° oven for about 30 minutes. **Serves 8.**

Shrimp Creole

2 tablespoons Seasoning Mix (see below)	2 tablespoons chopped garlic	¼ cup dry white wine
3 tablespoons olive oil	1 cup Seafood Stock (see page 133)	2 large bay leaves
2 cups chopped onions	1 15-ounce can of tomato purée	2 pounds raw, medium shrimp, peeled and de-veined
1 cup chopped bell pepper	1 teaspoon Worcestershire sauce	Cooked rice
1 cup chopped celery	1 tablespoon lemon juice	Chopped fresh parsley and green onions
1 cup peeled chopped tomatoes		

To make the Seasoning Mix, in a mixing bowl combine all of the Seasoning Mix ingredients and mix well. You may prepare this in advance and store in an airtight jar in a cool, dry place.

In a large skillet heat the olive oil and begin to sauté the onions, bell pepper, celery, and tomato. Add 1 tablespoon of the garlic and 1 tablespoon of the Seasoning Mix. Cook until the vegetables are soft. Add the stock, tomato puree, Worcestershire sauce, lemon juice, wine, the rest of the garlic and Seasoning Mix, and bay leaves. Simmer for at least 45 minutes. Remember: the longer this simmers, the more flavorful it will become, so 1 to 2 hours of cooking would be fine.

When the sauce is done to your taste, add the shrimp and cook until they are just pink, about 2 minutes. Serve over a bed of fluffy rice with some freshly chopped parsley and freshly chopped green onions. **Serves 4.**

Seasoning Mix

Use 2 tablespoons of your favorite Cajun/Creole seasoning blend or:

- 1 teaspoon sweet paprika
- 2 teaspoons dried thyme
- 2 teaspoons dried sweet basil leaves
- ½ teaspoon salt
- 1 teaspoon garlic powder
- 1 teaspoon onion powder
- ¼ teaspoon cayenne pepper
- ¼ teaspoon black pepper
- ¼ teaspoon white pepper

Cook's Note

You can add a new dimension to this dish by sautéing the shrimp separately before putting them in the sauce. To do this, melt 1 tablespoon of butter and 1 tablespoon of olive oil in a skillet. Add the shrimp and about 2 to 3 tablespoons of Seasoning Mix. Add fresh chopped garlic and about 3 to 4 tablespoons of dry white wine. Sauté until the shrimp are just turning pink, about 2 to 3 minutes, then add them to the sauce.

Shrimp Clemenceau

3 tablespoons Seasoning Mix (see below)

Vegetable oil for frying

2 raw medium potatoes peeled and diced small

3 tablespoons butter

2 tablespoons olive oil

1 cup chopped onions

½ cup chopped red bell peppers

½ cup chopped green bell peppers

1 cup sliced mushrooms

2 pounds medium or large shrimp peeled and de-veined

1 teaspoon Worcestershire sauce

1 tablespoon fresh–squeezed lemon juice

¼ cup dry white wine

2 tablespoons fresh chopped garlic

2 tablespoons fresh chopped parsley

2 tablespoons fresh chopped thyme

2 tablespoons fresh chopped sweet basil

1 teaspoon fresh chopped mint

1 cup green peas (if using fresh, precook them first)

To make the Seasoning Mix, in a mixing bowl combine all of the Seasoning Mix ingredients and mix well. You may prepare this in advance and store in an airtight jar in a cool, dry place.

Cover the bottom of a heavy skillet with vegetable oil. Warm the oil over medium heat to about 350°. Fry the diced potatoes with 1 tablespoon Seasoning Mix, stirring occasionally until they are a nice light golden brown. When done, remove the potatoes from the skillet and drain on paper towels.

In another large skillet heat the butter and olive oil over medium heat and sauté the onions, bell peppers, and mushrooms until they are soft. Add the shrimp, the remainder of the Seasoning Mix, Worcestershire sauce, and lemon juice and continue to cook, stirring occasionally. When the shrimp have just turned pink, deglaze the pan with the white wine and add the garlic, fresh herbs, and green peas, cover and simmer for about 1 minute. Remove the cover after about a minute and allow the liquid to reduce in the pan, usually about another 1 to 2 minutes. Mix in the fried potatoes, and you are ready to serve.

Goes great with some crusty French bread and a glass of your favorite wine. **Serves 4.**

Seasoning Mix

Use 2 to 3 tablespoons of your favorite Cajun/ Creole seasoning blend or:

1 teaspoon sweet paprika

1 teaspoon dried thyme

1 teaspoon dried sweet basil leaves

1 teaspoon dried parsley

½ teaspoon salt

½ teaspoon cayenne pepper

½ teaspoon black pepper

½ teaspoon white pepper

½ teaspoon garlic powder

½ teaspoon onion powder

Creole Barbecued Shrimp

This originally comes from Pascal's Manale Restaurant in New Orleans. There is nothing "barbecued" about this dish; it is basically shrimp cooked in a pound of butter and a can of beer, and it is absolutely heavenly!

The best way to make this is to use very large shrimp, unpeeled, with their heads still on. That way the sauce will acquire more flavor from the shrimp. If you cannot get shrimp with their heads still on, use very large unpeeled shrimp. This is a very messy dish to eat since you cook the shrimp still in its shell, but it is worth all the mess and work to eat it!

2 tablespoons Seasoning Mix (see below)	2 pounds fresh jumbo shrimp (raw and un- peeled with heads on)	8 ounces (1 cup) warm beer
1 pound (4 sticks) butter	2 tablespoons chopped garlic	1 tablespoon lemon juice
		1 teaspoon Worcestershire sauce

To make the Seasoning Mix, in a mixing bowl combine all of the Seasoning Mix ingredients and mix well. You may prepare this in advance and store in an airtight jar in a cool, dry place.

In a large skillet melt ¼ pound (1 stick) of butter over medium heat and sauté the shrimp for about 1 minute, continuously shaking the pan. Cut the remaining butter into little chunks. (You will also want to shake the pan while making this dish as opposed to stirring it.) Add the garlic, Seasoning Mix, beer, and more butter and continue to shake the pan until the butter has melted. Finally, add the lemon juice, Worcestershire sauce, and the rest of the butter and continue to cook, still shaking the pan occasionally until all of the butter has melted and the sauce is creamy. Serve with lots of crusty French bread to dunk in the sauce. **Serves 4.**

Seasoning Mix

Use 2 tablespoons of your favorite Cajun/Creole seasoning blend or:

- 1 teaspoon sweet paprika
- 1 teaspoon dried thyme
- 1 teaspoon dried sweet basil leaves
- 1 teaspoon dried parsley
- ½ teaspoon salt
- ½ teaspoon cayenne pepper
- ½ teaspoon black pepper
- ½ teaspoon white pepper
- ½ teaspoon garlic powder
- ½ teaspoon onion powder

Trout Marguery

6 trout fillets

4 ounces (1 stick) butter, melted

Salt and pepper to taste

½ pound lump crab meat, thoroughly cleaned of shell

1½ cups Classic White Cream Sauce (see page 93)

½ cup homemade bread-crumbs

½ cup grated white Ched-dar cheese

3 sprigs parsley, finely chopped

Preheat the broiler. Grease a shallow baking pan with butter. Arrange the fish fillets side by side in the pan. Using a pastry brush paint the trout liberally with melted butter and season with salt and pepper to taste. Slide the pan under a preheated broiler for 5 minutes only; remove from heat. Leave oven on.

Top each fillet with crab, Cream Sauce, breacrumbs, and cheese. Slide the fish back under the broiler for another 5 minutes. The fish is done when it flakes and the topping is gently bubbling.

Garnish with parsley. **Serves 6.**

Creole-Style Tuna Fish Salad

2 tablespoons Seasoning Mix (see below)	2 tablespoons chopped green onions	¼ cup chopped roasted pecans
14 ounces Albacore tuna packed in water	1 teaspoon fresh minced garlic	1 tablespoon olive oil
¼ cup chopped bell pepper	¼ cup chopped celery	½ cup mayonnaise

To make the Seasoning Mix, in a mixing bowl combine all of the Seasoning Mix ingredients and mix well. You may prepare this in advance and store in an airtight jar in a cool, dry place.

Open and drain the tuna, place in a mixing bowl, and break up with a fork. Add the bell pepper, green onions, garlic, celery, pecans, and Seasoning Mix. Stir well and add the olive oil and mayonnaise. Continue to stir this mixture very well until thoroughly mixed and smooth and creamy. Taste and adjust the seasoning if necessary. Refrigerate for 1 hour to let the spices and flavors meld. Then enjoy! This is a small recipe, but it can easily be doubled. **Serves 2.**

Seasoning Mix

Use 2 tablespoons of your favorite Cajun/Creole seasoning blend or:

1 teaspoon sweet paprika

2 teaspoons dried thyme

2 teaspoons dried sweet basil leaves

½ teaspoon salt

½ teaspoon garlic powder

½ teaspoon onion powder

¼ teaspoon cayenne pepper

¼ teaspoon black pepper

¼ teaspoon white pepper

Redfish Courtbouillon

Courtbouillon (pronounced coo-bee-yon) is a traditional Cajun Country fish-based soup similar to a French Bouill-abaisse, usually made with Louisiana redfish. It is very flavorful and delicious. If you cannot get these types of fish, you can substitute red snapper or any type of firm fish that you wish.

For the Broth:

¼ cup olive oil	2 large tomatoes, peeled, chopped	¼ teaspoon freshly ground black pepper
1 large onion, chopped	1 teaspoon sugar	¼ teaspoon white pepper
1 medium red bell pepper, chopped	2 bay leaves	½ teaspoon cayenne pepper
1 medium green bell pepper, chopped	1 teaspoon dried oregano leaves	1 quart Seafood Stock (see page 133)
2 large celery stalks, chopped	1 teaspoon dried sweet basil leaves	1 teaspoon Worcestershire sauce
4 large cloves garlic, chopped	1 teaspoon dried thyme leaves	1 tablespoon fresh lemon juice
	½ teaspoon dried parsley leaves	½ cup dry red wine

To make the broth, in a large ovenproof Dutch oven (a cast-iron 5- or 7-quart pot is perfect), heat ¼ cup of olive oil over medium heat and sauté the onions, bell peppers, celery, and garlic, stirring occasionally, until vegetables are slightly wilted and transparent, about 5 minutes. Add the tomatoes, sugar, seasonings, Seafood Stock, Worcestershire sauce, lemon juice, and wine. Stir and let the broth come to a gentle boil. Reduce the heat to low, cover, and simmer for about 25 minutes, stirring occasionally.

For the Fish:

6 redfish fillets (or any type of small fish fillets or fish steaks)	¼ cup (½ stick) unsalted butter	1 medium green bell pepper, chopped
About 4 cups all-purpose flour	¼ cup all-purpose flour (for roux)	1 celery stalk, chopped
2 cups olive oil	1 large onion, chopped	Minced parsley, preferable flat-leaf
		Lemon wedges

While the broth is simmering, in a large, heavy, 12-inch skillet heat 1 cup of olive oil over medium heat. Dredge the fish in flour, turning to coat well; shake off any excess flour. When the oil is hot, add the fish and sear quickly on both sides just long enough to form a crispy crust. Drain on paper towels.

Preheat the oven to 375°F.

In another large, heavy, 10-inch skillet melt the butter over medium heat, add ¼ cup of flour, and begin to make a roux by stirring it constantly with a wire whisk until a dark brown color. Add the onion, bell pepper, and celery, and cook for about 5 minutes, stirring constantly. Remove the pan from the heat.

Bring the broth mixture to a rolling boil and spoon in the roux a spoonful at a time. Reduce the heat to a simmer and cook for about 5 minutes. Remove the pot from the heat and add the fried fish. Bake until the fish turns from transparent to opaque, about 15 minutes.

To serve, place a whole fish or fillet in each soup plate, spoon some vegetables over the top, and add a generous amount of broth to each serving. Garnish with parsley. Serve hot. **Serves 6.**

Pecan-Crusted Catfish with Mushroom Sauce

For the Catfish:

- 3 tablespoons Seasoning Mix (see below)
- 4 catfish fillets
- ½ cup all–purpose flour
- 3 large eggs plus ¼ cup milk to make an egg wash
- 1 tablespoon of milk
- 2 cups Seasoned Bread–crumbs (see facing pg.)
- 1 cup finely chopped pecans
- ½ cup grated Parmigiano Reggiano cheese
- Peanut oil (enough to cover the bottom of the pan)

To make the Seasoning Mix, in a mixing bowl combine all of the Seasoning Mix ingredients and mix well. You may prepare this in advance and store in an airtight jar in a cool, dry place.

Mix the flour, cheese, pecans, and breadcrumbs together. Lightly season the catfish on both sides with 2 teaspoons of Seasoning Mix. Dredge the fish in the seasoned mixture. Dip the fish in the egg wash mixture, and then in the seasoned breadcrumbs mixture again. Refrigerate for about 30 minutes.

In a heavy skillet heat the peanut oil to about 350° and fry the catfish until it is a golden brown color, about 10 to 15 minutes over medium heat.

Seasoning Mix

Use 2 to 3 tablespoons of your favorite Cajun/ Creole seasoning blend or:

- 1 teaspoon sweet paprika
- 2 teaspoons dried thyme
- 2 teaspoons dried sweet basil leaves
- 1 teaspoon dried parsley
- ½ teaspoon salt
- ½ teaspoon cayenne pepper
- ½ teaspoon black pepper
- ½ teaspoon white pepper
- ½ teaspoon garlic powder
- ½ teaspoon onion powder

For the Mushroom Sauce:

- 2 tablespoons clarified butter
- 1 tablespoon olive oil
- 2 green onions, finely chopped
- 6 cloves fresh chopped garlic
- ¼ cup dry white wine
- ¼ cup heavy whipping cream
- 1 10½–ounce can mushroom soup
- 1 teaspoon Worcestershire sauce
- 1 tablespoon Cajun/Creole seasoning
- 1 small sprig each of parsley, sweet basil, and thyme, finely chopped

In a small saucepan heat the butter and olive oil, and sauté the onions and garlic until soft. Deglaze the pan with the white wine and add the cream, soup, Worcestershire sauce, and the seasoning. Mix well with a wire whisk and then add the fresh herbs. Simmer over low heat for about 20 minutes. Serve over the catfish and *bon appetit!* **Serves 4.**

Fried Creole Mustard Catfish

6 large catfish fillets
Peanut oil for frying
2 cups Creole mustard
3 organic, free–range eggs, well beaten
1 teaspoon Worcestershire sauce

1 cup finely ground yellow cornmeal
1 cup all–purpose flour
1½ cups seasoned bread–crumbs (see below)
1 teaspoon salt
1 teaspoon garlic powder

½ teaspoon cayenne pepper
1 teaspoon freshly ground pepper
1 teaspoon paprika
1 teaspoon onion powder
1 teaspoon ground thyme

Wash and dry the fish with paper towels and set aside. In a medium bowl combine mustard, eggs, and Worcestershire sauce. Pour the mixture into a shallow dish. In another medium bowl mix the flour, cornmeal, seasonings, and breadcrumbs, and pour into another large shallow dish. Dredge the fish in the mustard mixture, coating all surfaces. Dip the fish in the cornmeal mixture, turning to coat well. Shake off the excess and set in the refrigerator for 1 hour to allow the coating to set.

In a 12-inch cast-iron skillet over medium heat, heat 1 inch of oil over to 350°. Gently place the fish in preheated oil and fry until nicely brown and crispy on each side. Remove the fish from the pan and drain on paper towels. **Serves 4 to 6.**

Seasoned Breadcrumbs

We feel that the best breadcrumbs are home-made. To make your own, start with a crusty loaf of French bread (make sure that it is hard and crusty on the outside). Break off a few hunks of bread and grind them in a food processor or blender until they are nice and fine. Add a couple of tablespoons of your favorite Cajun/Creole seasoning, and you have seasoned breadcrumbs!

Shrimp or Crawfish Étouffée

For the Sauce:

2 tablespoons Seasoning Mix (see below)	1 cup chopped bell pepper	2 teaspoons lemon juice
½ cup (1 stick) butter	1 cup chopped celery	2 tablespoons Worcester-shire sauce
½ cup flour	2 tablespoons chopped garlic	
2 cups chopped onions	1½ cups Seafood Stock (see page 133)	½ cup dry white wine

To make the Seasoning Mix, in a mixing bowl combine all of the Seasoning Mix ingredients and mix well. You may prepare this in advance and store in an airtight jar in a cool, dry place.

In a large, heavy skillet or a large pot melt the butter over medium heat, being careful not to burn. Add the flour and stir constantly with a wire whisk to make a medium brown roux. Add the onions, bell pepper, celery, garlic, and 2 tablespoons of Seasoning Mix (this will cause steam, so turn the heat down to low and be careful not to splash any roux on yourself). Stir the roux well, blending all the ingredients together. Add the stock, lemon juice, Worcestershire sauce, wine, and 2 more tablespoons of Seasoning Mix. Reduce the heat to low, cover, and simmer for 30 minutes.

For the Seafood:

¼ cup olive oil	2 teaspoons lemon juice	2 tablespoons Seasoning Mix (see below)
2 pounds raw peeled and deveined shrimp	1 tablespoon Worcestershire sauce	1 recipe Basic Louisiana Tasty Rice (see page 156)
2 pounds crawfish or tails	1 tablespoon chopped garlic	
2 cups sliced mushrooms		Chopped fresh green onions and parsley
⅓ cup sweet white wine (Riesling)		

In a skillet heat the olive oil over medium heat and add the shrimp, crab meat, and mushrooms. Stir-fry this with the wine, lemon juice, Worcestershire sauce, garlic, and 2 tablespoons of Seasoning Mix. When the shrimp are just pink, about 2 minutes, add them to the sauce. Serve over Basic Louisiana Tasty Rice with some chopped fresh green onions and chopped fresh parsley. **Serves 4.**

Seasoning Mix

Use 2 tablespoons of your favorite Cajun/Creole seasoning blend or:

2	teaspoons dried thyme
2	teaspoons dried sweet basil leaves
1	teaspoon sweet paprika
1	teaspoon dried parsley
½	teaspoon salt
½	teaspoon garlic powder
½	teaspoon onion powder
¼	teaspoon cayenne pepper
¼	teaspoon black pepper
¼	teaspoon white pepper

Blackened Redfish

This dish has become a modern classic! It was originally created by Chef Paul Prudhomme, owner of K-Paul's Louisiana Kitchen in New Orleans. The key to this cooking technique is using a red-hot cast-iron skillet and a seasoning blend that you really like. It's best to cook it outdoors on a gas grill because it makes a tremendous amount of smoke.

4 large fish fillets (prefer-ably redfish, pompano, or tuna) at least ½ inch thick	1 pound (4 sticks) unsalted butter, melted	1 working fire extinguisher!
	1 jar Cajun/Creole sea-soning	

Heat a dry, heavy cast-iron skillet on an outdoor or gas grill until it is glowing white hot, about 15 minutes. It is important that the skillet is dry. (For more information about blackening, see page 33.)

Immerse the fillets in the melted butter, being sure to coat all sides. Cover the fish in seasoning, again coating all sides. Place fish in a hot skillet and cook 2 minutes on each side. **Serves 4.**

New Orleans–Style
Spinach and Crab Meat Casserole

- 2 tablespoons Seasoning Mix (see below)
- 2 tablespoons unsalted butter
- 1 tablespoon olive oil
- 1 cup chopped onions
- 1 cup chopped red bell pepper
- 4 cloves garlic, chopped
- ½ pound medium shrimp, peeled and deveined
- ¼ cup dry white wine
- 2 10–ounce packages frozen spinach, thawed, drained, and squeezed of excess moisture
- 1 pint sour cream
- 1 14–ounce can artichoke hearts, drained
- 1 teaspoon Worcestershire sauce
- ½ cup mix of chopped fresh parsley, sweet basil, and thyme
- ½ cup grated Parmigiano Reggiano cheese
- 1 pound lump crab meat, thoroughly checked for shell
- ½ cup Seasoned Bread-crumbs (see below)

To make the Seasoning Mix, in a mixing bowl combine all of the Seasoning Mix ingredients and mix well. You may prepare this in advance and store in an airtight jar in a cool, dry place.

Preheat oven to 350°.

In a heavy skillet heat the butter and olive oil and sauté the onions, bell pepper, and garlic over medium heat until soft. Add the shrimp and the Seasoning Mix, and continue to sauté for 1 to 2 minutes. Deglaze the pan with the white wine and add the spinach, sour cream, artichoke hearts, Worcestershire sauce, fresh herbs, and Parmigiano Reggiano cheese. Stir this gently to get a creamy consistency and then gently fold in the lump crab meat. When the mixture is combined, pour it into a 2-quart casserole dish and sprinkle the top with the seasoned breadcrumbs. At this point you may refrigerate the casserole until needed or bake in the oven for 30 to 40 minutes or until the breadcrumbs are lightly browned. **Serves 4.**

Seasoned Breadcrumbs

We feel that the best breadcrumbs are homemade. To make your own, start with a crusty loaf of French bread (make sure that it is hard and crusty on the outside). Break off a few hunks of bread and grind them in a food processor or blender until they are nice and fine. Add a couple of tablespoons of your favorite Cajun/Creole seasoning, and you have seasoned breadcrumbs!

Seasoning Mix

Use 2 tablespoons of your favorite Cajun/Creole seasoning blend or:

- 1 teaspoon sweet paprika
- 1 teaspoon dried thyme
- 1 teaspoon dried sweet basil leaves
- 1 teaspoon dried parsley
- ½ teaspoon salt
- ½ teaspoon cayenne pepper
- ½ teaspoon black pepper
- ½ teaspoon white pepper
- ½ teaspoon garlic powder
- ½ teaspoon onion powder

Louisiana-Style Boiled Shrimp

4	quarts water	tered and mashed	8 fresh new potatoes
3	pounds fresh raw shrimp	2 tablespoons Worcester-	4 small ears of corn
1	whole lemon, quartered	shire sauce	3 sprigs each of fresh pars-
1	whole onion, peeled and	1 bay leaf	ley, sweet basil, and
	quartered	1 package Louisiana Crab	thyme
1	whole garlic bud quar-	Boil Seasoning	

Put the water in a large stockpot and bring to a boil with the lemon, Worcestershire sauce, Bay leaf, and crab boil seasoning. Once the water has come to a good rolling boil, add the onions and new potatoes and let them boil until they are tender when you pierce them with a fork (about 20 minutes, depending on your stove). Add the shrimp and let the water come back to a good rolling boil. Turn the heat off and let the shrimp sit for about 2 minutes and absorb all of the flavors in the pot. Remember that the longer that you let the shrimp sit in the water the harder they will become so if you like your shrimp nice and tender you might just want to let them sit in the water for just a minute or two after you have shut off the heat. Drain everything in the sink, dump it all on a table covered with newspaper, and pig out! **Serves 4.**

Cook's Note

If you prefer cold shrimp, once the water has come to a boil and you have put in all of the seasonings, take out about 1 quart of water and put it in a bowl with some ice in it. Then when the shrimp are done and you drain them from the pot, put them into the seasoned ice water and let them sit for about 2 to 3 minutes. Then you can enjoy them seasoned, but cold.

Dipping Sauces

Cajun/Creole Seasoned Mayonnaise

Mix 1 cup of mayonnaise with 1 tablespoon of your favorite Cajun/Creole seasoning blend. Stir it well and enjoy a simple and tasty dipping sauce for your boiled shrimp. **Makes 1 cup.**

Quick n' Easy Cocktail Sauce

1	cup ketchup
1	tablespoon Cajun/Creole seasoning
2	teaspoons Worcestershire sauce
1	teaspoon lemon juice

In a small bowl mix all of the ingredients. Taste to see if you need to adjust the seasoning (i.e. if you would like more lemon juice or more Worcestershire sauce). Serve with your boiled shrimp and enjoy! **Makes 1 cup.**

Boiled Crawfish

2	3–ounce packages crab and shrimp boil	2 lemons, quartered
½	cup sea salt	¼ cup cayenne pepper
2	large bay leaves	6 sprigs each of parsley, thyme, and sweet basil
1	large garlic bulb, crushed	
5	gallons water	
20	pounds live crawfish	

In a 10-gallon stockpot combine the crab and shrimp boil and all other seasonings. Add the water and bring to a boil over high heat. Add crawfish. Bring the water back to a boil. Boil for 10 minutes. Remove and drain the crawfish. Serve hot. **Serves 4**.

Creole Shrimp and Crab Meat Quiche

This quiche has lots of hardy crab meat and shrimp, so even real men will eat it.

- 2 tablespoons Seasoning Mix (see below)
- 3 large organic, free-range eggs
- 1 cup heavy cream
- 2 tablespoons unsalted butter
- 1 pound medium shrimp, peeled and deveined
- 8 ounces fresh lump crab meat, picked through for shell
- 1 deep-dish, flaky 9-inch piecrust pastry shell
- 1 cup grated Gruyère cheese

To make the Seasoning Mix, in a mixing bowl combine all of the Seasoning Mix ingredients and mix well. You may prepare this in advance and store in an airtight jar in a cool, dry place.

Preheat oven to 350°.

In a large mixing bowl whip the eggs with heavy cream using a wire whisk until thoroughly mixed. In a heavy skillet melt the butter over medium heat and sauté the shrimp with 1 tablespoons of the Seasoning Mix for about 2 minutes. Remove the shrimp from the pan and set aside. Evenly distribute the shrimp and crab meat around to cover the bottom of the piecrust. Sprinkle about ½ cup of the Gruyère cheese over the seafood. Now pour in the egg and cream mixture, sprinkle with the remaining Gruyère cheese, and sprinkle the remaining Seasoning Mix on top.

Bake for 45 to 50 minutes. Remove the quiche from the oven and let sit it for about 5 to 10 minutes before serving.

Garnish with a little fresh chopped parsley. Enjoy! **Serves 6.**

Seasoning Mix

Use 2 tablespoons of your favorite Cajun/Creole seasoning blend or:

- 2 teaspoons dried thyme
- 2 teaspoons dried sweet basil leaves
- 1 teaspoon sweet paprika
- ½ teaspoon salt
- ½ teaspoon garlic powder
- ½ teaspoon onion powder
- ¼ teaspoon cayenne pepper
- ¼ teaspoon black pepper
- ¼ teaspoon white pepper

Louisiana-Style Shrimp Stir-Fry

2 tablespoons Seasoning Mix (see below)	1 small green bell pepper, julienne cut	2 pounds raw shrimp peeled and deveined
2 tablespoons olive oil	1 small yellow bell pepper, julienne cut	1 teaspoon Worcestershire sauce
2 tablespoons butter	5 to 6 large mushrooms, sliced	1 teaspoon lemon juice
1 medium onion, julienne cut (long thin strips)	1 tablespoon fresh minced garlic	¼ cup dry white wine
1 small red bell pepper, julienne cut		Basic Louisiana Tasty Rice (see page 156)

To make the Seasoning Mix, in a mixing bowl combine all of the Seasoning Mix ingredients and mix well. You may prepare this in advance and store in an airtight jar in a cool, dry place.

In a large skillet heat the olive oil and butter over medium heat until the butter is melted. Sauté the onion, bell peppers, and mushrooms until they are soft, about 3 minutes. Add the garlic, shrimp, and the Seasoning Mix and begin to stir them in the skillet. When the shrimp are just beginning to turn pink, add the Worcestershire sauce, lemon juice, and wine, and cover the skillet with a lid. Let this steam for about 1 to 1½ minutes. Serve over mounds of Louisiana Tasty Rice. **Serves 4.**

Seasoning Mix

Use 2 tablespoons of your favorite Cajun/Creole seasoning blend or:

2 teaspoons dried thyme
2 teaspoons dried sweet basil leaves
1 teaspoon sweet paprika
½ teaspoon salt
½ teaspoon garlic powder
½ teaspoon onion powder
¼ teaspoon cayenne pepper
¼ teaspoon black pepper
¼ teaspoon white pepper

Trout Amandine

2	tablespoons Seasoning Mix (see below)	2	cups all–purpose flour		Juice of 1 lemon
1	pound (4 sticks) unsalted butter	3	organic, free–range eggs	2	tablespoons dry white wine
8	ounces thinly sliced almonds	1	cup milk		
		6	large trout fillets		
		1	tablespoon fresh parsley chopped		

To make the Seasoning Mix, in a mixing bowl combine all of the Seasoning Mix ingredients and mix well. You may prepare this in advance and store in an airtight jar in a cool, dry place.

In a large heavy skillet over medium heat melt 4 ounces (1 stick) of butter and toast the almonds. When the almonds are toasted, they will have a nutty smell. Remove the almonds from the pan and set aside.

In a large bowl combine the flour, salt, pepper, and Seasoning Mix and mix thoroughly. In a separate bowl beat the eggs with the milk. Dip the trout in the egg wash and then dredge it in the flour mixture.

Melt 4 additional ounces of butter in the skillet. Place the trout in the skillet and cook until the crust is crispy and golden brown on both sides. Remove the trout from the skillet, drain, on paper towels. Add the remaining butter to the skillet along with the parsley, lemon juice, and wine and stir constantly with a wire whisk until it turns brown.

To serve, drizzle with butter sauce and sprinkle with toasted almonds. **Serves 6.**

Seasoning Mix

Use 2 tablespoons of your favorite Cajun/ Creole seasoning blend or:

- 2 teaspoons dried thyme
- 2 teaspoons dried sweet basil leaves
- 1 teaspoon sweet paprika
- ½ teaspoon salt
- ½ teaspoon garlic powder
- ½ teaspoon onion powder
- ¼ teaspoon cayenne pepper
- ¼ teaspoon black pepper
- ¼ teaspoon white pepper

Crawfish Pie

1 tablespoon Seasoning Mix (see below)	1 rib of celery chopped	½ cup chopped green onion tops
½ cup (1 stick) butter	¼ cup Seafood Stock (see page 133)	½ cup chopped parsley
½ cup all–purpose flour	2 pounds of peeled crawfish tails	1 9–inch flaky baked pie shell
1 large onion, chopped		
1 bell pepper, chopped		

To make the Seasoning Mix, in a mixing bowl combine all of the Seasoning Mix ingredients and mix well. You may prepare this in advance and store in an airtight jar in a cool, dry place.

Preheat the oven to 350°.

In a large, heavy skillet melt the butter over medium heat. Add the flour and stir constantly to make a light brown roux. Add the onion, bell pepper, and celery, and cook until the onions are soft. Reduce heat to simmer. Add Seafood Stock, crawfish, and green onion tops and cook approximately 10 minutes. Add parsley and Seasoning Mix and pour into the baked pie shell. Bake at 350° for 20 minutes. **Serves 6.**

Seasoning Mix

Use 1 tablespoons of your favorite Cajun/Creole seasoning blend or 1 tablespoon of the following blend:

  1 teaspoon dried thyme
  1 teaspoon dried sweet basil leaves
  1 teaspoon sweet paprika
  ½ teaspoon salt
  ½ teaspoon garlic powder
  ½ teaspoon onion powder
  ¼ teaspoon cayenne pepper
  ¼ teaspoon black pepper
  ¼ teaspoon white pepper

Crawfish Fettuccine

2 tablespoons Seasoning Mix (see below)	1 medium green bell pepper, chopped	3 tablespoons all-purpose flour
3 cups Seafood Stock (see page 133)	3 cloves of garlic, minced	3 pounds peeled crawfish tails
4 cups heavy cream	1 tablespoon minced fresh basil	6 green onions, chopped
½ cup (1 stick) unsalted butter	3 tablespoons unsalted butter	1 pound fettuccine, cooked
1 medium onion, chopped		Grated Parmigiano Reggiano cheese

To make the Seasoning Mix, in a mixing bowl combine all of the Seasoning Mix ingredients and mix well. You may prepare this in advance and store in an airtight jar in a cool, dry place.

In a large saucepan over medium heat melt 2 tablespoons of butter, add the flour, and combine with a wire whisk to make a blonde roux. Stir in the vegetables and herbs and cook for 5 minutes. Add the Seafood Stock and cream and bring to a boil, stirring continuously until thickened. Reduce heat and simmer for 5 minutes. Add the crawfish tails and Seasoning Mix. Cook for 2 to 3 minutes, stirring continuously. Stir in the green onions and remove pan from heat.

To serve, spoon over a bed of cooked spinach fettuccine and top with Parmigiano Reggiano cheese. **Serves 4.**

Seasoning Mix

Use 2 tablespoons of your favorite Cajun/ Creole seasoning blend or 1 tablespoon of the following blend:

- 1 teaspoon sweet paprika
- 2 teaspoons dried thyme
- 2 teaspoons dried sweet basil leaves
- ½ teaspoon salt
- ½ teaspoon garlic powder
- ½ teaspoon onion powder
- ¼ teaspoon cayenne pepper
- ¼ teaspoon black pepper
- ¼ teaspoon white pepper

Crab and Shrimp Étouffée

2 tablespoons Seasoning Mix (see below)

¼ cup unsalted butter

¼ cup all–purpose flour

2 cups chopped onions

1 cup chopped bell pepper

½ cup chopped celery

½ cup dry white wine

½ teaspoon Worcestershire sauce

2 tablespoons chopped garlic

2 cups Seafood Stock (see page 133)

2 pounds peeled and deveined shrimp

1 pound crab meat, thoroughly checked for shell

Cooked Basic Louisiana Tasty Rice (see page 156)

¼ cup chopped parsley

¼ cup chopped green onions

To make the Seasoning Mix, in a mixing bowl combine all of the Seasoning Mix ingredients and mix well. You may prepare this in advance and store in an airtight jar in a cool, dry place.

In a large, heavy skillet heat the butter over medium heat and add the flour, stirring the roux constantly until it reaches a dark brown color. Add the onions, bell pepper, and celery to the pan and mix all very thoroughly with a spoon. Add the white wine, Worcestershire sauce, garlic, and Seasoning Mix, and continue to cook for 1 minute. Add the Seafood Stock and continue to cook, stirring constantly, until the sauce thickens. Add the shrimp to the pan, reduce the heat to a simmer, and cook for about 3 minutes, stirring constantly. Gently fold in the crab meat to preserve the chunks of crab.

When ready serve, spoon over a bed of Tasty Rice, cover with sauce, and garnish with fresh chopped parsley and green onions. **Serves 4.**

Seasoning Mix

Use 2 tablespoons of your favorite Cajun/Creole seasoning blend or:

2 teaspoons dried thyme leaves

2 teaspoons dried sweet basil leaves

1 teaspoon dried oregano leaves

1 teaspoon sweet paprika

½ teaspoon salt

½ teaspoon garlic powder

½ teaspoon onion powder

¼ teaspoon black pepper

¼ teaspoon white pepper

¼ teaspoon cayenne pepper

Shrimp-Stuffed Mirlitons

Mirlitons are a member of the cucumber family. They are also known as Chayote or vegetable pears.

1 tablespoon Seasoning Mix (see below)	½ cup chopped red bell pepper	1 organic free–range egg, beaten
4 whole mirlitons	¾ pound raw shrimp, peeled and deveined	¼ cup chopped parsley
3 tablespoons butter		Additional seasoned bread–crumbs for topping
1 onion, chopped	1 cup seasoned breadcrumbs (see below)	
1 tablespoon minced garlic		1 tablespoon butter

To make the Seasoning Mix, in a mixing bowl combine all of the Seasoning Mix ingredients and mix well. You may prepare this in advance and store in an airtight jar in a cool, dry place.

In a large pot bring enough water to cover the mirlitons to a boil and add a couple of pinches of salt and the mirlitons. Cook until tender, approximately 45 minutes. Remove the mirlitons from the pot, drain, cut in half, and remove the seeds. Using a teaspoon, scoop out the pulp, preserving the shell with about ¼ inch of meat, and reserve the pulp.

In a large skillet melt the butter over medium heat and sauté the onion, garlic, red bell pepper, and shrimp until the shrimp just begin to turn pink. Add the Seasoned Breadcrumbs, mirliton pulp, and 1 tablespoon of Seasoning Mix and continue to cook for about 5 minutes, stirring occasionally. Remove the pan from the heat and allow to cool to touch. Add the egg and parsley and thoroughly combine.

Fill the mirliton shells with the shrimp stuffing, sprinkle the tops with breadcrumbs, and place a dot of butter on each. Place the stuffed mirlitons in a well-greased baking dish. Bake at 375° for about 20 minutes or until the tops are golden brown. **Serves 8.**

Seasoning Mix

Use 1 to 2 tablespoons of your favorite Cajun/ Creole seasoning blend or:

- 1 teaspoon dried thyme
- 1 teaspoon dried sweet basil leaves
- 1 teaspoon dried parsley
- ½ teaspoon salt
- ½ teaspoon sweet paprika
- ½ teaspoon garlic powder
- ½ teaspoon onion powder
- ¼ teaspoon cayenne pepper
- ¼ teaspoon black pepper
- ¼ teaspoon white pepper

Seasoned Breadcrumbs

We feel that the best breadcrumbs are home-made. To make your own, start with a crusty loaf of French bread (make sure that it is hard and crusty on the outside). Break off a few hunks of bread and grind them in a food processor or blender until they are nice and fine. Add a couple of tablespoons of your favorite Cajun/Creole seasoning and you have seasoned breadcrumbs!

Cajun Fried Crawfish Tails

2 tablespoons Seasoning Mix (see below)	2 cups all–purpose flour	1 cup cornmeal
2 tablespoons olive oil	3 organic, free–range eggs, beaten	Vegetable oil for frying
2 pounds crawfish tails	½ cup milk	

To make the Seasoning Mix, in a mixing bowl combine all of the Seasoning Mix ingredients and mix well. You may prepare this in advance and store in an airtight jar in a cool, dry place.

In a medium bowl combine the olive oil and 1 tablespoon of the Seasoning Mix and whisk together. Add the crawfish tails and toss well to coat. Refrigerate for 1 hour to allow the flavors to mingle.

Gather 3 medium bowls to create a production line!

In the first bowl combine the flour and the remaining Seasoning Mix. In the second bowl combine the beaten egg and milk, whisking them thoroughly to make an egg wash. Put the cornmeal in the third bowl, which should be closest to the stove.

In a large, heavy pot heat 3 inches of vegetable oil to 350°. Remove the crawfish from the refrigerator. Individually dredge the crawfish in the seasoned flour, then dip them in the egg wash and then in the cornmeal. Carefully place the crawfish in the hot oil and fry until golden brown. Be careful not to overcrowd the pot, or the crawfish will clump together.

When the crawfish are done, remove them from the pot and drain on paper towels. **Serves 4.**

Seasoning Mix

Use 2 tablespoons of your favorite Cajun/Creole seasoning blend or:

- 2 teaspoons dried thyme
- 2 teaspoons dried sweet basil leaves
- 1 teaspoon dried parsley
- ½ teaspoon salt
- ½ teaspoon sweet paprika
- ½ teaspoon garlic powder
- ½ teaspoon onion powder
- ¼ teaspoon cayenne pepper
- ¼ teaspoon black pepper
- ¼ teaspoon white pepper

Trout Meuniere

2 tablespoons Seasoning Mix (see below)	4 trout fillets	4 sprigs parsley, finely chopped
2½ cups vegetable oil	½ cup unsalted butter	1 tablespoon chopped fresh thyme
1 cup all–purpose flour	1 tablespoon minced garlic	
3 organic, free–range eggs	½ cup white wine	1 tablespoon chopped fresh sweet basil
1 cup milk	1 lemon, sliced	

To make the Seasoning Mix, in a mixing bowl combine all of the Seasoning Mix ingredients and mix well. You may prepare this in advance and store in an airtight jar in a cool, dry place.

In a large, heavy skillet heat the oil over medium heat to 350°. In a large bowl combine the flour and Seasoning Mix and mix thoroughly. In a separate bowl beat the eggs with the milk. Dip the trout in the egg wash and then dredge it in the flour mixture. Place the trout in the skillet and cook until the crust is crispy and golden brown on both sides. Remove the trout from the skillet, drain, and rest on paper towels.

In a small saucepan over low heat melt the butter and sauté the garlic. Stir in the white wine and warm thoroughly.

To serve, place the trout on a plate, pour the butter and wine sauce over the trout, and garnish with the lemon slices and parsley. **Serves 4.**

Seasoning Mix

Use 1 to 2 tablespoons of your favorite Cajun/ Creole seasoning blend or:

- 1 teaspoon dried thyme
- 1 teaspoon dried sweet basil leaves
- 1 teaspoon dried parsley
- ½ teaspoon salt
- ½ teaspoon sweet paprika
- ½ teaspoon garlic powder
- ½ teaspoon onion powder
- ¼ teaspoon cayenne pepper
- ¼ teaspoon black pepper
- ¼ teaspoon white pepper

Crab Meat Ravigote

The term "ravigote" means to invigorate.

---

2 tablespoons Seasoning Mix (see below)	1 tablespoon chopped fresh parsley	¼ cup Dijon mustard
3 pounds fresh lump crab meat, thoroughly checked for shell	4 green onions, finely sliced	3 tablespoons dry white wine
	1 cup sour cream	1 teaspoon freshly ground black pepper
	1 cup mayonnaise	

To make the Seasoning Mix, in a mixing bowl combine all of the Seasoning Mix ingredients and mix well. You may prepare this in advance and store in an airtight jar in a cool, dry place.

Preheat the oven to 350°.

In a medium bowl combine the crab meat, parsley, green onions, and Seasoning Mix. In a second bowl combine the sour cream, mayonnaise, mustard, wine, and pepper, and mix together. Fold the crab meat gently into the cream mixture. Divide this mixture into 4 ramekins. Chill and serve with green salad. **Serves 4.**

Seasoning Mix

Use 2 tablespoons of your favorite Cajun/Creole seasoning blend or:

2 teaspoons dried thyme

2 teaspoons dried sweet basil leaves

1 teaspoon dried parsley

½ teaspoon salt

½ teaspoon sweet paprika

½ teaspoon garlic powder

½ teaspoon onion powder

¼ teaspoon cayenne pepper

¼ teaspoon black pepper

¼ teaspoon white pepper

Desserts and Candy

<table>
<tr><td>1. Red Velvet Cake</td><td>10. Riz au Lait</td></tr>
<tr><td>2. Spiced Fig Cake</td><td>11. Chocolate Silk</td></tr>
<tr><td>3. Mardi Gras King Cake</td><td>12. New Orleans Bread Pudding</td></tr>
<tr><td>4. Satsuma Cake</td><td>13. Bananas Foster</td></tr>
<tr><td>5. Cajun Cane Syrup Cake</td><td>14. Oreilles de Cochon</td></tr>
<tr><td>6. Praline Cheesecake</td><td>15. Cajun Tac Tac</td></tr>
<tr><td>7. Pecan Pie</td><td>16. Creole Pecan Pralines I</td></tr>
<tr><td>8. Sweet Potato Pecan Pie</td><td>17. Creole Pralines II</td></tr>
<tr><td>9. Tarte à la Bouillie</td><td>18. Christmas Creole Toffee</td></tr>
</table>

Creole Pecan Pralines I, page 256

Photo by Keith Dunn.

Red Velvet Cake

The origin of red velvet cake is cloaked in mystery. Theories abound! Traditionally it contains a small amount of cocoa powder, but we think this version has a better texture and will be pleasing in both presentation and taste. See what y'all think.

For the Cake:

- 1½ cups sugar
- 2 cups vegetable oil
- 2 organic, free–range eggs
- 2 ounces red food coloring
- 2½ cups cake flour
- 1 teaspoon baking soda
- 1 teaspoon salt
- 1 cup buttermilk
- 1 teaspoon vanilla extract

For the Frosting:

- 8 ounces cream cheese, softened
- ½ cup (1 stick) unsalted butter
- 1 teaspoon vanilla extract
- 1 1–pound box confection–ers' sugar, sifted

Preheat the oven to 350°.

In a large bowl cream the sugar and oil together. Add the eggs one at a time and beat well. Sift the dry ingredients onto waxed paper, add to the liquid mixture, and then add the buttermilk, vanilla, and red food coloring. Pour the batter into 2 9-inch round pans. Bake for 25 minutes or until a cake tester inserted in the center comes out clean. Cool in the pan for 10 minutes. Turn out onto a cooling rack.

Place the cream cheese in the bowl of an electric mixer. Soften the butter and add to the cream cheese along with the vanilla. Beat well. Add the confectioners' sugar, continuing to beat until smooth. Frost the cooled cake. **Serves 8 to 12.**

Spiced Fig Cake

Fig trees abound in the South and many gifted cooks make delicious fig preserves. This is an excellent way to use the fruit before the birds eat them all! For Easter we like to dust the cake with powdered sugar and fill the center with mini chocolate eggs. Watch the young'uns eyes go wide!

½ cup plus 1 tablespoon un–salted butter	1 11½–ounce jar fig pre–serves	1 teaspoon cinnamon
1 cup fine white sugar	3 organic free–range eggs, lightly beaten	¼ teaspoon nutmeg
1 teaspoon vanilla extract		¼ teaspoon ginger
¼ cup whole milk	1¼ cups cake flour	1 cup chopped toasted pecans
	2 teaspoons baking powder	1 cup chopped dried figs

Preheat the oven to 350°.

Grease and lightly flour a 12-cup Bundt pan. Set aside. In a large bowl cream the butter and sugar until light and fluffy. Add the vanilla and milk. (Resist the urge to eat this mix because it is yummy.) Add the fig preserves and mix well. Add the eggs gradually, mixing well after each addition. In a separate bowl sift all dry ingredients together. Fold into the wet ingredients. Lastly, fold in the chopped pecans and figs. Gently pour into the prepared Bundt pan. Bake for 40 to 45 minutes or until a cake tester inserted in the center comes out clean and the cake springs back when lightly touched. Cool in the pan for 10 minutes and then turn out onto a cake or wire rack. Slice and serve with vanilla ice cream or whipped fresh cream. **Serves 10 to 12.**

Mardi Gras King Cake

The King Cake has long been a Mardi Gras tradition. A sweet bread covered in white icing, it is decorated with purple, green, and gold sprinkles that represent the official colors of Mardi Gras, which date back to 1872 (purple = justice, green = faith, gold = power). The cake has a small plastic baby hidden within it and is served at a King Cake Party. Whoever gets the slice with the baby is crowned the King/Queen of the party, and then throws another party with another King Cake before the end of the carnival season.

For the Cake:

- ½ cup (1 stick) plus 1 tablespoon butter
- ⅔ cup evaporated milk
- ½ cup sugar
- 2 teaspoons salt
- 2 packages dry yeast
- ⅓ cup warm water (110°)
- 4 organic, free-range eggs
- 2 tablespoons grated lemon zest
- 6 cups all-purpose flour
- 2 plastic babies (¾-inch)

In a medium saucepan melt ½ cup of butter with the milk, ⅓ cup of sugar, and salt and cool to lukewarm. In a large mixing bowl combine 2 tablespoons of sugar, the yeast, and water. Let stand until bubbly, about 5 to 10 minutes. Beat the eggs into the yeast; then add the milk mixture and zest. Stir in the flour, ½ cup at a time, keep 1 cup to flour the kneading surface. Knead the dough until smooth. Place in a large mixing bowl greased with 1 tablespoon of butter; rotate the dough once to grease the top. Cover and let rise in a warm place until doubled in size, about 1⅓ to 2 hours.

For the Filling:

- ¾ cup firmly packed dark brown sugar
- ½ cup granulated sugar
- 2 tablespoons cinnamon
- 1 cup white raisins
- 1 tablespoon allspice

For the Icing:

- ½ cup (1 stick) unsalted butter, softened
- 4 tablespoons unsalted butter
- About ¼ cup whole milk
- 1 1-pound box confectioners' sugar, sifted
- 1 cup sugar, colored (⅓ cup each of yellow, purple, and green)*

For the filling, in a small bowl mix the sugars, cinnamon, butter, raisins, and allspice. Set aside.

For the icing, in large heatproof bowl melt the butter. Add the milk and stir. Gradually add sifted confectioners' sugar until icing has a smooth consistency that will make it easy to spread.

*Cook's Note

Tint the sugar by mixing food coloring until desired color is reached. For purple, use equal amounts of blue and red. A food processor aids in mixing and keeps the sugar from being too moist.

When the dough has doubled, punch it down and divide it in half. On a floured surface, roll half into a 22 x 12-inch rectangle. Repeat with other half.

Divide the filling between the two rectangles, spreading over the surface of the dough, leaving a 1-inch border.

Roll each rectangle up like a jelly roll, beginning with the longest side. Place each roll seam side down on two lightly greased baking sheets, each forming a ring and pinch the ends together.

Cover with a damp cloth and leave in a warm place to rise and again double in size (about 1 hour).

Preheat the oven to 350°. Place baking sheets in the oven and bake for 20 minutes or until golden. When cool, hide one baby inside each cake (do not bake the baby in the cake), ice, and sprinkle each with alternating colored sugar. **Makes 2 cakes.**

Satsuma Cake

Satsumas are small oranges that grow in South Louisiana. They are deliciously sweet, but if you can't find them use mandarin oranges instead.

For the Cake:

8¾ ounces (2 sticks plus 1½ tablespoons) butter, softened

1¾ cups sugar

Finely grated zest of 2 Satsuma mandarin oranges (reserve fruit segments for decoration)

3 organic, free-range eggs, beaten

2 cups cake flour

½ teaspoon pumpkin pie spice (mixture of cinnamon, ginger, nutmeg, and allspice)

1½ teaspoons baking powder

1 cup sour cream

1 teaspoon vanilla extract

2 teaspoons orange extract

1¼ cups finely chopped pecans

For the Icing:

3 cups confectioners' sugar, sifted

¼ cup (½ stick) unsalted butter

¼ cup orange juice with pulp

Preheat the oven to 325°. Butter and flour 2 9-inch round cake pans, shaking out all excess flour.

In a large bowl of an electric mixer combine the butter, sugar, and orange zest and cream until light and fluffy. Add the eggs one at a time, beating well after each addition. In a separate bowl sift the flour, pumpkin pie spice, and baking powder. In another bowl combine the sour cream, vanilla, and orange extract. Alternate adding the dry ingredients and sour cream mixture into creamed butter and eggs, mixing well after each addition. Remove from the mixer beater and fold in the chopped pecans.

Pour the batter into the cake pans. Bake for 45 minutes or until the cake springs back when touched or a cake tester inserted into the center comes out clean. Cool in the pan for 10 minutes. Turn out onto a wire or cake rack and cool completely.

To make the icing, in a large bowl beat all of the icing ingredients with an electric mixer until fluffy and well combined. If needed, add additional juice, a splash at a time, until the icing is spreadable.

To assemble, place one layer on a cake plate and spread with approximately half of the icing. Top with the other layer and ice with the remaining icing. Decorate with reserved orange segments. **Serves 8 to 12.**

Cajun Cane Syrup Cake

For best results, use Steen's Pure Cane Syrup. This standard Louisiana product has been made in an open kettle in Abbeville since 1880.

1 cup (2 sticks) butter	3 cups cake flour	¼ teaspoon allspice
1 cup pure cane syrup	Pinch salt	½ cup raisins
3 organic, free-range eggs, beaten	1 tablespoon baking powder	Whipped cream
	1 teaspoon cinnamon	

Preheat oven to 375°.

Lightly grease a 9-inch square baking pan. In the bowl of an electric mixer cream the shortening until light and fluffy. Beat in the cane syrup. Add the eggs one at a time, beating well after each addition. On a sheet of waxed paper sift the flour together with a pinch of salt and the baking powder. Add the dry ingredients to the syrup mixture. Add the cinnamon and allspice. Fold in the raisins and pour the mixture into the prepared pan. Bake for about 40 minutes, until a cake tester inserted into the center of the cake comes out clean. Allow to cool in the pan. Cut into squares and serve with whipped cream. **Serves 8.**

Praline Cheesecake

Brown sugar and pecans give this delicious cheesecake a taste reminiscent of Louisiana pralines. When served with a praline sauce, the brown sugar flavor blends to a mouth-watering experience.

For the Crust:

- 1¼ cups graham-cracker crumbs
- ¼ cup firmly packed light brown sugar
- ¼ cup chopped pecans
- 4 tablespoons unsalted butter, melted

For the Filling:

- 3 8-ounce packages cream cheese, at room temperature
- 1 cup firmly packed light brown sugar
- ⅔ cup evaporated milk
- 2 tablespoons all-purpose flour

- 1½ teaspoons vanilla extract
- 3 organic, free-range eggs
- Cinnamon sugared pecan halves
- Freshly whipped cream
- Fresh whole strawberries
- Praline Sauce (see page 105)

Preheat the oven to 350°. Grease a 9-inch springform pan.

To prepare the crust, in a small bowl combine the crumbs, ¼ cup of brown sugar, and pecans. Stir in the melted butter. Press into the bottom and 1½ inch up sides of the prepared pan. Bake for 10 minutes. Set aside to cool.

When ready to use, cover the bottom and sides of the pan with a piece of extra-wide, heavy-duty aluminum foil.

To prepare the filling, in the bowl of an electric mixer combine the cream cheese, 1 cup of brown sugar, milk, flour, and vanilla and beat at medium speed. Add the eggs and beat on low speed just until blended. Pour into the baked crust. To prevent cracking, prepare a water bath by adding hot water to a large roasting pan to come halfway up the side of the springform pan. Place the pan in the water bath. Very carefully place the pan into the oven. Bake for 50 to 55 minutes, until set. Remove the cheesecake from the water bath and place on a wire rack. Cool in the pan for 30 minutes. Carefully remove the outside of the springform pan and let the cheesecake completely.

Arrange cinnamon-sugared pecans on top of cake with mounds of freshly whipped cream. Surround the cheesecake with fresh strawberries and serve with Praline Sauce. **Serves 8.**

Pecan Pie

Don't be shocked, but this is not a traditional Southern pecan pie. This version, however, with its ground pecans and hint of maple flavoring, will provide a delicious ending to any meal. The flavors blend even better when refrigerated overnight.

2 organic, free-range eggs	1 cup sugar	1 9-inch pie shell, unbaked
3 organic, free-range egg whites	¼ cup pure maple syrup (no substitute)	½ cup pecan halves
½ teaspoon vanilla extract	7 ounces pecans, ground in food processor	1 cup whipping cream
½ cup (1 stick) butter		

Preheat the oven to 350°.

In a medium bowl beat the eggs, egg whites, and vanilla until frothy. Set aside. In a large pot bring the butter, sugar, and maple syrup to a boil, stirring continuously. Very slowly, add the hot mixture into the eggs in a slow trickle, being careful not to curdle the eggs. Stir with a whisk until well combined. Add the ground nuts and pour mixture into the unbaked pie shell. Arrange pecans halves on top of the pie in a decorative fashion. Bake for 35 to 40 minutes. Serve with whipped cream. **Serves 6 to 8.**

Sweet Potato Pecan Pie

This easy recipe combines two of our favorites!

For the Filling:

- 2 tablespoons unsalted butter, melted
- 1 cup cooked, mashed sweet potatoes
- 2 organic, free-range eggs, slightly beaten
- ¾ cup firmly packed light brown sugar
- 1 teaspoon ground ginger
- ½ teaspoon allspice
- 1 teaspoon ground cinnamon
- ½ teaspoon freshly grated (or ground) nutmeg
- 1 teaspoon vanilla extract
- ½ teaspoon salt
- ½ cup dark corn syrup
- 1 cup evaporated milk
- 1½ cups coarsely chopped pecans
- 1 deep-dish, flaky, home-style pie crust

For the Topping:

- 1 teaspoon vanilla
- 1 pint (2 cups) whipping cream
- 3 tablespoons sifted confectioners' sugar

Pecan halves

In a large bowl mix together the butter and sweet potatoes. Add the remaining filling ingredients except the chopped pecans; blend well. Fold in the pecans.

Pour the sweet potato filling into the unbaked pie crust. Bake at 350° for 40 to 45 minutes, until the filling is set and a fork inserted into the center comes out clean. Cool in the pan on a rack to room temperature.

To prepare the topping, in the bowl of an electric mixer combine the cream, confectioners' sugar. Beat until soft peaks form. Spread the topping over the cooled pie. Top with pecan halves. **Serves 8.**

Tarte à la Bouillie

(Custard Pie)

⅔ cup sugar	2 cups milk	2 teaspoons vanilla extract
6 tablespoons all–purpose flour	½ cup seedless blackberry fruit spread	Fresh, whole blackberries for garnish
¼ teaspoon salt	1 deep–dish, flaky, home–style pie shell	Whipped cream
2 eggs, beaten		

Preheat the oven to 350°.

In a large bowl mix the sugar, flour, and salt. Add the eggs and beat well. Bring the milk to a boil; add the egg mixture and cook over medium heat until thick. Set aside to cool. Spoon the fruit spread onto the bottom of the pie shell. Add the vanilla to the custard and carefully pour into the pie shell. Bake for 30 to 35 minutes or until golden brown. Decorate with blackberries and serve warm with mounds of whipped cream. **Serves 8.**

Riz au Lait
(Rice Custard)

3 cups whole milk	3 organic, free–range egg yolks	3 cups half and half
½ teaspoon cinnamon		1½ teaspoons vanilla extract
¾ cup long–grain white rice	¾ cup white sugar	1 cup raisins

In a heavy saucepan heat the milk and cinnamon. Bring to boil over medium-high heat. Dribble in rice and stir once or twice while returning to a boil. Reduce the heat, cover, and cook for 30 to 45 minutes, until the rice is tender and the milk is completely absorbed.

In a medium bowl beat the heck out of the egg yolks and sugar, add the half and half, and stir well. Stir in the cooked rice. Return the mixture to the saucepan. Cook, stirring constantly, until the mixture is thick enough to coat a spoon. Remove from the heat and add the vanilla and raisins. Serve hot or chilled. **Serves 4.**

Chocolate Silk

1 cup heavy cream	12 ounces high–quality semi–sweet chocolate, cut into pieces	2 tablespoons sugar
2 tablespoons unsalted butter		

In a medium saucepan heat the heavy cream, butter, and sugar, stirring constantly with a wire whisk until the cream just comes to a boil (be careful not to let this over boil). Place the chocolate pieces in a large mixing bowl. Pour the hot cream over them. Let this sit for about 30 seconds, then gently stir the mixture with a spoon, mixing until nice and creamy. Pour this into a mold, glass, or pie shell and refrigerate to set for about 2 hours to set. Remove it from the refrigerator about 30 minutes before serving to let it warm up to room temperature.

Serving suggestions: Spoon the silk into a Martini glass or parfait glasses and decorate with piroulines or strawberries or other fruit.

Spoon the mixture into a chocolate cups and decorate with whipped cream or fruit.

Spoon the mixture into a graham cracker crust and decorate with whipped cream and/or fruit.

Serves 6.

New Orleans Bread Pudding

Don't worry about the milk-and-egg mixture being too sweet or the spices being too strong; they will be absorbed by the bland bread during baking. The result is a magnificent pudding.

4 organic, free–range eggs	1½ cups whole milk	¼ cup chopped dried apricots
1 cup sugar	1 cup heavy cream	½ cup raisins
1½ teaspoons vanilla extract	1 French baguette, stale	½ cup dried cherries
1 teaspoon ground nutmeg	and cut into ¼–inch slices	¼ cup sweetened flaked
1½ teaspoons cinnamon	(with crust)	coconut

Preheat the oven to 350°.

In a 2-quart measuring cup combine the eggs, sugar, vanilla, spices, milk and cream. Mix well with a wire whisk. Layer the bread slices in a greased 2-quart casserole dish and top with half of the dried fruits. Pour about half the custard mixture over the bread and fruit. Repeat, using the remaining bread, fruit, and custard. Set aside for 40 minutes to let the bread absorb the liquids. Sprinkle the top with flaked coconut. Bake for 45 to 55 minutes or until lightly browned. Serve with rum sauce or whipped cream. **Serves 6.**

Bananas Foster

¼ cup (½ stick) unsalted butter	2 ounces banana liqueur	Ground cinnamon to taste
1 cup firmly packed dark brown sugar	2 bananas, sliced	Ice cream
	4 ounces (½ cup) dark rum	

In a skillet melt the butter and add the brown sugar to form a creamy paste. Let this mixture caramelize over the heat for about 5 minutes. Carefully stir in the banana liqueur, bananas, and rum. *Never* pour liquor straight from the bottle into flames as fire can climb up the stream of liquor into the bottle and explode. Ignite the mixture and gently stir it to keep the flame burning. (Please do not stand over the pan when you light it.) While it is burning, add a pinch or so of the cinnamon and note the sparks that fly. (This is a neat effect when the lights are out.) To stop the flame, merely stop stirring and it will go out. Serve it over some ice cream and enjoy! **Serves 4.**

Oreilles de Cochon

(Pastries shaped like pig's ears)

1 egg	¼ teaspoon allspice	2 cups sugar cane syrup
½ cup milk	¼ teaspoon cinnamon	1 cup chopped roasted
2 cups all–purpose flour	½ teaspoon salt	pecans
2 teaspoons baking powder	Vegetable oil for frying	

In a large bowl beat the egg; add the milk and blend. On a sheet of waxed paper sift the flour, baking powder, allspice, cinnamon, and salt together twice; add to egg mixture and blend. Cut off small portions of dough, form into small balls, and roll on a lightly floured board until very thin. Drop each piece into hot oil at 350° and give each piece a twist from the top with a fork; fry until light brown and drain on paper towels.

In a saucepan boil the sugar cane syrup until it forms a soft ball in cold water. Dunk the pastry very carefully in syrup. While syrup is still hot, drop chopped pecans onto the pastries. **Makes 4 dozen.**

Cajun Tac Tac

| 1½ cups sugar cane syrup | 1 tablespoon butter | 16 cups or 4 quarts popped |
| Pinch salt | ¾ cup chopped pecans | popcorn |

In a heavy saucepan combine the syrup and salt and cook until a drop forms a hard ball in a cup of cold water. Remove from the heat, add butter and nuts and mix. Quickly pour the syrup in a small stream over the popcorn, stirring to mix well. Shape into popcorn balls and place on a greased cookie sheet to harden. **Makes 1 dozen.**

Creole Pecan Pralines I

Here is the first of two variations of pecan pralines, a well-loved candy of the South. Both recipes are guaranteed to melt in your mouth—and into your heart. You'll need a candy thermometer for this recipe.

1½ cups unsalted butter, melted

½ cup firmly packed dark brown sugar

½ cup firmly packed light brown sugar

1 cup granulated sugar

1 cup whole milk

½ cup heavy cream

2 tablespoons vanilla extract

2 teaspoons water

1 cup chopped and roasted, unsalted pecans

In a heavy saucepan combine the butter, sugars, milk, and heavy cream and bring to a boil, stirring constantly with a wire whisk. Simmer the mixture until the color is deep golden brown, stirring constantly, for about 20 minutes. The mixture will be ready when it registers 250° on a candy thermometer or forms a hard ball when a small amount is dropped into ice water. Add the vanilla, water, and pecans, and stir well until creamy. Drop by tablespoonfuls onto a well-greased cookie sheet. The candy will flatten out and harden as it cools. **Makes 24 pralines.**

Creole Pecan Pralines II

The praline was, we believe, originally made with cane syrup. This old-fashioned recipe is an attempt to recreate what the original might have tasted like.

1 cup sugar	$\frac{1}{8}$ teaspoon salt
2 cups light brown sugar	$1\frac{1}{4}$ cups whole milk
3 tablespoons pure sugar cane syrup	2 cups unsalted pecan halves

In a saucepan mix the sugars, cane syrup, salt, and milk. Stirring constantly, heat to about 235° to 250° on a candy thermometer or until a little of the mixture forms a soft ball when dropped in cold water. Remove from the heat and allow to cool to lukewarm. Stir in the pecans; beat until the mixture begins to thicken. Drop quickly, a spoonful at a time, onto the cookie sheet. Eat when firm!
Makes 2 dozen.

Christmas Creole Toffee

Every year since we were kids, we look forward to Harriett Wright's Christmas toffee. It just wouldn't seem like Christmas without this delectable Creole confection. Thank you, Mrs. Wright!

1 cup chopped pecans	1 cup firmly packed brown sugar	4 ounces sweet milk chocolate
1 cup (2 sticks) butter		

Spread ½ cup of pecans on a cookie sheet. Place the butter in a heavy skillet. Add the brown sugar and mix together thoroughly. Bring to a boil and boil 12 minutes. Reduce the heat to medium, stirring constantly. (Will usually boil on medium.) Pour the butter-sugar mixture over pecans in a thin sheet. Break the milk chocolate over the top, and as it melts spread it evenly over the toffee. Sprinkle the remaining chopped pecans over the chocolate. When cool, break into pieces. Should be crunchy and delicious.

Cook's Note
Do not make the toffee when raining.

Appendixes

Cajun/Creole Cooking Resources

The New Orleans School of Cooking and Louisiana General Store
Many of the products mentioned in this book, such as seasoning blends, sauces, and mixes are available here.

524 St. Louis Street (between Charters Street and Decatur Street)
New Orleans, Louisiana 70130
(800) 237-4841 or (504) 525-2665
www.nosoc.com

K-Paul's Louisiana Kitchen
Chef Paul Prudhomme is famous worldwide for his restaurant and his "magic" seasoning blends. In addition, he has a mail order business that ships Cajun Andouille sausages and tasso.

500 Mandeville St., New Orleans, Louisiana 70117
(800) 654-6017
www.chefpaul.com

Conrad Rice Mill
Famous throughout Louisiana for its Konriko brand of rice mixes, seasonings, and in particular its wonderfully delicious tasting Wild Pecan Rice.

307 St. Ann Street, New Iberia, Louisiana 70560
(800) 551-3245
www.conradricemill.com

Lodge Manufacturing Company
Well-known manufacturer of high-quality cast-iron cookware.

P.O. Box 380, South Pittsburg, Tennessee 37380
(423) 837-7181
www.lodgemfg.com

Steen's Pure Ribbon Cane Syrup
Authentic Louisiana cane syrup made in Abbeville, Louisiana.
> P.O. Box 339, 119 North Main Street, Abbeville, Louisiana 70510
> (800) 725-1654
> *www.steensyrup.com*

Savoie's Real Cajun Food Products
Produces an excellent variety of Cajun Andouille sausages, boudin, and mixes.
> 1742 Highway 742 Opelousas, Louisiana 70570
> (337) 942-7241
> *www.savoiesfoods.com*

Bootsie's Southern Seasonings
An excellent Cajun brand of seasonings, sauces, mixes, and even bottled roux.
> 206 Burgess, Broussard, Louisiana 70518
> (800) 879-5129
> *www.louisianaspice.com*

Chef John Folse and Company
Chef Folse has a tremendous operation in Gonzales, Louisiana, including a bakery division, a dairy division, the Lafitte's Landing restaurant, the White Oak Plantation Bed and Breakfast, and an on-line store where you'll find Creole cream cheese, sausages, seafood, meats, his own line of seasonings, cookbooks, you name it!
> Corporate office:
> 2517 South Philippe Avenue, Gonzales, Louisiana 70737
> (225) 644-6000
> *www.jfolse.com*

Louisiana Seafood Exchange
Will ship both fresh and frozen seafood including fish, shrimp, crawfish, crabs, alligator meat, and sausage all over the world.
> 428 Jefferson Highway, Jefferson, Louisiana 70121
> (800) 969-9394
> e-mail: Len4fish@msn.com

Jacob's Andouille Sausage
Will ship about 30 different types of sausages and meats all over the country, including andouille, smoked sausage, tasso, and others.
> 505 West Airline Highway, La Place, Louisiana 70068
> (985) 652-9080
> *www.cajunsausage.com*

Aunt Sally's Pralines

Makes a wide variety of *delectable* pralines for those of you who have a sweet tooth. They ship all over the world as well!

810 Decatur Street, New Orleans, Louisiana 70116

(504) 524-3373

www.auntsallys.com

Colonel Paul's Cajun/Creole Seasonings

That's right. The Colonel has his own brand of Cajun and Creole seasonings made in Opelousas, Louisiana. Colonel Paul's seasonings are all natural and have a wonderfully delicious herb combination using only those herbs and spices that are traditionally used in Cajun and Creole cuisine. The Colonel's Cajun seasoning comes in Mild, Medium, or Hot n' Spicy so you can have authentic Cajun flavor at whatever heat level is right for you. In addition, he also makes a delightful Creole Spice which has a very delicate flavor and can be used right at the table instead of salt or pepper. The Colonel's Seasonings are distributed by:

Paul Products Inc., P.O. Box 36835, Birmingham, Alabama 35236.

(205) 988-0788

www.colonelpaul.com

Cajun and Creole Restaurants, Nightclubs, and Dance Halls

There are numerous Cajun and Creole restaurants, nightclubs, and dance halls in Louisiana where one can experience some of the very best that our culture has to offer. Following is a partial list of some of our favorite establishments around the state.

Restaurants of New Orleans

The French Quarter

Antoine's

The oldest restaurant in New Orleans, going back to 1840. Antoine's is one of the "old line" restaurants in the city that have stood the test of time. The menu is in French and the service is white tablecloth. Antoine's is especially known for catering large parties and social functions giving them great service and an excellent meal. The restaurant is famous for creating Oysters Rockefeller, which comes highly recommended. Wonderfully fancy Creole dining in a very historic atmosphere.

> 713 Rue St. Louis
> (504) 581-4422

Arnaud's

Arnaud's is a unique restaurant with a history dating back to the 1920s. Arnaud's has wonderful Creole cuisine in a very interesting atmosphere. They even have a Mardi Gras museum on the premises. The restaurant is famous for a dish called Shrimp Arnaud, which comes highly recommended. A charming and delectable dining experience.

> 813 Rue Bienville
> (504) 523-5433

Brennan's

Owned by the Brannan family since the 1930s, people all over the world come to New Orleans to have "breakfast at Brennan's." They have excellent service and one of the most beautiful courtyards in the French Quarter. Brennan's has created some classic breakfast dishes and the Eggs Houssarde come highly recommended. A deliciously elegant Creole breakfast experience.

>   417 Rue Royale
>   (504) 525-9711

Galatoire's

Galatoire's is an old Creole favorite in New Orleans. The atmosphere is very European and the food is fabulous. It is formal dress and they do not take reservations so you had better get in line early, but it is well worth it. This restaurant is truly an exquisite Creole dining experience. The Crabmeat Ravigote is very highly recommended.

>   209 Rue Bourbon
>   (504) 525-2021

The Gumbo Shop

An excellent restaurant to sample traditional Creole delicacies for a reasonable price. It has a casual atmosphere with a quaint Creole courtyard. No reservations are required. If you have never tried Creole cuisine before, this restaurant is a great place to sample traditional dishes. The combination platter, which comes with a sample of red beans & rice, shrimp Creole, and jambalaya, is highly recommended. Get a bowl of gumbo to go with it and you can sample four traditional Creole dishes for under $20. Very deliciously prepared meals.

>   630 Rue St. Peter
>   (504) 525-1486

The Napoleon House

This is one of the most charming little restaurants in all of New Orleans. The house is an historic home with a European atmosphere and plays beautiful classical music while you eat. It has a very quaint courtyard and a nice "light lunch" type of menu. It is very reasonably priced and is a wonderful place to eat on a hot day and relax and soak in the Creole ambience. Their muffuletta sandwich is highly recommended.

>   500 Rue Charters
>   (504) 524-9752

K-Paul's Louisiana Kitchen

Opened in 1979 by Chef Paul Prudhomme, K-Paul's has become a dining mecca for gourmets the world over. The food is truly phenomenal, with subtle yet complex flavors in every bite. Reservations are taken one month in advance. They will seat you if you show up at the door, but reservations are seated first. This restaurant is a true gastronomic treat and well worth waiting in line for. The Blackened Redfish is most highly recommended.

416 Rue Charters

(504) 524-7394

Le Café Du Monde

This place is famous all over the world for the only two things that it sells: café au lait and beignets (pronounced *ben-yays*). Beignets are small, square doughnuts without a hole that are lightly fried and served covered in powdered sugar. They are absolutely delicious served with a glass of milk or some nice hot café au lait (coffee and boiled milk). The restaurant is a New Orleans institution and is open 24 hours a day, 7 days a week. At any given time of the night or day you will find it packed with people enjoying this Creole delicacy.

813 Rue Decatur

(504) 581-2914

Uptown

Commander's Palace

This is absolutely one of the finest restaurants in North America. Opened in 1880 and now owned by the Brennan family, Commander's sets the standard for elegant dining and exceptional service. Situated in the heart of the New Orleans Garden District, Commander's Palace is known for creating the jazz brunch, which is offered on Sundays. Their menu is truly wonderful, and the bread pudding soufflé is most highly recommended.

1427 Washington Avenue

(504) 899-8221

Pascal's Manale

This Uptown restaurant is a real local favorite in New Orleans. It features wonderfully prepared Creole cuisine. Pascal's is famous for creating Nawlins-style Barbequed Shrimp, which if you have not tried you have missed out on one of the finest dishes on the planet. The restaurant is casual for lunch and dinner. An old local favorite since 1913.

1838 Napoleon Avenue

(504) 895-4877

The French Quarter

The Old Absinthe House Bar

A very interesting Bourbon Street bar. Legend has it that if you sign a dollar bill and tack it on the wall that you will return to get another drink. Consequently, there are dollar bills and business card tacked up all over the walls. The bar plays live jazz and rhythm & blues every night. A very popular night spot.

309 Bourbon Street

(504) 523-3181

Pat O'Brien's

Any place that is known as "the world's most popular bar" has to be visited at least once. The building was the first Spanish theatre in New Orleans and goes back to 1792. There are several bars within it all nestled around a central patio that is very beautiful. Pat O'Brien's is famous for a drink known as the "hurricane," which is basically a rum punch made with a passion fruit cocktail mix and served in a very distinctive tall glass that is shaped like an old style kerosene lantern. Their slogan is "Have Fun" and as the slogan implies, it is usually very crowded in this place.

718 St. Peter Street

(504) 525-4823

Preservation Hall

This is one of the most famous jazz clubs, sought out by jazz enthusiasts the world over. The price for admission is $8.00. You can sit on the floor or on a bench, or stand. It is very small and does not serve any food or drinks . . . just jazz. But it is one of the best places in the world to go and hear traditional New Orleans Dixieland jazz. Several different bands play there each night and this place features some of the oldest living Dixieland jazz musicians. It is a real treat for anyone who is into Dixieland and is usually very crowded, so get there early and line up.

726 St. Peter Street

(504) 522-2841

Fauburg Marigny

Snug Harbor

Situated just outside of the French Quarter on Frenchman Street, Snug Harbor is a real nice supper club. The restaurant serves fine Creole cuisine and some of the premier bands in New Orleans perform here. This establishment is very popular with the locals and is an excellent place to listen to some of the new kind of jazz coming out of the city.

626 Frenchman Street

(504) 949-0696

Uptown

Tipitina's

Tipitina's is one of the finest clubs in New Orleans according to most locals. It is very popular and usually very crowded. The best bands in the state perform here and the music ranges from jazz, to rock & roll, zydeco, blues, Cajun, you name it. Nice big dance floor. A wonderful place to hear all different sorts of music and some excellent local talent.

> 501 Napoleon Avenue
> (504) 895-8477

The Maple Leaf Bar

This is a very popular local nightspot with live music most every night. It is very small and cozy inside and features a nice dance floor and an excellent selection of local talent. You can hear all sorts of different styles of music and really have a great time here.

> 8316 Oak Street
> (504) 866-9359

Cajun Country Dance Halls

If you have never visited the Cajun country of South Louisiana then you have missed out on one of life's great experiences. It is a truly wonderful part of the world, with some of the nicest people and best food and music that you will ever find anywhere. A trip there is a real downhome family experience and should not be missed. Here is a short list of some of our favorite Cajun restaurants and dance halls around the state.

Mulate's Cajun Restaurant

Mulate's is one of the most famous and popular Cajun restaurants and dance halls in all of Louisiana. The best Cajun and zydeco bands in the state play here. Everything about it is great. Wonderful food, wonderful people, and fantastic music. It can get very crowded on the weekends.

> 325 Mills Street
> Breaux Bridge, Louisiana
> (800) 42-CAJUN

Randol's

One of the most popular restaurants and dance halls in all of Lafayette. It has a big dance floor, excellent Cajun cuisine, and great bands that play every night. A very fun place indeed.

> 2320 Kaliste Saloom Road
> Lafayette, Louisiana
> (337) 988-0216

Slim's Y-Ki-Ki

Slim's is a legendary zydeco dance hall deep in the heart of Cajun country. It is a very popular dance hall where some of the best zydeco bands in the state play.

> Highway 182/167
> Opelousas, Louisiana
> (318) 942-9980

Fred's Lounge

The renowned Fred's Lounge is famous the world over for good beer, boudin, and Cajun music and dancing every Saturday morning. The place is *only* open on Saturday morning from 7:00 till about 2:00 and a live radio show is broadcast from the lounge from 9:00 till noon. It is *very* popular and a real institution in the state. One of the best times you can have on a Saturday morning anywhere. Lots of good food, music, and fun! Ask for Tante Sue.

> 420 6th Street
> Mamou, Louisiana
> (337) 468-5411

La Poussiere

This is a very authentic and charming Louisiana dance hall. Open on Saturday nights from 7:00 to 11:00 and Sunday afternoons from 3:00 to 7:00. It is possible to go to this dance hall and never hear a word of English spoken from the crowd. Very friendly people and wonderful music. Everyone is most warmly welcomed and you will have a *great* time there for true!

> 1301 Grand Point Road
> Breaux Bridge, Louisiana
> (337) 332-1721

Prejean's

Prejean's is famous not only for great live Cajun music but also for having a very innovative restaurant. Wonderful Cajun cuisine. A real popular Cajun restaurant and dance hall that should not be missed on your next trip.

> 3480 I-49 North
> Lafayette, Louisiana
> (337) 896-3247

Famous Festivals of Louisiana

Louisiana is famous for its *joie de vivre* and for its many wonderful festivals celebrating good times. We have a saying that in Louisiana there is a festival somewhere in the state every day of the year! As with all Louisiana festivals you have lots of food, music, dancing, and good down-home family fun! Here are a few of some of the more popular festivals around the state.

March

The Black Heritage Festival

African-American culture is celebrated in this three-day festival held in Lake Charles every March. The festival features incredible music from jazz to gospel, blues, and zydeco along with many educational and cultural activities and *wonderful* food. It is a most unique celebration of the significant cultural contributions made by African Americans to the state, and a *very* fun festival.

April

The New Orleans Jazz and Heritage Festival

Since its creation in 1968, the New Orleans Jazz and Heritage Festival (known as Jazzfest to the locals) has grown to become one of the premier music festivals in the country. Held every year on the last weekend of April and the first weekend of May, this festival promotes music from around Louisiana and the world. You can literally hear *any* kind of music from jazz to blues, gospel, country, Cajun, zydeco, rock n' roll, folk, and anything else. Big name bands and celebrities from around the world flock to Jazzfest, and it is a tremendously large and popular festival featuring not only music but also wonderful food, arts and crafts, and cultural activities. Jazzfest is a tradition that highlights the city of New Orleans, which gave birth to so much incredible music!

The Strawberry Festival

Now if you happen to like strawberries, then this is the festival for you! Held in Pontchatoula every April (the strawberry capital of the world), you can find all sorts of "strawberry stuff" from jams and jellies to frozen drinks, pies, cakes—you name it. They also have rides for the kids, great food, music, dancing, and lots of berry pickin' fun!

May

The Crawfish Festival

Now this festival is for the *real* crawfish lover. Held in Breaux Bridge every May, here you can find crawfish *anything*! Crawfish are available prepared in every conceivable manner known to man. It is a true celebration of our state's national delicacy. There are crawfish races, cooking and eating contests, and the music is phenomenal! They have a Cajun music workshop for those who would like to learn how to play Cajun music, and a dance contest as well. A very popular and fun-filled festival in the Crawfish capital of the world!

The Jambalaya Festival
Held in Gonzales every Memorial Day weekend. It is a celebration of the state's other famous dish, jambalaya. Lots of food, music, dancing, rides, games, activities, and a wonderful time for all!

July

The Louisiana Catfish Festival
This festival, held in Des Allemand every July, is the ultimate fish fry for true! Literally thousands of pounds of catfish are fried up for the catfish connoisseur along with all kinds of other seafood. Lots of fish, fun, food, music and great family times can be had by all!

August

French Music Festival
This festival, held in Lafayette every August, is a real gem and celebrates music from throughout the French-speaking world. Here you will hear top bands from not only Louisiana but Canada, Africa, the Caribbean, and anywhere else that was once a former French colony. Lots of wonderful food, music, and very interesting cultural activities highlight this one-of-a-kind festival.

October

Festival d'Acadien (Cajun Music Festival)
This is the festival to attend for the avid Cajun/zydeco music lover. The best Cajun and zydeco bands in the state regularly attend this festival, which is held in Lafayette on the second weekend of October every year. This festival is a real fun family time that celebrates all things Cajun from food to music to culture. The music is truly awesome and features musicians from the very old to the very latest.

The Gumbo Festival
Held in Bridge City every year in October. This festival celebrates not only Louisiana's famous gumbo but also Cajun/Creole cuisine as a whole. There's tons of food, from gumbo to jambalaya, étouffée, and anything Cajun. There will be lots of wonderful music, dancing, food, fun, and even a 5k run! A great festival in the gumbo capital of the world!

November

The Los Isleno Festival
This festival held in St. Bernard every November celebrates and honors the culture and traditions of the Isleno people, who came to Louisiana from the Canary Islands off of the coast of Spain in the late eighteenth century. The festival highlights their unique culture and features Isleño dancing, music, boat building, and food. It is a uniquely Spanish festival that honors Isleño traditions and their strong sense of community.

Tables, Measurements, and Equivalents

Dry Measurements

1 teaspoon	= 5ml			
3 teaspoons	= 1 tbsp	= ½ ounce	= 14.3 grams	
1 tablespoon	= 15ml			
2 tablespoons	= ⅛ cup	= 1 ounce	= 28.3 grams	
4 tablespoons	= ¼ cup	= 2 ounces	= 56.7 grams	
5⅓ tablespoons	= ⅓ cup	= 2.6 ounces	= 75.6 grams	
8 tablespoons	= ½ cup	= 4 ounces	= 113.4 grams	
12 tablespoons	= ¾ cup	= 6 ounces	= 170 grams	= .375 pound
32 tablespoons	= 2 cups	= 16 ounces	= 453.6 grams	= 1 pound
64 tablespoons	= 4 cups	= 32 ounces	= 907 grams	= 2 pounds

Liquid Measurements

1 cup	= 8 ounces	= ½ pint	= 240ml
2 cups	= 16 ounces	= 1 pint	= 470ml
4 cups	= 32 ounces	= 1 quart	= 946ml
2 pints	= 32 ounces	= 1 quart	= .95 liters
4 quarts	= 128 ounces	= 1 gallon	= 3.8 liters

Selected Bibliography

Adai, James. *Adair's History of the American Indians*. London, 1775. Reprinted from the original by Samuel Cole Williams. New York, 1930.

Asbur, Herbert. *The French Quarter*. New York: Thunder Mouth Press, 1936.

Brasseaux, Carl A. *The Founding of New Acadia: The Beginnings of Acadian Life in Louisiana, 1795–1803*. Baton Rouge: Louisiana State University Press, 1987.

Brown, Virginia Pounds and Laurella Owens. *The World of Southern Indians*. Birmingham, AL: Beechwood Books, 1990.

Cast Iron Classics. South Pittsburg, TN: Lodge Press, 2004.

Chambers, Henry E. *Mississippi Valley Beginnings*. New York: Putnam, 1922.

Clark, John G. *New Orleans 1718–1812 An Economic History*. Baton Rouge: Louisiana State University Press, 1970.

Davis, Edwin Adams. *Louisiana: A Narrative History*. Baton Rouge: Claitor's Publishing, 1971.

Eccles, W. J. *The Canadian Frontier 1534–1760*. Albuquerque: University of New Mexico Press, 1983.

Hall, Gwendolyn Midlo. *Africans in Colonial Louisiana: The Development of Afro-Creole Culture in the Eighteenth Century*. Baton Rouge: Louisiana State University Press, 1992.

Hamilton, Peter J. *Colonial Mobile*. Reprinted from the 1910 edition and revised and edited by Charles G. Summersell. Tuscaloosa, AL: University of Alabama Press, 1976.

Hearn, Lafcadio. *Lafcadio Hearn's Creole Cook Book*. Revised reprint of the 1885 edition. Gretna, LA: Pelican Publishing, 1990.

Higginbotham, J. *Old Mobile: Fort Louis de la Louisiane 1702–1711*. Tuscaloosa, AL: University of Alabama Press, 1977.

Holder, Katy, and Gail Duff. *A Pinch of Herbs*. London, Chartwell Books, 1997.

Holmes, Jack D. L. *A Guide to Spanish Louisiana 1762–1806*. New Orleans: A. F. Laborde, 1970.

_____. *New Orleans Drinks and How to Mix Them*. New Orleans: Hope Publications, 1973.

Holmes, Jack D. L., and Raymond J. Martinez. *New Orleans Facts and Legends*. New Orleans: Hope Publications.

Huber, Leonard V. *New Orleans A Pictorial History.* Gretna, LA: Pelican Publications, 1991.

Hudson, Charles. *The Southeastern Indians.* Knoxville: University of Tennessee Press, 1976.

Keville, Kathi. *Herbs: An Illustrated Encyclopedia.* New York: Friedman and Fairfax Publishers, 1994.

Leavitt, Mel. *A Short History of New Orleans.* San Francisco: Lexikos, 1982.

McWilliams, Richebourg Gaillard, trans. and ed. *Iberville's Gulf Journals.* Tuscaloosa, AL: University of Alabama Press, 1981.

Milioni, Stefano. *The Columbus Menu: Italian Cuisine after the First Voyage of Christopher Columbus 1492–1992.* New York: Italian Trade Commision, 1992.

Miller, Mark. *The Great Chile Book.* Berkeley: Ten Speed Press, 1991.

Mitchell, Patricia B. *An Affair of the Heart: America's Romance with Louisiana Food.* Chatham, VA: Mitchells Publications, 1999.

_____. *French Cooking in Early America.* Chatham, VA: Mitchells Publications, 1991.

_____. *The Good Land: Native American Early Colonial Food.* Chatham, VA: Mitchells Publications, 1991.

_____. *Plantation Row Slave Cabin Cooking: The Roots of Soul Food.* Chatham, VA: Mitchells Publications, 1998.

_____. *Soul On Rice: African Influences on American Cooking.* Chatham, VA: Mitchells Publications, 1993.

Nau, John Fredrick. *The German People of New Orleans 1850-1900.* University of South Mississippi Publications, 1958.

Norman, Jill. *The Complete Book of Spices.* London: Dorling Kindersley, 1990.

Ortiz, Elizabeth Lambert. *The Encyclopedia of Herbs, Spices & Flavorings.* New York: Dorling Kindersley, Inc, 1994.

Peckham, Howard H. *The Colonial Wars 1689–1762.* Chicago: University of Chicago Press, 1964.

Picayune's Creole Cook Book, The. Sesquicentennial edition. Revised reprint of the 1901 edition. New Orleans: Times-Picayune, 1987.

Roberts, W. Adolphe. *Lake Pontchartrain.* Indianapolis: Bobbs-Merrill Company, 1946.

Roboni, Frances D. and Peter J. *French Cooking in the New World: Louisiana Creole and French Canadian Cuisine.* Garden City, NY: Double Day, 1967.

Rushton, William Faulkner. *The Cajuns from Acadia to Louisiana.* New York: Farrar Straus Giroux, 1979.

Historical Louisiana Cookbook References

Louisiana is world famous for its brilliant chefs and exceptionally fine cookbooks. In the writing of our own cookbook, we researched many outstanding Louisiana cookbooks to find classic recipes that we felt best reflected Louisiana's Cajun/Creole cuisine. We were greatly influenced and inspired by the following list of cookbooks.

It is with the utmost respect and admiration that we proudly recommend the following list of Louisiana cookbooks. Any of these would be a great addition to your own personal culinary library.

Cajun-Creole Cooking, Terry Thompson.

The Encyclopedia of Cajun & Creole Cuisine, John D. Folse.

Cajun Cuisine, Beau Bayou Publishing Company.

Creole Feast, Nathaniel Burton & Rudy Lombard.

Jambalaya, The Junior League of New Orleans.

Chef Paul Prudhommes Louisiana Kitchen, Chef Paul Prudhomme.

The Commander's Palace New Orleans Cookbook, Ella & Dick Brennan.

The Picayune Creole Cook Book, The Times-Picayune.

Gumbo Shop, Richard Stewart.

La Bouche Creole, Leon Soniat.

Step By Step Creole Cooking, Gallery Books.

Step By Step Cajun Cooking, Gallery Books.

Better Homes and Gardens Cajun Cooking, Better Homes and Gardens.

Lafcadio Hearn's Creole Cook Book, Lafcadio Hearn.

Lache pas la Patate!, Joeann McLemore.

Index

Alligator Sauce Piquant, 206

Appetizers and Dips, 117–30

Artichoke Bisque, Oyster and, 139

Asparagus Soup, Cream of, 150

Bananas Foster, 253

Barbequed Ribs, Cajun-Style, 186

Basic Louisiana Tasty Rice, 156

beans

    Congri, 167

    Creole Red Beans and Rice, 166

    Creole String Beans, 171

Béarnaise Sauce, 96

Béchamel Sauce, 97

beef

    Beef Bordelaise, 190

    Beef Stock, 135

    Cajun "Dirty" Rice, 161

    Daubé Glacé, 191

    Grillades and Grits, 110

    Marinated Steak with Mushrooms, 182

    Natchitoches Meat Pies, 129

    Pecan-and-Herb-Encrusted Prime Rib Roast, 185

    Pot-au-Feu à la Creole, 148

    Steak Louisiane, 180

Beignets, Crawfish, 130

Blackened Redfish, 225

blackening, about, 33

Boiled Crawfish, 228

Bordelaise Sauce, 92

Bouillabaisse Louisiane, 143

Brabant Potatoes, 177

bread

    Beignets, 109

    Bread Pudding, New Orleans, 252

    Hush Puppies, 174

    Pain Perdu, 116

Breakfast Dishes, 107–16

Brown Rice, 157

Cabbage, Smothered, 178

Cajun Cane Syrup Cake, 245

Cajun Collard Greens, 163

Cajun Corn Pudding, 162

Cajun Coush-Coush, 116

Cajun-Style Barbeque Ribs, 186

Cajun-Style Pumpkin Soup, 152

Cajun "Dirty" Rice, 161

Cajun Fried Chicken, 203

Cajun Fried Crawfish Tails, 236

Cajun Jambalaya, 188

Cajun Maque Choux, 158

Cajun Pork Roast, 192

Cajun Potato Fries, 169

Cajun Roasted Duck, 209

Cajun Sauce Piquant, 100

Cajun Tac Tac, 255

Cajun Venison Roast, 208

Cajun/Creole Seafood Dip, 125

cakes

    Cajun Cane Syrup Cake, 245

    Mardi Gras King Cake, 242

    Red Velvet Cake, 240

    Satsuma Cake, 244

    Spiced Fig Cake, 241

Calas, 108
cast-iron cookware
    caring for, 9
    cooking with, 8–11
    seasoning, 9
catfish
    Fried Creole Mustard Catfish, 223
    Pecan-Crusted Catfish with Mushroom
        Sauce, 222
Cheesecake, Praline, 246
Chicken, 195–204
    Cajun Fried Chicken, 203
    Cajun Jambalaya, 188
    Chicken Étouffée, 199
    Chicken Espagnole, 198
    Chicken Florentine, 204
    Chicken in White Wine Sauce, 202
    Chicken Jean Laffite, 201
    Chicken Sauce Piquant, 197
    Chicken Sausage Gumbo, 144
    Chicken Stock, 132
    Creole Chicken Salad, 196
    New Orleans Creole Jambalaya, 189
    New Year's Day Hoppin' John, 173
    Pecan-Crusted Chicken with Cream Sauce,
        200
cheese
    Cheese Grits, 111
    Shrimp and Crabmeat au Gratin, 214
Cocktail Sauce, 227
Chocolate Silk, 251
Christmas Creole Toffee, 258
Classic Sauces, 91–105
Classic White Cream Sauce, 93
Cochon de Lait, 193
Collard Greens, Cajun, 163
Congri, 167
corn
    Cajun Maque Choux, 158
    Corn and Crabmeat Soup, 152
    Cajun Corn Pudding, 162
cooking techniques, Cajun/Creole, 32

cooking tips, basic, 14–17
Coush-Coush, Cajun, 116
Cotelettes Creole de Cochon, 184
crab
    Cajun-Style Pumpkin Soup, 152
    Crab and Shrimp Étouffée, 234
    Crab Meat Ravigote, 238
    Creole Crabmeat Omelet Filling, 115
    Creole Shrimp and Crab Meat Quiche, 229
    Louisiana Crab Cakes, 121
    New Orleans–Style Spinach and Crab Meat
        Casserole, 226
    Seafood-Stuffed Bell Peppers, 175
    Shrimp and Crab Meat Bisque, 140
    Shrimp and Crabmeat au Gratin, 214
    Spinach and Crabmeat Dip, 128
cream cheese, Creole, about, 41
crawfish
    about, 37
    Boiled Crawfish, 228
    Cajun Fried Crawfish Tails, 236
    Crawfish Beignets, 130
    Crawfish Bisque, 142
    Crawfish Fettuccine, 233
    Crawfish Pie, 232
    Shrimp or Crawfish Boulettes, 124
    Shrimp or Crawfish Étouffée, 224
Cream of Asparagus Soup, 150
Creole Barbecued Shrimp, 217
Creole Chicken Salad, 196
Creole Cocktail Sauce, 104
Creole Crabmeat Omelet Filling, 115
Creole French Onion Soup, 153
Creole Hollandaise Sauce, 98
Creole Mayonnaise, 101
Creole Meuniere Sauce, 98
Creole Panéed Veal, 187
Creole Pecan Pralines I, 256
Creole Pecan Pralines II, 257
Creole Potato Soup, 149
Creole Red Beans and Rice, 166
Creole Sauce, 95

Creole Shrimp and Crab Meat Quiche, 229
Creole Stewed Okra and Tomatoes, 159
Creole String Beans, 171
Creole-Style Tuna Fish Salad, 219
Creole Stuffed Shrimp, 122
Creole Vegetable Soup, 141
Creole Zucchini and Tomatoes, 164
culinary terms, 33–35
custard
    Riz au Lait, 250
Daubé Glacé, 191
deep frying, 33
Desserts and Candy, 239–58
duck
    Duck and Sausage Gumbo, 154
    Cajun Roasted Duck, 209
Eggplant, Stuffed, 176
eggs
    Eggs Creole, 114
    Eggs Hussarde, 113
    Eggs Sardou, 112
Fig Cake, Spiced, 241
filé, about, 23, 39
Fried Creole Mustard Catfish, 223
Fried Okra, 165
Fried Sweet Potatoes and Onion, 170
Game, 205–10
green beans
    Creole String Beans, 171
Grillades and Grits, 110
Grits, Cheese, 111
gumbo, defined, 34. *See also* Soups and Gum-
    bos
Gumbo Z'Herbes, 146
herbs, 21–23
hot sauce, about, 36
Hush Puppies, 174
jambalaya
    Cajun, 188
    defined, 34
    New Orleans Creole, 189
Lapin au Sauce Piquant, 207

Lemon Butter Sauce, 104
Louisiana Crab Cakes, 121
Louisiana-Style Boiled Shrimp, 227
Louisiana-Style Shrimp Stir-Fry, 230
Louisiana Turtle Soup, 138
Marchand de Vin Sauce, 99
Mardi Gras King Cake, 242
Marinated Steak with Mushrooms, 182
Mayonnaise, Cajun/Creole Seasoned, 227
Mayonnaise, Creole, 101
Meat Entrées, 179–93
Mirlitons, Shrimp-Stuffed, 235
mushrooms
    Marinated Steak with Mushrooms, 182
    Stuffed Mushrooms, 120
Natchitoches Meat Pies, 129
New Orleans Bread Pudding, 252
New Orleans Creole Jambalaya, 189
New Orleans–Style Spinach and Crab Meat
    Casserole, 226
New Year's Day Hoppin' John, 173
okra
    and gumbo, 73
    Creole Stewed Okra and Tomatoes, 159
    Seafood Okra Gumbo, 145
omelets
    Creole Crabmeat Omelet Filling, 115
onions
    Creole French Onion Soup, 153
    Fried Sweet Potatoes and Onion, 170
oranges
    Satsuma Cake, 244
Oreilles de Cochon, 254
oysters
    Bouillabaisse Louisiane, 143
    Natchitoches Meat Pies, 129
    Oyster and Artichoke Bisque, 139
    Oysters Bienville, 126
    Oysters Mosca, 127
Pain Perdu, 116
pasta
    Crawfish Fettuccine, 233

pastries
    Oreilles de Cochon, 254
pecans
    Creole Pecan Pralines I, 256
    Creole Pecan Pralines II, 257
    Pecan Rice, 168
    Pecan-and-Herb-Encrusted Prime Rib Roast, 185
    Pecan-Crusted Catfish with Mushroom Sauce, 222
    Pecan-Crusted Chicken with Cream Sauce, 200
    Roasted Pecan and Sausage Stuffing, 172
    Sweet Potato Pecan Pie, 248
peppers, 24–26
peppers, bell
    Beef-Stuffed Bell Peppers, 160
    Seafood-Stuffed Bell Peppers, 175
pepper sauce, about, 37
pies
    Pecan Pie, 247
    Sweet Potato Pecan Pie, 248
    Tarte à la Bouillie, 249
Pompano en Papillote, 212
popcorn balls
    Cajun Tac Tac, 255
pork
    Cajun Pork Roast, 192
    Cajun-Style Barbeque Ribs, 186
    Chicken Sausage Gumbo, 144
    Cochon de Lait, 193
    Cotelettes Creole de Cochon, 184
    Duck and Sausage Gumbo, 154
    New Year's Day Hoppin' John, 173
    Pork Stock, 134
    Roasted Pecan and Sausage Stuffing, 172
potatoes
    Brabant Potatoes, 177
    Cajun Potato Fries, 169
    Creole Potato Soup, 149
    Pot-au-Feu à la Creole, 148

pralines
    about, 40–41
    Creole Pecan Pralines I, 256
    Creole Pecan Pralines II, 257
    Praline Cheesecake, 246
    Praline Sauce, 105
pudding
    Chocolate Silk, 251
    New Orleans Bread Pudding, 252
Pumpkin Soup, Cajun-Style, 151
Quail Étouffée, 210
rabbit
    Lapin au Sauce Piquant, 207
Red Beans and Rice, Creole, 166
redfish
    Blackened Redfish, 225
    Redfish Courtbouillon, 220
Red Velvet Cake, 240
Rémoulade Sauce, 94
ribbon cane syrup, about, 39
rice
    about, 20
    Basic Louisiana Tasty Rice, 156
    Beef-Stuffed Bell Peppers, 160
    Brown Rice, 157
    Cajun "Dirty" Rice, 161
    Creole Red Beans and Rice, 166
    Pecan Rice, 168
    wild pecan rice, about, 39
Riz au Lait, 250
Roasted Pecan and Sausage Stuffing, 172
roux, 17–19
Sassy Lemon Sauce, 99
Satsuma Cake, 244
Sauce Espagnole, 103
sauces, 91–105
    about, 31
Seafood, 211–38. *See also* specific kinds
    Bouillabaisse Louisiane, 143
    Pompano en Papillote, 212
    Seafood Dip, Cajun/Creole, 125
    Seafood Filé Gumbo, 147

Seafood Okra Gumbo, 145
Seafood Stock, 133
Seafood-Stuffed Bell Peppers, 175
seasoning blends, Cajun/Creole
    about, 26–28, 35
    Colonel Paul's, 28, XXX
shrimp
    Crab and Shrimp Étouffée, 234
    Creole Barbecued Shrimp, 217
    Creole Shrimp and Crab Meat Quiche, 229
    Creole Stuffed Shrimp, 122
    Louisiana-Style Boiled Shrimp, 227
    Louisiana-Style Shrimp Stir-Fry, 230
    Seafood Okra Gumbo, 145
    Shrimp and Crab Meat Bisque, 140
    Shrimp and Crabmeat au Gratin, 214
    Shrimp Clemenceau, 216
    Shrimp Creole, 215
    Shrimp or Crawfish Étouffée, 224
    Shrimp or Crawfish Boulettes, 124
    Shrimp Rémoulade, 118
    Shrimp-Stuffed Mirlitons, 235
slow cooking, 32
Smothered Cabbage, 178
Soups and Gumbos, 137–154
Spiced Fig Cake, 241
spinach
    New Orleans–Style Spinach and Crab Meat
        Casserole, 226
    Spinach and Crabmeat Dip, 128
Soups and Gumbos, 137–54
stainless steel cookware, 12
Steak Louisiane, 180
Stocks, 131–36
    how to make basic stock, 28–30
Stuffed Eggplant, 176
Stuffed Mushrooms, 120
sweet potatoes
    Fried Sweet Potatoes and Onion, 170
    Sweet Potato Pecan Pie, 248
Tarte à la Bouillie, 249
Toffee, Christmas Creole, 258

tomatoes
    Creole, about, 38
    Creole Stewed Okra and Tomatoes, 159
    Creole Zucchini and Tomatoes, 164
trinity, 30
trout
    Trout Amandine, 231
    Trout Marguery, 218
    Trout Meuniere, 237
Tuna Fish Salad, Creole-Style, 219
Turtle Soup, Louisiana, 138
utensils, essential for cooking, 11–14
veal
    Grillades and Grits, 110
    Creole Panéed Veal, 187
Vegetable Dishes, 155–78
Vegetable Soup, Creole, 141
Vegetable Stock, 136
Venison Roast, Cajun, 208
Whiskey or Rum Sauce, 102
White Wine Sauce, 105
wines and liquors, cooking with, 30–31
Zucchini and Tomatoes, Creole, 164

Colonel Paul's Cajun Seasonings

In Mild, Medium, and Hot n' Spicy!

Colonel Paul's Cajun Seasoning is unique to all others in that it is the only Cajun seasoning made in Louisiana to come in mild, medium, or hot.

    Colonel Paul's Cajun Seasoning is coarsely ground and leafy, blended together with lots of garlic, thyme, and sweet basil to give it a marvelous herby flavor. Wonderful on meats, seafood, vegetables, or anything. It comes in shaker container that holds 5.6 ounces (159 g).

Authentic Louisiana Flavor at Your Own Heat Level!!

COLONEL PAUL'S MILD CAJUN SEASONING - Offers authentic Cajun flavor with just a little spice for those who don't want it too hot.

COLONEL PAUL'S MEDIUM CAJUN SEASONING - Offers a great balance of flavor and heat. Our most popular seasoning.

COLONEL PAUL'S HOT N' SPICY CAJUN SEASONING - Made exclusively for those who want a real good "bite" but with lots of flavor.

For more information:
Visit the Colonel online at:
www.colonelpaul.com
e-mail: colonelpaul@colonelpaul.com

The Colonel's products are distributed by:
Paul Products Inc.
P.O. Box 36835
Birmingham, Alabama 35236
(205) 988-0788
Fax: (205) 733-0107